Tick...Tick...Tick...

Tick...Tick...Tick

The Long Life
and Turbulent Times
of 60 *Minutes*

David Blum

HarperCollins*Publishers*

Designed by Elliott Beard

ISBN 0-7394-5325-4

For Sam and Annie

Contents

Tick...Tick...Tick...

Prologue

On the Tuesday afternoon before his final *60 Minutes* broadcast on May 30, 2004, Don Hewitt's belongings are being removed, against his will, from his corner office. All of his possessions have been packed away: his Emmy statuettes, his framed, autographed photographs with presidents from Truman to Bush, his Thomas Kent wall clock, even his huge, glass-topped office desk—the one at which he'd lately been telling everyone he wanted to die. After returning from lunch, the 81-year-old Hewitt had been summoned to Screening Room 164 for what he thinks will be his last look at a *60 Minutes* segment. Instead, the correspondents and a few dozen staffers greet him for a champagne toast out of plastic glasses. It is a sad, surreal surprise party hastily arranged to commemorate his final day of work at the show he created in 1968 that has earned $2 billion in profits for CBS, the network that has now removed his personal effects to make room for a new generation. The end of his 36-year reign as executive producer has finally come.

This was Hewitt's screening room; these were his hallways, his offices, his editing rooms and telephones. These were the men and women who worked tirelessly, day and night, to execute his vision. Here on the ninth floor of a nondescript office building on New York's West 57th Street near the Hudson River, above a BMW dealership, he

ruled over a show that shook up television—a show that took viewers into the private worlds of Katharine Hepburn and Lena Horne, that
opened a window into the minds of Richard Nixon and Bill Clinton,
that got Lenell Geter out of jail in 1983 and put dozens of others behind bars. For just another few hours, this remains the kingdom of Don
Hewitt's creation; he is the ruler of all that he surveys.

When Hewitt enters the screening room, his eyes mist up as he rec-
ognizes the reporters he has alternately loved and loathed—a Mount
Rushmore–like gathering of the *60 Minutes* correspondents, lined up
against the wall to say good-bye. There stands 86-year-old Mike Wallace, looking dapper in a gray business suit, flanked by Lesley Stahl
in a pink leather jacket and Steve Kroft in an open-collar shirt. At the
other side of the room stands Ed Bradley in his usual dark T-shirt. Morley Safer is away on vacation in Spain.

"I'm not going anywhere," Hewitt says, after a brief round of applause dies down. "I'm going downstairs." He is referring to the spa-
cious office directly below his current one that will be his new home
as an executive producer of CBS News, the consulting gig the network
gave him in return for letting go, at last, of his estimated $7-million-
a-year full-time job.

"You gonna put a spiral staircase in?" asks Bradley.

"I'm never coming up here again," Hewitt says.

"You've had it with us," says Stahl.

"I've seen the last of this floor," Hewitt agrees, and looks around the
room, tears glistening in his eyes. "Gee whiz. I don't know what to say."

"Ordinarily, Don, in the screening room," Wallace quickly rebuts,
"you know what to say."

Wallace is referring to the countless tempestuous, screaming battles between Hewitt and his correspondents that have defined life at
60 Minutes—and, in particular, the dysfunctional, passion-filled 36-
year marriage between Hewitt and Wallace. The two men have been
yelling at each other since they first began working together in 1968,
the improbable pairing of a rough-edged whiz kid from New Rochelle
and an elegant, well-spoken former Broadway actor from a leafy Boston

suburb who together produced some of the most memorable journalism of the twentieth century—and some of the most legendary fights
in this room.

"I don't know about you," Stahl interjects with sarcasm. "He's wonderful to the rest of us."

It has been over a year since Hewitt reluctantly signed the contract
that forced him to at last cede control of his show to Jeffrey Fager, a
comparatively mild-mannered, 49-year-old former *60 Minutes* producer. The agreement followed months of battling between Hewitt and
CBS executives, with the correspondents—frustrated by Hewitt's
weakened physical condition and his continued tantrums—struggling
between their loyalty to their boss and their desire to protect the show's
future. Privately, several of the correspondents expressed a desire to
see Hewitt move on; they knew it made no sense to have a tired old
man, now only working three days a week, as executive producer. But
now that the day has finally come, their conflicted emotions surface
as they see Hewitt still stewing over CBS's decision to remove him.

"Without you, none of us would be here," says Josh Howard, Hewitt's genial 49-year-old second-in-command, sensing the need for someone to express some actual gratitude to Hewitt. "And there are a lot of
cars and houses and college educations that we have you to thank for."

The moment of sincerity is short-lived. "Psychotherapists as well,"
comes the crack from an unidentifiable voice behind the correspondents.

"Do you want to tell that to Andrew and Betsy?" Hewitt says, referring to CBS News president Andrew Heyward and his deputy, senior vice president Betsy West, the architects of the succession plan.
"They have a different idea about this whole thing."

Stahl steps forward and faces Hewitt. "There's just sort of this un-
reality about all this," she says, standing on the spot where she and
Hewitt have shouted at each other so many times over the last 13 years.

"But it is," Hewitt says. "That's the way they wanted it."

"You're dead, son—get yourself buried," the journalist J. J. Hunsecker
counsels Sidney Falco in *Sweet Smell of Success*. Only a few yards away

from the screening room, workmen are applying Hunsecker's advice to Hewitt; cartons of papers sit outside his office waiting to be moved downstairs, where CBS News has stashed him in digs befitting an exiled king. Hewitt knows he is being cast off but desperately wants to keep anyone from thinking of his career as finished. That, perhaps, is why he has chosen this moment to announce to his *60 Minutes* family his latest idea for a TV show—news he has shared with no one else until now.

"I'm going to be doing something right now that the network has bought lock, stock, and barrel," Hewitt says. "We're going to start nineteen shows on the nineteen owned and operated affiliates—called *30 Boston Minutes, 30 New York Minutes, 30 San Francisco Minutes, 30 Dallas Minutes, 30 Miami Minutes.* Instead of saying *60 Minutes,* it'll say *30 Minutes.* And I'm going to do the pilot in San Francisco, probably in about two weeks." (As usual, Hewitt has exaggerated; in fact, CBS has authorized the making of the pilot but will not approve the launch until it sees the results.)

There's a moment of stunned silence in the room as everyone collectively considers the latest improbable notion of a man who has had several million of them in his career—most notably, of course, the idea for *60 Minutes* itself.

Stahl finally breaks the silence. "That's fabulous," she says. "Who's going to be on camera?" The laughter that follows has something to do with Stahl's well-known desire for face time on television, and with the fact that only days earlier she'd reportedly lost a part-time job as host of *48 Hours Investigates* that had been supplementing her *60 Minutes* exposure and salary. Hewitt explains that local correspondents will be filling the on-air jobs.

His decision to spill the news of his future plans has created some discomfort in a roomful of people gathered to pay tribute, not to wish Hewitt well on his next cockeyed crusade. There's a noticeable silence in response to his announcement. His longtime assistant, Beverly Morgan—sensitive as always to Hewitt's mercurial moods—urges everyone to begin the toasts and turns to a Safer assistant to read that 72-year-old correspondent's faxed tribute to his fallen boss.

"Don, I do not expect much to change except for an address," Safer has written. "We will now have to go to the eighth floor to bitch and moan. You are and always will be the DNA of this broadcast. I will always expect those calls at 5, 6 or 7 A.M. and for sure at 7:59 P.M. on Sunday. I still expect those harebrained ideas and those flashes of brilliance. Will I miss the screening room mutual-torture sessions? No. Will I miss the kiss-and-make-up ten minutes later? Yes. Do I expect a weekly critique? Of course. Is this the end of the Hewitt era? Never. Yours with the usual mix of anxiety and frustration and, despite all, deep and abiding respect and affection. Morley."

Had Safer been able to predict the awkwardness of this event, he might not have bothered. Ed Bradley follows with a toast not to Hewitt at all, but to Morgan, Hewitt's assistant, who will also be leaving. After that, Kroft offers a lukewarm tribute. "No matter what happens in anybody else's career," Kroft predicts confidently, "I think at the end of it we'll all remember when we worked with Don Hewitt."

"Cheers!" Stahl says.

"Anybody want to go down and tell that to Heyward?" Hewitt says, almost as though he hasn't heard what anyone has been saying. "Frazier Moore of the AP asked me the other day, Why are they doing this? I said, nobody ever explained it to me. I have never had an explanation. Never. But it happened."

Hewitt's evident bitterness—running on a seemingly endless loop in his brain—causes an anguished moment, until Stahl breaks the silence.

"So you *have* gotten over it," Stahl deadpanned.

As the laughter dies down, the unmistakable voice of Mike Wallace returns the party to rapt attention.

"Thirty-six years ago," Wallace says, casting his eyes over the crowd of young assistants and producers, many of them barely born when *60 Minutes* began. "Out of a job. In a room about a quarter the size of this room. With a good-looking assistant—what was her name?"

"Suzanne Davis," Hewitt says.

"That's right. Suzanne Davis. He effectively had been fired. Told,

'Hey, come up with an idea.' They'd already gotten rid of him because of some of his ideas. And on a Sunday he said, 'Can I come over?' And he came over to 74th Street. And we went upstairs. . . . He said, 'Listen. I've got an idea. I've got an idea for a show.'

"I wanted to go to the White House," Wallace goes on. "I hadn't the slightest desire . . . but I figured, what the hell. I felt sorry for him."

"Who was president then?" Stahl interjects. "Coolidge?"

Wallace continues, unamused. "Nixon," he says. "Nixon. In any case, this man . . . somebody said it before. He put our kids through school. He made some of us much richer than we should be. But mainly, we had such a ball. For the first ten or fifteen years. We worked seven days a week, twelve hours a day. Everybody saw everybody else's piece in the screening room. It was . . . Jesus, it was . . ."

Wallace stops, his reverie finished in midthought. He has remembered enough. Hewitt doesn't mind; he's dying to repeat for the millionth time his own memory of the early days, when the two men who still call each other "kid" really were just kids, playing with the power of television.

"One day, Mike calls me and he says, 'Kid, guess what? Leonard Garment just called me, they're offering me the job of Nixon's press secretary.' I said, 'Are you out of your mind? You don't take a job like that after you've been Mike Wallace. You take a job like that so after it's over you can get to be Mike Wallace.' "

The two titans stare at each other from across the room, their eyes as cloudy as their memories. Their final moment together at *60 Minutes* has come, and with it the uncertainty of a future without each other to yell at, laugh with, or love. Wallace clears his throat; he has one final question to ask his boss.

"What's going to happen to this broadcast?" he asks.

"I don't know," Hewitt says. "I don't know. I don't know."

At last the champagne begins to flow; staffers head toward the makeshift bar for a badly needed drink. But Wallace puts down his glass and makes his way quickly through the crowd to the door of the screening room. For him, the party is over.

Chapter 1

What-a-Vision

It was a Saturday afternoon in March 1931, and an 8-year-old boy named Donald Shepard Hewitt had taken the profits from his part-time job selling magazines in the tree-trimmed New York suburb of New Rochelle and bought himself a frozen Milky Way bar and a trolley car ticket to the neighborhood movie house. That day's feature was *The Front Page,* which had opened to rave reviews—an adaptation of the Ben Hecht–Charles McArthur play about a big-city newspaper and the people who worked there. *The Front Page* had had a great run on Broadway in 1928 and done plenty to glamorize the journalism profession into which young Don had been born. Don's dad wasn't a reporter, exactly; he sold classified advertising, and not even for a New York newspaper, and these days he was selling ad circulars. But that was the black-and-white real world; in the wide-screen, Technicolor world inside young Don's head—where even the best story could stand a little exaggeration—Ely Hewitt might as well have been the editor of the *New York Herald Tribune.* Plus the kid loved the movies, and a comedy about the newspaper business was one he did not intend to miss.

The Front Page introduced the world to one of the great archetypes in the short history of the movies: Hildy Johnson, the freewheeling, rule-breaking Chicago newspaper reporter preparing to leave the chaotic news business for marriage and a more respectable career in advertising. His last day on the courthouse beat, hell-bent on breaking one last story, Johnson spends every penny of his $260 in honeymoon booty to buy an exclusive on the prison escape of convicted murderer Earle Williams. With his crusty but benign editor Walter Burns—another archetype built to last—he manages to grab Williams and stash him inside a rolltop desk in the courthouse press room until their scoop is assured.

The movie made a fortune at the box office and resulted in multiple remakes (including Howard Hawks's classic 1940 comedy, *His Girl Friday*) and contributed an enduring stereotype to the culture: Hildy Johnson defined the hard-drinking, intrepid newshound in his broad-brimmed fedora, feet up on the pressroom desk, wisecracking about dames, pols, and the latest big story. He would stand for decades as Hollywood's ultimate reporter—a little shady around the edges, no holds barred—at least until Robert Redford and Dustin Hoffman came along and sanctified journalism as a serious business for ethical, hard-working professionals who never stretched the truth.

From the moment young Don stepped out of the theater into the March sunlight, he knew exactly what he wanted to do when he grew up—to get the story, no matter what it took.

It didn't take Hewitt long to find a way to turn his Hildy obsession into coin. In the seventh grade, while his pals were playing baseball and chasing girls, the opinionated and boisterous teenager won a *Junior Scholastic Magazine* contest for "best editorial" with a piece he'd titled, "Press Drives Lindbergh to Self-Exile." He put his moviegoer's sense of story and drama to use in the student paper at New Rochelle High School, in a sports column with the somewhat catchier title of "Athlete's Footnotes." After that he set his media obsession aside just long enough to join the track team and earn an athletic scholarship to New York University.

At 19, Hewitt's already well-developed short attention span got the best of him; he dropped out of NYU and found what looked like his dream job—night copyboy at the fabled *New York Herald Tribune*. But sharpening pencils for other Hildy Johnsons wasn't quite the fulfilling experience Hewitt had dreamed of back in the movie house. After several months racing around the newsroom in the service of other reporters' stories, Hewitt found a ticket to bigger and more exciting opportunities: World War II. He enrolled at the Merchant Marine Academy in Kings Point, New York, in 1943, and by the next year he was working public relations for the Merchant Marine in London. There he finally got the chance to work with real reporters—among them two young journalists named Andy Rooney and Walter Cronkite.

"He was a young fellow, as we all were, much younger than we are now, anyway," Cronkite remembers. "It seemed that he was enjoying hanging out with the news people more than he was busy. . . . I think many of us questioned whether he was busy doing anything, except kind of enjoying the war." Andy Rooney's recollections were a bit more specific: "He used to come into the *Stars and Stripes* office all the time. . . . He was very good, he did good pieces for us. He submitted pieces about the Merchant Marine, and we often ran them."

One night near the end of the war, in his capacity as a Merchant Marine correspondent, Hewitt was a passenger in a supply convoy in the Atlantic Ocean taking heavy enemy fire. All around him, ships were sinking; as the night wore on and the battle raged, Hewitt watched helplessly as one ship after another disappeared beneath the ocean surface. By dawn, according to Hewitt's own highly theatrical account, his was the only boat still afloat, the only one to escape enemy fire. Then came two Royal Air Force planes out of Scotland—and the realization that rescue was near.

"Where's the music?" Hewitt said to himself as he watched the planes head toward them. "This can't be happening unless Dimitri

Tiomkin writes the score." Even in the middle of a war, Hewitt figured
the action could be more thrilling with just a few small improvements.

Hewitt may not have quite realized it that night, but despite all his
fantasies of a career as a dashing correspondent, he seemed to be missing the basic reporter gene. He had the flamboyant personality and the
wild ideas, and he liked being near the action. But he appeared to shy
away from the hard, gritty work that came with the job description.
While his pals Rooney and Cronkite—and other future TV stars like
Edward R. Murrow and Eric Sevareid—tore up the continent with
their confidence and tenacity, Hewitt hurried back to the United States
and got himself a job as the night editor of the Associated Press bureau in Memphis, Tennessee.

It was in Memphis in 1945 that Hewitt met his first wife, Mary Weaver,
who had the ambition to prod him out of that $50-a-week dead-end
job to take a position as editor-in-chief of the *Pelham Sun,* a suburban
New York weekly he'd been writing for before the war. It wasn't the
Herald Tribune, but it gave Hewitt some geographic proximity to the
world he'd dreamed of as a kid.

Six months later he found his way back inside the New York city
limits, with a job as night telephoto editor of Acme Newspictures. His
job was to choose and write captions for photographs to be sent out
on the Associated Press wire. But he quickly discovered that he'd
traded one boring job for another—again—and this was the worst one
yet. When a friend told him about a job at CBS News, he was interested, even though he'd never exactly heard of CBS News before.

"Not radio," the friend explained. "Television."

"What-a-vision?" Hewitt asked (or so he's claimed repeatedly ever
since).

Hewitt got the job—taking a $20-a-week cut in pay—and in Au-
gust 1948, at the age of 25, went to work for the fledgling news division of the network, then headquartered in the rafters above Grand
Central Station, in the heart of New York City.

*　　*　　*

At 6:45 every weeknight in those days, a mild and unassuming gentleman named Douglas Edwards sat at a desk in Studio 41 above Grand Central Terminal and read the news. This was before market research revealed to TV executives that "mild and unassuming" were two characteristics viewers didn't want in their TV newsreaders. Edwards read headlines off a script and into a camera, resulting in a resoundingly dull broadcast seen only by the tiny handful of Americans who owned televisions—1.4 million people watching 254,000 TV sets in 12 large American cities. *Douglas Edwards With the News* began broadcasting on August 15, 1948. Each show was supposed to last 15 minutes, but who was going to complain if they ran over a little bit?

These were the dark ages of television. It wasn't until much later that 1948 emerged as a turning point in the history of the medium. Sure, new cities and sets were constantly being added to the coaxial cable, delivering the programs of CBS, NBC, ABC, and DuMont. But Douglas Edwards was typical of the personalities that TV attracted at that point—pedestrian types with little glamour or star power. On June 20, 1948, a few weeks before Hewitt got hired, CBS gave a Sunday-night timeslot to a variety show hosted by a squat, greasy *New York Daily News* gossip columnist named Ed Sullivan, whose singular lack of charm did not preclude a 23-year career on CBS as an entertainment ringmaster.

CBS handed Hewitt the title of associate director and hoped that this hyperkinetic young man might jazz up their nightly newscast a little bit. (He shared the title with some other talented young men, including actor Yul Brynner and future movie directors Sidney Lumet and John Frankenheimer.) In those days videotape wasn't in wide use—the broadcast was redone live every night at 9:45 P.M. for the West Coast audience.

Hewitt was in his element at last. His idea-a-minute personality perfectly suited a fledgling medium in need of new ideas. Even better, no one cared if he broke the rules; in 1948, there weren't any rules to break. It was as close to Hildy Johnson's chaotic newsroom as Hewitt had yet come.

*   *   *

One of Hewitt's first missions as a TV news director was to find a way to keep Douglas Edwards from spending the entire newscast staring dully at the script in front of him.

At first Hewitt tried to cajole Edwards into memorizing the text. When this didn't work out (Edwards not being a trained Shakespearean actor capable of committing 15 minutes' worth of news copy to memory every night), Hewitt had the script written on poster cards held by a technician just to the side of the camera. It would look like Edwards had it memorized, even if he was in fact reading it. And it worked well enough.

But one morning Hewitt arrived at work with yet another brainstorm: What about braille? If Edwards could learn braille, he could just run his fingers over the script while looking directly into the camera. Hewitt's colleagues reacted with stupefaction and annoyance. Edwards wasn't about to learn braille, and CBS News wasn't about to pay for the conversion of scripts into braille on deadline.

With his braille proposal, Hewitt revealed not only a propensity for offbeat and impractical ideas but also an inordinate loyalty to them in the face of rejection. He pushed the notion for years; even Walter Cronkite heard the pitch. "Gosh, he was serious but nobody else took it very seriously," Cronkite remembers. "But it sure shook everybody up for a while." Ultimately, in the early 1950s the TelePrompTer was invented—a running strip of text that would appear directly above the camera lens. That sent the braille idea into the dustbin of television history, along with several other Hewitt brainstorms.

Nevertheless, Hewitt kept impressing people with his energy and ideas. In June 1951, Edward R. Murrow and his producer, Fred Friendly (born with the slightly less amicable name of Ferdinand Friendly Wachenheimer), agreed to move their popular *Hear It Now* radio show to TV, and they hired Hewitt to run the control room. *See It Now* debuted on November 18, 1951, with Murrow admitting to his audience, "This is an old team trying to learn a new trade." Hewitt, who after three years in television was one of its most experienced directors, appeared on camera during that show's control room opening; but it was Murrow and Friendly, not the 28-year-old Hewitt, who determined the show's direction.

See It Now was a show that needed only one boss—not a good arrangement for Hewitt, who was already accustomed to calling the shots. And further complicating matters, Hewitt, with his push-the-limits style, and Friendly, the ultraserious documentarian, hated each other instantly. "Don Hewitt's idea of news," Friendly used to say, "is an elephant on water skis in Cypress Gardens."

One morning during the 1952 Democratic Convention in Chicago, Hewitt went for breakfast in a local diner, and as he sat at his table his eyes lit on the blackboard listing that day's specials. The restaurant had mounted white letters onto the black background, and it occurred to Hewitt—staring at the word "hamburger"—that if he pointed a camera in the direction of such a sign, and then superimposed that shot onto a picture of a hamburger, the black background would "disappear" and only the white letters would show. "What if we did the same thing with, say, Adlai Stevenson?" he wondered. Hewitt immediately convinced himself that he'd come up with another idea to change television forever. His new technique would enable the viewer at home to know the identity of the presidential candidate on screen without the help of the on-air correspondent, freeing up considerable time for commentary and making broadcasts easier to follow.

"I'll have the board," Hewitt told the perplexed waitress when she asked for his order, or so he recalled in his 2002 memoir, *Tell Me a Story*. Paying $45, he walked out the door with the blackboard and carried it back up to the CBS News broadcast booth at the convention.

"Hey, look at this!" Hewitt shouted to his colleagues, lifting up the blackboard. Within minutes, a camera had filmed his new possession with names of various Democratic dignitaries now listed upon it; technicians then superimposed those shots onto the screen as the politicians showed up. By the end of the day, Hewitt's breakfast brainstorm had become an essential ingredient of all news broadcasting. Eventually this technique would come to be called a "chyron," or "super."

Hewitt understood the need for shorthand terms in a fast-paced industry—and either dreamed them up himself or popularized them to the point where people assumed they were his creations. For years, his colleagues recall he took credit for applying the relay-racing term "anchorman" to the role Cronkite played at the 1952 conventions—the notion being that while other reporters roamed the convention hall in search of stories, he would remain "anchored" to the news desk. "He always said it was his term, even though we all heard different stories," recalls Sanford Socolow, who joined CBS News as a news writer in 1956 and later worked as a producer alongside Hewitt on the *CBS Evening News*. Hewitt now backs off the claim; Cronkite himself credits the term to a junior CBS News producer named Paul Levitan. "Hewitt would be glad to take credit for that, but it's not so," Cronkite says firmly. "He may have picked it up instantly and made it the word that was used, but it was used in conversation before that."

Nonetheless, these household words would never have emerged from backstage without Hewitt to promote them. He knew the value of quick, catchy terms like "anchorman" for the nascent TV viewer. As producer, Hewitt was the advocate for the guy at home—the one in the Barcalounger, with the beer and the potato chips and the short attention span to rival his own. Hewitt wanted that guy, and he was always ready to do whatever it took to get him.

Chapter 2

You Son of a Bitch!

Don Hewitt flew to Iowa with the noblest of intentions. It was September 1959, and he was now the most powerful man at CBS News. As executive producer of *Douglas Edwards and the News*, the frenzied Hewitt made all the crucial decisions governing each night's broadcast and shaped the network's coverage of news events more than any other employee. At 37, Hewitt's dogged personal style colored every aspect of CBS's daily coverage; he often held two telephones to his ears at once, the better to bark commands at underlings. His terrified but fiercely loyal team of reporters worked nonstop to deliver better pictures, bigger scoops, and fresher stories to their demanding boss. That said— all the power and noise notwithstanding—CBS was losing to NBC's more popular newscast anchored by emerging stars Chet Huntley and David Brinkley. And Hewitt didn't like to lose.

He traveled to corn country that September with Harry Reasoner and Charles Kuralt, two of the most formidable young members of the CBS News reporting team. They were going to cover the first visit of Nikita Khrushchev, then premier of the Soviet Union, to the farm of Roswell Garst of Cumberland, Iowa. A Soviet leader was touring the

United States for the first time since the advent of communism and the explosion of television, and he cleverly saw the potential for creating goodwill through a staged media event.

Khrushchev's trip to the heartland handed TV networks the chance to vie for a new kind of broadcast coup—a contest seemingly made for Don Hewitt, who loved nothing more than the adrenaline rush of fighting over a breaking news story with great pictures.

On Friday, shortly after Hewitt got to Cumberland, he and his colleagues dropped in on the local police chief to say howdy. They were also looking for help in finding a driver to take them around town and hoped the officer might oblige. He connected them with the recently retired chief of police, who happily signed on for the job and agreed to wear his old uniform—giving Hewitt the benefit of a badge in making his way around town. Hewitt could barely contain his excitement, and then he pushed his luck even further. "What should we do when he's not available?" he gently inquired of the police chief.

"Oh, we'll make you honorary sheriff," the chief replied and gave Hewitt a badge.

The next day, Hewitt ran into an NBC camera crew from Omaha sent to help with that network's coverage and flashed his badge. "Howdy, folks," Sheriff Hewitt said as he approached the crew, who had no idea who he was.

"Morning, Sheriff," a crew member said to Hewitt.

"Mornin', boys," Hewitt replied. "What's goin' on?"

Whereupon the camera crew began to outline the details of NBC's coverage plans—until an NBC executive spotted Hewitt from a distance. Hewitt quickly excused himself and raced to spill the secrets to his CBS pals.

On the Saturday morning Khrushchev was to arrive, Hewitt roused his two correspondents before dawn and loaded them into a car, along with a young desk assistant named Robert Wussler, who went on to become president of CBS. They began driving around Cumberland in search of fresh new angles for the story.

"What's that over there?" he asked, as they drove along a dirt road alongside the Garst farm. He'd spotted a large truck parked in the distance. The side of the truck was clearly marked with the letters "NBC." Noting its size, Hewitt quickly deduced that the truck contained the mobile control room his primary competitor would need to broadcast its own coverage live.

Hewitt parked his car and walked over with Reasoner and Kuralt to take a look. "Hey, look," he said. "The keys are inside!"

Hewitt looked at Wussler and smiled.

"You wouldn't dare," Wussler said.

"Try me."

"You wouldn't have the guts."

"I have the guts, but what in hell would we do with it?"

"Hide it in a cornfield," said Wussler. "They won't find it until they harvest the corn in August."

With his reporters watching incredulously, Hewitt opened the door on the driver's side of the truck and hopped in. He turned the key and the engine started. With a big smile for his colleagues, Hewitt prepared to drive the short distance down the road, to an area of trees big enough to camouflage the truck. (It was as though Hewitt was hoping to duplicate, in spirit, the famous scene from *The Front Page* in which Hildy Johnson stashes the prisoner in the rolltop desk.) Only at the last minute did he reconsider and return to his own vehicle. Wussler wiped Hewitt's fingerprints off the steering wheel, and the four men drove off.

Of course, the news division executives were apoplectic over Hewitt's various stunts. But how do you punish your top producer, particularly when he was delivering great TV to a growing audience? A stern reprimand was all he ever got. And as frequently as Hewitt annoyed his bosses with his antics, he also pushed his notions of news as entertainment by devising ingenious ways to circumvent the normal methods of news gathering. His methods ranged from the benign to the extreme—from hiring a Navy plane to film the sinking of the *Andrea Doria* in 1956 to making an off-camera obscene gesture at prisoners to get them angry enough to re-create the scene of a New Jersey prison riot for film cameras, after the riot had already been quelled. Hewitt had an image in his mind of news that didn't always conform to the pictures he got.

Hewitt rankled most of his bosses, from Sig Mickelson, who ran CBS News in the 1950s, to his replacement, Richard Salant, a lawyer for CBS who had no previous news experience when he took over the news division in 1961. With his literate memos and aggressive adherence to ethical standards, Salant was a gentlemanly adversary for Hewitt, who wasn't about to change his ways. And despite the controversy around Hewitt, there was no doubting his talents as a visionary news producer who was attracting attention to a news show that desperately needed it.

To Salant, Hewitt's primary failing as a showman was his allegiance to Douglas Edwards, the stolid anchorman of the broadcast who couldn't compete with the combined charisma of Chet Huntley and David Brinkley, NBC's more successful news anchors. It seemed to Salant and others that Hewitt championed Edwards because the anchorman never contradicted Hewitt's own demanding point of view. "Edwards was Don's puppet," recalls Dan Rather, who joined CBS News as a reporter in 1961, just before Edwards was replaced in April 1962 with a popular TV journalist from Missouri by the name of Walter Cronkite.

Hewitt agreed to continue as executive producer of the *CBS Evening News* with Walter Cronkite, but neither man was overjoyed with the prospect. Radically different in their approach, the two men had already worked together a number of times since their days in London during World War II. Cronkite, a former United Press war correspondent and one of the fabled "Murrow's boys," was yet another CBS News employee with little patience for Hewitt.

On the night of Tuesday, April 5, 1960, Hewitt was in the control room calling the shots as Walter Cronkite sat behind the broadcast desk in the studio of CBS's Milwaukee affiliate, reporting on the returns from the all-important Wisconsin primary, which Senator John F. Kennedy had just won with 56 percent of the vote—bolstered by the state's substantial Catholic population.

Religion was a hot media topic that spring, as pundits and reporters speculated about how Kennedy's Catholic heritage would help or hurt his campaign, given that no Catholic had ever been elected president. Kennedy had grown sensitive on the subject, declaring in West Virginia at one point, "I don't think my religion is anyone's business." On this primary day in Wisconsin, Hewitt had assigned reporters to canvass voters in two key precincts—one Catholic, one not—to compare the candidates' strengths in these areas.

Earlier in the evening, Cronkite had already told viewers that Kennedy had shown unusual strength among Catholic voters—but he was looking forward to sharing the findings with Senator Kennedy himself. In a deal brokered by the senator's brother and campaign manager, Bobby Kennedy, Hewitt had arranged for Kennedy to meet with Cronkite live in the studio.

With Bobby Kennedy in the control room alongside Hewitt, Cronkite held an early TV interview with the presidential candidate. "Senator, tell me something." he said at one point, leaning in toward Kennedy. "We have some interesting returns here from a Catholic district and a non-Catholic district."

Kennedy froze. Leaning back in his chair and glaring across the desk, he said nothing. Cronkite, mystified by his reaction, continued to press the question. "And we're showing so far that there seems to be a very definite religious preference," Cronkite went on. "The Catholics are voting almost solidly for you, and the non-Catholics are voting almost solidly for Humphrey."

"Well, that's interesting," Senator Kennedy offered curtly.

"Do you think that'll carry around the country?" Cronkite asked.

"I discussed that in Houston this past week," was Kennedy's clipped response.

"Well, I was just going to ask you—" Cronkite blurted, before Kennedy cut him off.

"I've answered the question," he snapped, standing up and removing his microphone. "Thank you very much." At which point he walked off the studio set, leaving a stunned Cronkite behind.

Bobby Kennedy, in the control room, turned to Hewitt. "You son of a bitch!" he screamed. "You told me you weren't going to ask him any questions on religion!"

"No, I didn't!" Hewitt yelled back.

Bobby Kennedy stormed out of the control room, grabbed his brother, and left the building. Hewitt walked out onto the set to talk to Cronkite.

"What the hell happened?" Cronkite asked. *"Did* you tell Kennedy I wouldn't ask the Catholic question?"

"I told him we were going to ask him the question," Hewitt said.

Cronkite looked at Hewitt; he didn't know what to think. He knew the producer's penchant for exaggeration and his desperation for a good interview, and wondered who was telling the truth. He hoped it might have been a misunderstanding, but harbored doubts that would linger for many years after.

When asked about it recently, Hewitt remembered the incident but says it was between Kennedy and Cronkite. "I know he and Bobby had a fight," Hewitt says of Cronkite. What about the promise Cronkite had described? "I never said that in my life," Hewitt replied. "Never ever said that in my life." In fact, Hewitt says, he took issue with those who predicted that "bingo games and confessionals" would follow the election of a Catholic to the White House. "I had nothing to do with any of this," Hewitt continues. "Bobby Kennedy and Cronkite . . . I had nothing to do with that. That was nothing [Cronkite] ever blamed me for." However, it was difficult to dismiss the Cronkite version; the Most Trusted Man in America told the story in a March 2003 interview with considerable recall of details.

During the same campaign, Hewitt the showman produced a singular event that forever changed the American political landscape. On September 26, 1960, he directed the first of two debates between the

Beautiful Homes™
2006

July

S	M	T	W	T	F	S
						1
2	3	4	5	6	7	8
9	10	11	12	13	14	15
16	17	18	19	20	21	22
23	24	25	26	27	28	29
30	31					

August

S	M	T	W	T	F	S
		1	2	3	4	5
6	7	8	9	10	11	12
13	14	15	16	17	18	19
20	21	22	23	24	25	26
27	28	29	30	31		

September

S	M	T	W	T	F	S
					1	2
3	4	5	6	7	8	9
10	11	12	13	14	15	16
17	18	19	20	21	22	23
24	25	26	27	28	29	30

October

S	M	T	W	T	F	S
1	2	3	4	5	6	7
8	9	10	11	12	13	14
15	16	17	18	19	20	21
22	23	24	25	26	27	28
29	30	31				

November

S	M	T	W	T	F	S
		1	2	3	4	
5	6	7	8	9	10	11
12	13	14	15	16	17	18
19	20	21	22	23	24	25
26	27	28	29	30		

December

S	M	T	W	T	F	S
					1	2
3	4	5	6	7	8	9
10	11	12	13	14	15	16
17	18	19	20	21	22	23
24	25	26	27	28	29	30
31						

#05

Beautiful Homes™
2006

January

S	M	T	W	T	F	S
1	2	3	4	5	6	7
8	9	10	11	12	13	14
15	16	17	18	19	20	21
22	23	24	25	26	27	28
29	30	31				

February

S	M	T	W	T	F	S
			1	2	3	4
5	6	7	8	9	10	11
12	13	14	15	16	17	18
19	20	21	22	23	24	25
26	27	28				

March

S	M	T	W	T	F	S
			1	2	3	4
5	6	7	8	9	10	11
12	13	14	15	16	17	18
19	20	21	22	23	24	25
26	27	28	29	30	31	

April

S	M	T	W	T	F	S
						1
2	3	4	5	6	7	8
9	10	11	12	13	14	15
16	17	18	19	20	21	22
23	24	25	26	27	28	29
30						

May

S	M	T	W	T	F	S
	1	2	3	4	5	6
7	8	9	10	11	12	13
14	15	16	17	18	19	20
21	22	23	24	25	26	27
28	29	30	31			

June

S	M	T	W	T	F	S
				1	2	3
4	5	6	7	8	9	10
11	12	13	14	15	16	17
18	19	20	21	22	23	24
25	26	27	28	29	30	

Beautiful Homes • 1716 Locust Street • Des Moines, Iowa 50309-3023 • BHMFLPP2

two presidential candidates, John F. Kennedy and Richard M. Nixon. Historians now generally concede that Kennedy changed the course of history that night. Theodore H. White, in *The Making of the President 1960,* described Nixon in the debate as "half-slouched, his 'Lazy Shaves' powder faintly streaked with sweat, his eyes exaggerated hollows of blackness, his jaws, jowls and face drooping," whereas the well-tanned Kennedy "appeared to be the pillar of robust good health." Hewitt had offered Nixon the services of a professional makeup artist; the dour Nixon had declined. Although the debate's production came under Hewitt's exclusive control, he ultimately had little to do with the course of that night beyond doing his job. But his presence there, recorded on film and in photographs (including one on the cover of his 2002 memoir), has nevertheless contributed to Hewitt's reputation as a part of television history.

The debate created the central story of the 1960 presidential campaign—and demonstrated yet again Hewitt's skill at being at the center of big stories and major news events. He had no trouble locating the nexus of drama, especially in politics.

In those days conventions could still alter the course of presidential politics, and Hewitt covered them more like a Hollywood movie than a political event. He positioned cameras everywhere on the convention floor, in the offices of the candidates, on the ground floors of the hotels, and outside for street scenes. He made sure no image was left unrecorded and then choreographed the coverage from inside the control room—choosing on the fly among dozens of shots to tell the ongoing, unscripted story. He monitored events and made sure that crucial characters stayed on screen. He developed roles for his correspondents, assigning them delegations and keeping them in place down on the floor with microphones and headsets, constantly reporting up to Cronkite in the anchor booth.

"I'm coming to you next!" Hewitt would yell to a reporter, ordering him to chase down a candidate or important delegate. If Senator Jacob Javits of New York was reported to be upset about something, Hewitt would scream to Harry Reasoner in the New York delegation: "Get over to see Javits! If you don't know the story I'll tell you but get Javits!" Blessed with encyclopedic recall, Hewitt kept reams of ever-shifting information in his head, weaving a story line that somehow transcended mere news and kept viewers glued to CBS to see what would happen next.

For the 1960 conventions, Hewitt had the smart-sounding idea of pairing Cronkite and Edward R. Murrow—a match that sounded great on paper to hapless CBS News executives who had no choice but to trust Hewitt's casting instincts and showbiz judgment. But the two titanic egos just didn't mesh on television, and the ratings showed that viewers still felt more comfortable with the Huntley-Brinkley team. The experience proved the difficulty of casting Hewitt's made-for-TV dramas: anchormen weren't actors, nor did they like being told how to perform by some maniacal producer swearing at them from on high in the control booth.

No drama ever compared to the one that kept Hewitt from going out to lunch on Friday, November 22, 1963, when he heard the bulletin that President John F. Kennedy had been shot in Dallas. Hewitt took control of the news coverage that afternoon and stayed firmly in charge until the network finally resumed regular programming the following Tuesday.

A few hours after the president was assassinated, Dan Rather (then a CBS reporter based in New Orleans) called Hewitt from Dallas with an astonishing scoop.

"Don! Somebody filmed it. The assassination. A man named Abraham Zapruder, he had a camera, he got the whole thing."

Hewitt was stunned; he recognized immediately the historical significance of what his reporter had just told him, and the incredible value of being able to have the film.

"Go to Zapruder's house!" Hewitt yelled at Rather, thinking fast—possibly too fast. He then recalled instructing Rather to sock him in the jaw, take him to the CBS affiliate in Dallas, copy it onto videotape, and let the CBS lawyers decide whether it could be sold or whether it was in the public domain.

A moment's silence at the other end. "Great idea, I'll do it," the 32-year-old reporter said obediently.

As Rather prepared to race across town to Zapruder's house and assault him, Hewitt sat in the control room and reconsidered his instructions. Giving in to a rare moment of self-doubt, he picked up the phone and called Rather back. "For Christ's sake, don't do what I just told you to," Hewitt said.

It ultimately took more than 30 years for the entire Zapruder film to be shown on network television, much to Hewitt's consternation.

No matter how many rules Hewitt broke or bent in the late 1950s and early 1960s, he was unable to tell stories the way he wanted to, thwarted by the primitive technology that just could not accommodate the complex pieces Hewitt yearned to produce.

One day in 1963, as he dealt yet again with the frustration of being stuck with good pictures that arrived with bad audio, he began tinkering and soon came up with a way to separate the sound track from the picture track—he called them the A and B rolls, terms that have survived to the present. It gave television, at last, a bit of leeway in playing with the mix of pictures and sound.

For Walter Cronkite, Hewitt's effort to make the news entertaining went counter to his own straightforward approach. Hewitt was executive producer of the *CBS Evening News with Walter Cronkite* from its debut in 1962 through its expansion to a 30-minute broadcast on September 15, 1963. Anticipating problems with Hewitt, Cronkite made sure he was given the title and duties of managing editor before he agreed to replace Edwards in 1962. Cronkite was far more hot-blooded than he appeared on television, prone at times to explosive rage. And by 1964 he was running out of patience with Hewitt's style.

At the same time, CBS News was losing in the ratings to NBC's *Huntley-Brinkley Report*, and CBS executives, now under the leadership of Richard Salant, figured they needed new leadership if they had any chance of beating the NBC juggernaut. As experienced as he was, Hewitt just wasn't delivering the numbers.

During preparations for the 1964 political conventions, Cronkite and Hewitt were in regular conflict. Adding to the tension was the fallout from Hewitt's latest stunt. An NBC news producer left an internal guide to the network's coverage of the Republican National Convention in San Francisco lying around within Hewitt's reach—and Hewitt promptly grabbed it. Once NBC realized what had happened, word leaked to the press, and Hewitt was called to task yet again by exasperated bosses.

It got worse. In the fall of 1964, Hewitt's archenemy Fred Friendly was brought in to replace Richard Salant as president of the ailing news division. That presented the perfect opportunity to get Hewitt out.

Four decades later (during which time Hewitt and Cronkite became friends), Cronkite has no trouble recalling their battles and how it was that he demanded Hewitt be removed as his executive producer. "[Hewitt] would not tell me things that were going into the broadcast until the very last minute, and it was too late to make any changes," Cronkite remembered. "And then this incident occurred and that confirmed for me that I didn't have control of this broadcast. There was a specific story that somebody had been promised. I forget the story now; it was not a terribly serious story. But it was serious in that Don had promised it was not going to be used, and then he did use it. The promise had been violated."

Friendly agreed with Cronkite. In December 1964, he called Don Hewitt into his office. This was it, everyone thought. Fred Friendly was going to fire him from CBS at last. After 16 years, Hewitt's time in television had come to an end.

Hewitt went to Friendly's office dragging his feet just a little; no encounter with this particular boss turned out pleasant.

"You know, I've been thinking about this," Friendly told Hewitt once he'd settled into his seat. "The *CBS Evening News* is not big enough for you. You're bigger than that broadcast. I'm going to set up a special unit that'll be yours, and yours alone. I want you to cover the world. You don't even have to check with anyone. Some big story breaks out, just go. You have my blessing. You have your own crews and your own editors. And that's what I want you to do."

Now this was a surprise. Hewitt didn't like Friendly, and vice versa. So why was the network news president talking about this fabulous new job? But then Hewitt, never much for introspection, just decided to accept his promotion with as much grace as he could muster.

"Sounds great, Fred," Hewitt said. "Sounds like a terrific setup. I wouldn't mind getting away from the daily grind." Hewitt told Friendly he'd be ready to switch roles immediately, they shook hands on it, and Hewitt headed back to the newsroom.

Along the way, Hewitt made a quick stop to see Bill Leonard, a good friend who had recently become a CBS News vice president. He barged into Leonard's office to tell him the good news. "Jesus, Bill, guess what?" he blurted. "Fred just decided to give me this great new organization, all mine."

Leonard looked up from his desk and stared at Hewitt, incredulous.

"Don," he said, "you just got fired."

"No, you don't understand, he's . . ."

Hewitt stopped talking and took a rare moment to consider his friend's comment.

"Shit."

"What?"

"You're right," Hewitt said, slowly. "It was Fred's way of sticking a knife in me. Making me think this is some sort of advancement in my career." Like many anecdotes from his life, Hewitt has repeated this one endlessly and with a fluid sense of detail. In his 1985 memoir, *Minute by Minute,* Hewitt attributes the "you just got fired" comment to his then-wife Frankie. But by the time Hewitt wrote his 2002 memoir, *Tell Me a Story,* he'd decided it was Leonard who broke the news.

But one detail is constant: Hewitt, heady with the aphrodisiac that long-term power affords, hadn't seen it coming. After nearly two decades designing the future of the TV news business, he'd just become part of its past.

Chapter 3

Did You Ever Think About *Two* Guys?

Inside the news division—under Friendly's brief, stormy leadership and later, after the return of Richard Salant to the president's office in 1966—the trend had moved away from Hewitt's news-gathering methods. Serious attention was given to making and obeying new rules to govern the growing influence of news coverage. As the technology changed (thanks in part to Hewitt's endless stream of ideas), reporters had new ways to make stories more interesting—at the possible expense of fairness and ethics. The leaders of the news division wanted to cover themselves in case of attack from the growing number of watchdogs and critics assigned to monitor television.

Hewitt had to watch all this from the sidelines, pacing impatiently as history was made, both inside CBS News headquarters and in the world at large. He'd been booted pretty far from the halls of power—the news division moved to new headquarters in a converted milk barn on West 57th Street near the Hudson River, and Hewitt's new office was about as far from Walter Cronkite as you could get. Most people figured that's where he'd stay.

*   *   *

Let other people do the serious documentaries about drugs and war and poverty; Don Hewitt turned his attention to Frank Sinatra.

There was little dispute that *Sinatra,* a one-hour Hewitt-produced profile of the singer that aired in November 1965, was the finest hour of TV he'd ever produced. He somehow recruited Cronkite as his interviewer and host; he got his World War II pal Andy Rooney to write the narration. Hewitt delivered Sinatra at a recording session, on a movie set, at a benefit party, crooning to prisoners, and relaxing at a New York saloon owned by his good friend Jilly Rizzo, with friends like Sammy Davis Jr. at the table. This was front-row access to the most famous man in America.

The interview at Sinatra's Palm Springs home had gone well enough at first. In fact, the two men were hitting it off so well that Hewitt, standing behind the camera, decided to push the performer a little. He stopped the filming and walked across the room. "Ask him about Mia Farrow," Andy Rooney recalled him whispering to Cronkite. The anchorman, unaccustomed to celebrity interviews of this nature, did as he was told.

At which point Sinatra glared over at Hewitt. "You broke the rules and I ought to kill you," Sinatra said, his blue eyes narrowing. (Sinatra later claimed that Hewitt had previously agreed not to include those questions—an agreement Hewitt once again denied having made.)

"With anyone else that's a figure of speech," Hewitt said. "You probably mean it."

"I mean it," Sinatra growled.

"Well, if I had a choice," Hewitt said, "I'd rather you didn't."

Hewitt was beginning to see the risk involved in his approach to journalism. Maybe it was more fun running a show than producing it. After all, he liked life in the power seat, shaping the work of others. So in spare moments between his prosaic producing chores, Hewitt started looking around for something else to do at CBS.

*   *   *

"Perhaps I have been mis-titling my proposal for a new Tuesday night concept," Don Hewitt conceded to his boss, CBS News vice president Bill Leonard, in the fall of 1967, in a memo riddled with typos and cross-outs. "It may be that 'magazine' is not the proper word," he added in a rare moment of modesty.

For months, Hewitt had bombarded Leonard with memos about his idea to create a weekly newsmagazine—a show that would allow pieces more complex than an evening news story but not worth a full hour. Hewitt knew he was staking out uncharted territory in a business still committed to the documentary form, and in his early memos, he hedged his bets. In one, he proposed putting together a staff to produce three 1-hour Tuesday night magazines a month—"every third one to be devoted to a single subject." In another, he proposed the notion of guest columnists. He also pitched a sensibility relatively untouched by anyone else in television at the time, except perhaps the producers of *Laugh-In* and *The Smothers Brothers Comedy Hour.*

"The magazine should be very 'with it,'" Hewitt wrote, "and in today's world being 'with it' connotes a certain amount of irreverence for established institutions."

But who would host this new show? Hewitt's first idea acknowledged his awareness of where he stood in the hierarchy of CBS News, reaching out to a correspondent who—like himself—had plateaued at a level of success that didn't match his own self-perception.

"I think Harry Reasoner should be the on-air editor of the magazine," Hewitt wrote, referring to the white-haired correspondent who was Cronkite's chief substitute as anchor of the *CBS Evening News.* Reasoner was an Iowa farm boy who'd risen through the ranks of radio and television by virtue of his classic middle-American manner and his clear intelligence. He smoked, drank, and fancied himself the dashing correspondent, even though he had a wife and children at home in Connecticut. He'd covered civil rights marches, space launches and political conventions for CBS News and ranked among the top TV news personalities of the day. But Reasoner was waiting for something bigger—like the day Cronkite would step aside and CBS would choose him to take over *CBS Evening News*. In 1967, that day was nowhere in sight and Reasoner was ready to consider other possibilities.

Meanwhile, Hewitt kept flooding his bosses with potential *60 Minutes* story ideas. At one point, he even suggested a segment called "Good Idea!" based on having seen travelers at the Copenhagen airport using scooters to get around. "I thought, 'What a good idea!'" Hewitt wrote. "And then I thought that all we'd have to do is film thirty seconds or so of people riding the scooters and label it this week's GOOD IDEA!" Okay, so it wasn't a good idea—but if you didn't like it, he had several thousand more.

Hewitt got the green light to make a rough pilot with Reasoner in early 1968, made up of edited portions of hour-long CBS documentaries, some never-used footage, and stale chunks of an old Charles Kuralt profile of Henry Ford. Hewitt showed it to everyone he could buttonhole in the hallway and drag into an editing room.

When the lights came up after Hewitt finally showed the pilot to management, there was modest enthusiasm. "Pretty damn good," Bill Leonard allowed. He looked over at Bob Chandler, a vice president working under Bill Leonard, who sat in on the screening.

"Did you ever think about *two* guys?" Chandler said.

"Yeah, like who?" Hewitt demanded.

"Mike Wallace," Chandler replied.

At the time of Chandler's suggestion, Mike Wallace wasn't particularly hot; in fact, the 49-year-old reporter was far less successful than Reasoner, having been pushed aside by a management team that found him too abrasive to be a major player in the TV news business. He was a general-assignment reporter for the *CBS Evening News*, and as he covered the early stages of what looked like a long-shot Nixon presidential campaign, no one considered him as the Next Big Anything. Like Hewitt, Mike Wallace was desperate for a way back to the top.

Hewitt immediately saw Chandler's point: *60 Minutes* might benefit from two hosts balancing off each other, a black hat–white hat arrangement that perfectly suited their sensibilities.

One weekend that spring, Hewitt visited Wallace at his apartment to pitch the possibility of joining *60 Minutes*. Wallace, then covering the early days of the Nixon presidential campaign, figured there was no harm in listening, even though he knew Hewitt had spent much of the last four years in purgatory and suspected CBS would never truly entrust an hour of its prime-time schedule to him. Besides, he didn't like the show's name: *60 Minutes* sounded too pedestrian, Wallace thought. But Hewitt could not be deterred.

"This is going to be a radical departure in both form and content," he told Wallace, as recounted in Wallace's memoir, *Close Encounters*. "Our documentaries are so damn stuffy. . . . Most subjects don't deserve the full hour treatment we give them." Hewitt barely seemed to be stopping for breath.

"You know as well as I do," he went on, "that television practically ignores what the newsmagazines call the back of the book—the arts and sciences and all that stuff. We'll be going into those subjects, and there will be features and profiles of personalities from all walks of life. The idea is to strike a balance between those pieces and the more serious, conventional stories we'll be doing. And Mike, listen to this: You'll have a chance to do your long interviews again. How about *that?*"

Wallace still wasn't convinced, but he was willing to let Hewitt shoot a second pilot with Reasoner and him. They slapped it together quickly—this time using old footage from a documentary about Bobby Kennedy, showing the New York senator on a ski trip with his family. Wallace didn't think very much of it; he later described it as a "banal pastiche of leftovers and outtakes from pieces that had already been on the air"—at least what he saw of it. He didn't even bother to watch the whole thing.

Wallace's path to the crossroads of *60 Minutes* couldn't have differed more from Hewitt's, yet somehow, he was just as anxiously in need of redemption. And so he figured, what the hell. He dropped off the Nixon campaign trail in August 1968 and went to work on Don Hewitt's new show.

*   *   *

Wallace and Hewitt both grew up in immigrant Jewish families, but that's where the similarity ends. While Hewitt, the kid from New Rochelle with the New York accent, scraped his way into journalism through the service entrance, the smooth-talking Wallace sauntered in through the front door in middle age, his notable gifts as an interviewer and television performer already well established.

Young Mike had shown an early interest in theater and spent summers at Interlochen, the fabled music and theater camp in upstate Michigan. By the time he started college at the University of Michigan in 1936, he'd suffered the ravages of teenage acne that he has referred to as disfiguring, though it never seemed to detract from people's desire to look at him. Wallace emerged from college with a degree in broadcasting and got himself a radio job in Grand Rapids, Michigan, which led to a job in Detroit, then one in Chicago. By then he'd married college sweetheart Norma Kaplan and fathered two sons, Peter and Chris.

In 1946, radio station WGN hired Wallace to host a celebrity-interview show called *Famous Names,* sponsored by Walgreens. That's where he chatted one morning with an actress named Buff Cobb, who had come to town to appear in Noel Coward's *Private Lives.* Wallace's marriage to Norma Kaplan skidded to a halt as he began a relationship with Cobb that resulted not only in marriage number two but also a professional partnership on a radio show dreamed up by Wallace called *The Chez Show,* broadcast from a Chicago nightclub.

In 1951, Wallace and Cobb packed up their lives and moved to New York and an afternoon television talk show on CBS called *Mike and Buff.* Built around the notion of the natural bickering between husband and wife, the show dwelled on the specific issues that faced a young married couple (Wallace was 33 when the show first aired). And it worked, at least for a while, allowing Wallace to adjust to a new medium, a new home, and the high-powered lifestyle that came with a network television show.

But after three years CBS pulled the plug on *Mike and Buff.* At the same time it became clear that the on-air bickering was a bit too real; Wallace and Cobb ended their marriage soon after the show was canceled.

That left Wallace at loose ends in the summer of 1954, until he auditioned for a Broadway show, got the gig, and embarked on yet another new career. He played the part of an art dealer in *Reclining Figure*, a comedy by Harry Kurnitz about an art collector who buys a forgery. In the *New York Times*, Brooks Atkinson noted that "Wallace does well with the part of a dealer who comes as close as possible to being on the level." Not exactly a career-launching notice, but it led Wallace into a series of TV commercials. One in particular would come back to haunt him 40 years later as a crusading correspondent for *60 Minutes*—hawking cigarettes for Philip Morris. He would later investigate the tobacco industry as part of a controversial segment about the addictive qualities of nicotine. "Where can you find a man's kind of mildness except in today's Philip Morris?" the suave Wallace asked, puffing smoothly on a cigarette. That became a trademark look for him, much as it had for the biggest star of network news at that moment, Edward R. Murrow.

Mike Wallace decided in 1955 that he belonged in Murrow's profession; little more than a year later, he was hosting *Night Beat* on NBC's New York affiliate. The show was an hour-long interview at 11:00 P.M. four nights a week, in which Wallace honed the in-your-face questioning style that would become his trademark. He loved hitting celebrities with provocative questions or, more often, provocative statements that they were invited to contradict. The first question Wallace asked on his first show (with New York's liberal Democratic mayor, Robert F. Wagner) was, "How do you feel when the *Herald Tribune* calls you a do-nothing mayor?" (Wallace's Republican leanings have since been well established.)

It only got more interesting. "Mrs. Roosevelt, I think you will agree," he said one night to Eleanor Roosevelt, widow of President Franklin D. Roosevelt, "that a good many people hated your husband." Given no room to move, Mrs. Roosevelt—and the audience at home—had little choice but to agree. Audiences loved Wallace's confrontational style; it caught on so fast that less than six months later, ABC hired him away to do a half-hour version of *Night Beat* for a national audience on Sunday nights. He quickly became a force to be reckoned with; comedians like Sid Caesar and Carl Reiner were doing parodies of Wallace, and major critics were writing essays about his impact on the medium. "In a very real sense [Wallace] is a pioneer in electronic journalism of substance," wrote the influential *New York Times* television critic Jack Gould. "He has shown how through the instrument of the TV close-up millions of set owners can gain a new insight into people and how and why they think as they do." But the forward-looking Gould also warned: "By building carefully on a sound journalistic foundation he could achieve a lasting place in national TV; his present risk is that by pushing too hard he may prove to be only a fleeting fad."

Gould's cautionary came true one year later, when ratings declined and Wallace's flagging show lost its sponsors, and the network rescinded its pledge to keep him on the air once a week in prime time. Wallace took *Night Beat* to Channel 13 (then a small independent station in New York). By 1961, it had fizzled completely.

In 1962, as his once-burgeoning career seemed to be settling into decline, Wallace was hit with a personal tragedy that would alter his career forever: the death of Peter, his oldest son. A 19-year-old Yale sophomore, Peter had been reported lost by friends while on summer vacation in Greece. Wallace went in search of him and finally found his body 50 feet below the ledge of a mountain where he had apparently fallen during a hike. The death devastated Wallace, forcing him into some deep soul-searching. Ultimately, with the encouragement of wife number three, a Haitian beauty named Lorraine Perigord, whom he'd met on vacation in Puerto Rico and married in 1955, Wallace disavowed entertainment programming entirely, committing himself to a career in serious journalism instead. "It's the only kind of work that makes you happy," Wallace recalled his wife saying after he told her of his decision. He wrote letters to the heads of the news divisions at

ABC, NBC, and CBS, and in March 1963, he received an offer from Richard Salant at CBS to join his staff as a reporter. Late that summer, after bouncing around the network for a few months in various capacities, Wallace was chosen to be the host of *The CBS Morning News,* a new venture that faced the challenge of competing with NBC's far more successful *Today Show.*

After three years, Wallace left the morning show and moved to a general-assignment reporting position for Cronkite's evening newscast; this took him briefly to Vietnam and the Middle East. By 1968, when he agreed to sign on to Hewitt's new show, he had yet to achieve the success he craved. It was expected that he'd play second banana in the new arrangement, this time to Harry Reasoner.

Reasoner had been at CBS since the mid-1950s, when he arrived as one of the first writers hired by the nascent network news division, after brief stints as a reporter and drama critic for the *Minneapolis Times,* and later as a local TV news director. Before that he'd taken a stab at novel writing: in 1946, at the age of 23, he published *Tell Me About Women.*

At CBS News, Reasoner's wry wit and laconic delivery caught on immediately; within a few years he became one of the network's most dependable reporters, dispatched at a moment's notice to places like Little Rock, Arkansas, where in 1958 he provided distinguished coverage of the school desegregation case. He hosted a network morning show called *Calendar* from 1961 to 1963; replaced by Wallace, Reasoner returned to the daily news beat, reviving his reputation as one of the network's brightest stars. By 1967, he was the anchorman of CBS's Sunday night newscast and the chief substitute for Walter Cronkite on the *CBS Evening News*—not to mention the boyfriend of movie star Angie Dickinson.

The rap on Reasoner—which he went to little effort to shake—was that he was lazy. He loved long lunches at Le Biarritz, a French bistro a couple of blocks from CBS, where he downed martinis before returning to the office for a nap. Between his marriage, his girlfriend, and his passion for food and drink, Reasoner simply didn't have time to devote to forging a future. His prodigious talents as a writer, reporter, and raconteur were keeping him afloat; in those days, such gifts were worth more than the cut of one's jaw line or even the number of reporting trips to foreign capitals.

Those talents were reflected at the end of a typical Sunday night newscast in March 1964, when he capped the news of the day with a bit of quintessential Reasoner drollery: "Elizabeth Taylor, the American actress, and Richard Burton, the Welsh actor, were married today in Montreal. They met two years ago while working on the movie *Cleopatra* in Rome and have been good friends ever since." Pause. "That's the news. This is Harry Reasoner, CBS News. Good night."

Reasoner was always considered good enough to keep skating by, but his options—beyond the anchorman's job—were limited. Reasoner and Hewitt were both far enough from the top that they needed each other, more perhaps than either wanted to admit. Each thought he was doing the other a favor, agreeing to merge talents on a venture that seemed certain to fail.

Chapter 4

The Symphony of the Real World

"Good evening, this is *60 Minutes*," Harry Reasoner said into the camera, then paused for a beat as though startled himself by the sound of it.

Mike Wallace sat stiff and motionless to Reasoner's right, as Reasoner continued: "It's a kind of a magazine for television, which means it has the flexibility and diversity of a magazine, adapted to broadcast journalism." It was 10:00 P.M. on Tuesday, September 24, 1968; perhaps 13 million Americans were watching as TV history was getting made. By the standards of 1968 television ratings, when hit shows routinely attracted 30 million viewers, it was a dismal performance. The sole sponsor of the first episode of *60 Minutes* was Alpo, "the all-meat dog food!"

Over on ABC that night, more Americans were watching *That's Life!* with Robert Morse, a musical comedy series with guest stars George Burns and Tony Randall; everybody else tuned in for Rock Hudson in *Blindfold,* the NBC Tuesday night movie. The debut of *60 Minutes* wasn't helped much by its own CBS lead-in, the leaden debut of *The*

Doris Day Show, in which the former film star played a widow who returns to her family ranch with her two young sons.

Perhaps Hewitt's years in purgatory had given him the stimulus to rush recklessly into the unknown; the opening moments of *60 Minutes* were not the work of a producer who understood the power of finding (rather than manufacturing) drama. Nor was much of what immediately followed. Reasoner segued to the show's first report, a look inside the hotel rooms of presidential candidates Nixon and Humphrey from that summer's political conventions. The story had been Wallace's idea, and Hewitt loved it. But the footage wasn't particularly groundbreaking or even all that revealing. Still, it struck viewers as entertaining to see these two powerful men behind closed doors, in a way that hadn't been shown before, and in a backhanded way it ended up revealing something of the show's intended personality. This wasn't the stuff of a documentary (it was far too inconsequential for that) but it made for far more interesting viewing than a typical campaign piece on the evening news. It was followed by some interstitial and odd humor from two silhouetted commentators.

Up next were three prominent European thinkers of the period — Malcolm Muggeridge of England, Luigi Barzini of Italy, and Peter Van Zahn of West Germany—who weighed in portentously with their thoughts on the American presidential campaign. (Humorist Art Buchwald then offered an American perspective.) The show's third piece, a Mike Wallace interview with Attorney General Ramsey Clark, was executed in the tough-guy mode of the former *Night Beat* host, though this time in the context of a broader story about the police. Gruff and confrontational, Wallace tried to provoke Clark, but the laconic Texan calmly held his ground.

WALLACE: I think Dick Gregory has said that today's cop is yesterday's nigger. Do you understand that?

CLARK: Yes, I understand that, and it's, you know, you've got to be able to recognize wisdom and truth where you find it.

Next came a bizarre vignette about the recent violence at the Democratic National Convention in Chicago, again presented by those two silhouetted figures—written by Andy Rooney, and given voice by him and the show's senior producer, Palmer Williams.

FIRST SILHOUETTE: I know how the cops feel.

SECOND SILHOUETTE: Not being a cop, you can't possibly know how they feel.

FIRST: Not being me, how do you know whether I know how the cops feel?

SECOND: Not being me, how do you know whether I know how you know or not?

FIRST: Thank you.

SECOND: Thank you.

This was followed by *Why Man Creates,* a short film from Saul Bass and commissioned by Kaiser Aluminum, after which Wallace and Reasoner returned for some self-promotional chat.

WALLACE: And there you have our first *60 Minutes* broadcast. Looking back, it had quite a range, as the problems and interests of our lives have quite a range. Our perception of reality roams, in a given day, from the light to the heavy, from warmth to menace, and if this broadcast does what we hope it will do, it will report reality.

Reasoner followed with a statement of odd, homespun media philosophy, perhaps the product of Rooney's typewriter:

REASONER: The reality, as we have suggested, is various; the symphony of the real world is not a monotone. This doesn't necessarily mean you have to mix it up all in one broadcast, but it seems to us that the idea of a flexible attitude has its attractions. All art is the rearrangement of previous perceptions, and we don't claim this is anything more than that, or even that journalism is an art, for that matter. But we do think this is sort of a new approach. We realize, of course, that new approaches are not always instantly accepted. . . .

WALLACE: We'll see. I'm Mike Wallace.

REASONER: We will indeed. I'm Harry Reasoner. *60 Minutes* will be back two weeks from tonight.

The reviews were mixed. "The stories were dated," said *Variety,* "and the magazine format, lifted from print, pretentious." As for its prospects, *Variety* concluded: "If it had been a newspaper, it would not have sold many copies."

The *New York Times* was kinder, calling it "something television has long needed," and said the first episode "explored only a few of the many possibilities open to an imaginative editor." Confirming the very point of Hewitt's concept, the review added: "Not all the segments were of equal interest, but one doesn't expect that in a magazine."

60 Minutes brought in low ratings, but CBS was happy enough to let it continue. It cost far less to produce than a drama show and offered the network a new show to add to the luster of the news division, still a point of pride for CBS chairman William Paley. And for the time being it was filling space.

At the beginning, the show operated with a skeleton staff: Each correspondent had three producers, and the management team consisted only of Hewitt and Palmer Williams, a CBS News producer brought in to run the mechanics of the show. Hewitt lacked any interest in the tedium of budgets and schedules and meetings; that became Williams's job. He preferred to make decisions on the way to the men's room—or *in* the men's room—and since the only women working on *60 Minutes* were secretaries, that didn't impede the process much. Williams had been brought to CBS in 1951 by Edward R. Murrow and Fred Friendly to help produce *See It Now,* after having produced documentaries for, among others, the legendary theater producer John Houseman. The two men worked side by side from the first day of work on *60 Minutes*, but they were fundamentally different; Hewitt aspired to an upper-class lifestyle and fancy friends, while Williams lived downtown in Greenwich Village and wore his bohemian tastes proudly. Like Wallace and Reasoner, they made an oddly perfect match.

By the second episode Hewitt already seemed to be finding the show's voice—an amalgam of Hildy and Hollywood. He offered what by any standard would be viewed as a piece of sensational tabloid journalism: the first of two parts of a Mike Wallace investigation into the secret development of biological weapons, including anthrax. With shots of an ominous building and tanks and, of course, Wallace's highly theatrical delivery underscoring it all as he stood on-camera wearing a scary-looking protective uniform, it screamed to the audience that danger lurked around every corner.

WALLACE: In wars of the future one breath could mean instant death. An invisible odorless cloud could be lethal. The uniform I'm wearing was especially designed to protect a man against nerve gas. The mask protects against both gas and biological agents. If chemical and biological weapons are used in wars of the future, a man will have to have a uniform like this just to stay alive in order to fight.

Wallace tempered neither the tone of his writing nor the timber of his voice as he reported in grim detail the dangers of these toxic substances. In doing so he foretold not only the frightening future of chemical weapons, but also the plan of *60 Minutes* to get noticed at any cost, by delivering stories that begged, even demanded, to be watched.

In that second episode, Wallace also sat down with Richard Nixon, the Republican presidential candidate, who would within a month win the presidency and offer Wallace a job as his press secretary. In that conversation, Wallace would create another ingredient that set *60 Minutes* apart: the newsmaker interview with gravitas. With his Republican leanings and known kinship with Nixon, Wallace used his seductive powers as an interviewer to draw out the inner Nixon. His patented methods still provoked his subject to respond with his own version of the truth, as happened with this telling exchange about Nixon's failed 1960 candidacy for the presidency:

WALLACE: There are those who suggest you were awed, almost overawed by Jack Kennedy's money, social grace, position.

NIXON: Oh, I don't buy that. . . . Believe me, when you've gone through the fires of having to work your way through school, of having to fight campaigns with no money, of having to do it all on your own, you come out a pretty strong man and you're not in awe of anybody.

WALLACE: There's been so much talk in recent years of style and of charisma. No one suggests that either you or your opponent, Hubert Humphrey, have a good deal of it. Have you given no thought to this aspect of campaigning and of leading?

NIXON: Well, when style and charisma connotes the idea of contriving, of public relations, I don't buy it at all. As I look back on the history of this country, some of our great leaders would not have been perhaps great television personalities, but they were great presidents because of what they stood for. . . . The most important thing about a public man is not whether he's loved or disliked but whether he's respected. And I hope to restore respect to the presidency at all levels by my conduct.

Once again, the show's ending and references to the next episode captured the quickly evolving nature of *60 Minutes*—not to mention the differences in style between Reasoner and Wallace.

WALLACE: And we'll have Part Two of that exclusive look that began tonight into the world of chemical and biological warfare.

REASONER: And other wonders, some perhaps as yet undreamed of.

For Wallace and Hewitt, this vastly improved second broadcast demonstrated their real potential as a television team—Hewitt in the screening room in New York, Wallace out in the field. Hewitt was begging for glitz from his correspondents, and Wallace understood how to provide it. He gathered the raw information; Hewitt packaged it for maximum impact. Unlike the plodding pilot, the second episode revealed the promise of real collaboration; it showed the symmetry of their thinking and the common thread that linked them.

"Tick . . . tick . . . tick . . ." was a sound nowhere to be found in the opening credits of *60 Minutes* on its first two episodes. Most of the discussions about the show's opening focused on creating the look of a magazine cover—known as "The Book"—as a backdrop. The show's director, Arthur Bloom, added the image of a Minerva stopwatch to the opening credits of episode 3, on October 22, 1968. (Hewitt has often claimed, incorrectly, that the ticking clock was heard over the closing credits in the first two episodes. "I keep telling him it's not true," Bloom said in May 2004.) After that, Bloom inserted the tick—which was, in fact, the sound of a grandfather clock he had found at a New York sound studio—in between pieces. A few episodes later, a swankier Heuer stopwatch replaced the Minerva. For years, the stopwatch posed significant technical difficulties. The clock had to be filmed in real time; during that process the watch would sometimes fall off its stand, or someone would forget to wind it, causing it to stop prematurely. In the late 1970s, it was replaced by an Aristo, which remains the template for the current stopwatch.

Through the fall of 1968, Wallace and Reasoner traveled around the world in pursuit of stories no one else was doing, or wanted to do. They were trying to figure out how to navigate this brave new world with only one rule to guide them: Make Hewitt happy.

The stories from the early part of that first season rarely rank among those described as classic *60 Minutes* pieces. Hewitt still couldn't settle on a format for the show or the kinds of stories he wanted. The pol-

icy over how to deal with breaking news seemed to shift from week
to week. After no news in the first two episodes, for example, the third
episode included commentary on that week's wedding between
Jacqueline Kennedy and Aristotle Onassis. The "humorous" interludes
of the two silhouettes continued as an interstitial device, even though
they were rarely amusing.

The meat of the broadcast continued to come from Wallace. This
heated Ping-Pong match between Wallace and third-party presidential candidate George Wallace proved the high point of episode 3:

GEORGE WALLACE: Let's get off of race. I'm not a racist. If every-
    body's a racist who's been called one, you're one. How do you
    explain your racism away? The Kerner Commission said that
    you're one and that's a presidential report.
MIKE WALLACE: Well, not me, you're not speaking—
GEORGE WALLACE: It said all the American people.
MIKE WALLACE: Oh, I see what you mean.
GEORGE WALLACE: You're an American.
MIKE WALLACE: Yes.
GEORGE WALLACE: Well, that got you.
MIKE WALLACE: Touché.
GEORGE WALLACE: Touché.

The fourth episode included a wrap-up of that week's election,
which put Richard Nixon into the White House, and a profile of football star Joe Namath. In the shows to follow, it was clear *60 Minutes*
hadn't yet found an identity. Interviews with politicians alternated
with such softballs as a Reasoner profile of *New York Times* food critic
Craig Claiborne.

Perhaps the most successful single feature was Reasoner's reading
of viewers' letters to the show; it provided a nice episode ender and
gave the two men a chance to relax in front of the camera, while gradually building a bond with each other and the audience. Based on the
mail read on episode 4, it was working:

REASONER: A fan at the University of Tennessee wrote: "*60 Min-utes* is wonderful. Does this mean that it will be dropped in a few weeks?" And lastly, this from a student at Catholic University: "Tell Mike Wallace if he continues to imitate David Brinkley he ought to go to NBC. I understand they have a va-cancy." *60 Minutes* returns two weeks from tonight. Good night, Mike.

WALLACE: Good night, Chet.

On Christmas Eve, 1968, Hewitt went for timing over substance. It included the first essay by Andy Rooney—"What Christ Looked Like," read by Reasoner—and was followed by the talking silhouettes—now known as Ipso and Facto, but still not very funny. The episode also included two contemporary icons: a Wallace visit to Martin Luther King Jr.'s family and Reasoner's interview with the widow of Senator Robert F. Kennedy. Perhaps the stories sacrificed weight for emotion, but in Hewitt's view, anything that seemed like it would connect the viewer to the broadcast was a good thing—even if the numbers rarely reflected an audience upsurge. Hewitt continued to trust his impulses as he always had, but in the absence of overt viewer interest it wasn't easy to figure out what worked and what didn't.

Part of what held *60 Minutes* back was the continuing technology constraints of television, which in 1968 remained relatively primitive. Videotape was still not in wide use, and Hewitt preferred the look of film, anyway—and there was no way for him to get film produced, processed, and ready for air without at least 24 hours' lead time. This meant that it was almost impossible for *60 Minutes* to cover breaking news stories, and worse, that the show might never have the feel of immediacy fantasized in its planning stages. Hewitt had little passion for "evergreens," those stories capable of sitting around for months with no news peg to justify their existence. He wanted stories hot off the press, Hildy style.

As fall turned to winter, *60 Minutes* began to find a hint of its own voice and a way to incorporate ongoing events into the show's weekly format. On the episode that aired on January 21, 1969 (only the show's ninth), Reasoner and Wallace illustrated the battle between Israel and Lebanon by telling the story from both sides in one week, with pieces from each correspondent. It may not have redefined TV news, but it was the kind of presentation that might eventually set *60 Minutes* apart from other news shows: the nightly newscasts rarely had room for conceptual thinking like that.

And from the beginning, the pieces had another distinguishing feature that reflected Hewitt's cinematic style: they showcased the correspondent as star. Reasoner and Wallace turned up front and center in early stories, often incorporating their own movements and reporting into the narrative. No one watching *60 Minutes*, even in the first season, would have had a moment's doubt about who was doing the reporting behind these pieces—it was Reasoner and Wallace, right? The viewers at home didn't have to trouble themselves with the disillusioning truth—which was that behind-the-scenes producers did the vast majority of the reporting, while the correspondents swooped in at the last minute to film the on-air interviews. This was a format made to order for a former actor like Wallace or a correspondent like Reasoner, who preferred to leave the heavy lifting to others.

This also left considerable room for humor, such as Wallace's introduction to a Reasoner piece about the Jack Daniel's distillery in Lynchburg, Kentucky, in which he made strong allusions to his costar's affection for liquor:

WALLACE: I think you can understand that as journalists who cover any and everything, there are certain stories that appeal to us more than others. Harry Reasoner has been working on a story for some time now. I don't believe that in all the years I've known Harry, I have ever seen him devote himself to a story more completely and with more apparent pleasure. Herewith that report.

On February 4, 1969, Reasoner weighed in with "Cottage For Sale," a typically laconic ramble that showed a glimpse of what the show could deliver, while defining the incalculable value of an on-site correspondent to pose pertinent and provocative questions. Essentially an interview with the Duke and Duchess of Windsor, the piece included this memorable interchange with the one-time monarch, who was now selling his French cottage years after having so famously abdicated the throne.

REASONER: How old were you, then, when you became king?
THE DUKE OF WINDSOR: Forty-two.
REASONER: And you were king for—
WINDSOR: Ten months.
REASONER: Is that long enough to be king?
WINDSOR: No.

Two weeks later, though, *60 Minutes* was back to its mix of the profound and the predictable, including a report about heavy snowstorms in the Northeast; a timely interview by Mike Wallace of Daniel Cohn-Bendit, the 23-year-old French student-rebel; and a piece by CBS sports reporter Heywood Hale Broun about the high cost of skiing, the kind of fluff one imagines being ordered up by some high-level CBS executive who'd recently been to Aspen and found himself horrified at the bill. The inclusion of Broun also showed a lack of fidelity to the show's basic concept of using only its full-time stars; while Broun had an on-screen persona perfected by years on the evening news, his presence on *60 Minutes* did nothing to enhance the show's intended point of view.

By the spring, as the show settled into a biweekly rhythm, its stories began to feel more in line with Hewitt's grand idea. The April 1, 1969, broadcast included stories about infants born addicted to heroin, Texas billionaire H. L. Hunt, and fatherless German war babies. Wallace, in particular, was hitting his stride, with his interviews demon-

strating a refreshingly pointed style. His Hunt interview elicited responses unlike any heard elsewhere on prime-time television.

WALLACE: Give us a horseback guess as to how much H. L. Hunt
is worth.

HUNT: Well, it would be so—so misleading no one would believe
it, so let's don't.

WALLACE: What do you mean—why misleading?

HUNT: Well, you see, they talk about that I have an income of a
million dollars a week.

WALLACE: Yes.

HUNT: And that is a lot of percent erroneous.

WALLACE: Is it erroneous? It's bigger or smaller than that?

HUNT: As far as I know, I would starve to death with an income
of a million dollars a week.

Hewitt sometimes ran out of original material in those early
episodes. Two weeks later, *60 Minutes* included another short film by
Saul Bass, alongside a freelance interview done for British television
with Teddy Roosevelt's oldest daughter, Alice Roosevelt Longworth,
now 85 years old. A livelier, homemade May 13, 1969, report focused
on young American draft resisters who moved to Canada. During the
final episode of the first season of *60 Minutes* on June 24, 1969, a look
at the slow, steady sinking of Venice into the sea was sensationally
(though perhaps with some prescience) called "The Death of Venice."

Hewitt, as always, wanted headlines. From his earliest days in television Hewitt knew and respected the capacity of print to promote the
cause. For all of television's supposed power, its impact couldn't be
quantified by the size of its audience. He wanted to see the impact of
his stories on the front page of the newspaper, with copious coverage
of his show and its ambitious agenda. He craved reviews and praise
but would just as soon settle for controversy and outrage—either pro-

duced headlines. It frustrated Hewitt that, for its first year, the show generated hardly any press at all.

But the mere existence of *60 Minutes* on the CBS schedule in the fall of 1969 for a second season somehow seemed to make the show more newsworthy—and perhaps its survival was itself amazing, considering how few people watched it. The show ranked 83rd out of 103 prime-time shows that season. But the network still had nothing more noteworthy to put in the Tuesday 10:00 P.M. slot, and this season ABC had developed a new medical drama with Robert Young that looked like it might work, a little something called *Marcus Welby, M.D.*

Repeating his first-season pattern, Hewitt launched the second year of *60 Minutes* with a yawn-inducing episode that tried too hard to attract attention—which in itself showed Hewitt's apparent bias toward Wallace, despite Reasoner's seniority.

The show opened with a Wallace investigation into a battle over valuable Alaskan land, which ended with Wallace reading a stanza from a Carl Sandburg poem. A piece followed about Moscow at night; then came another Wallace report about a soldier confined to a sweatshop at Camp Pendleton (based on a story previously published in *The Nation*), and, finally, a Reasoner story on racial discrimination by labor unions. But this time the show played better with the newspaper boys. "A varied TV magazine, as it were," the *New York Times* raved, "with almost limitless potentialities in electronic journalism."

Two months later, the *Times* put a *60 Minutes* story on its front page for the first time—an interview by Mike Wallace with Paul Meadlo, a 22-year-old Vietnam veteran who said he had been part of the team of soldiers ordered by Lt. William Calley Jr. to kill men, women, and children in a March 1968 attack on the Vietnamese village of Songmy. The scoop resulted from reporting done by freelance journalist Seymour Hersh, who went on to win the Pulitzer Prize for the story—and who used *60 Minutes* as a way of promoting his account. (The *Times* story raised a rumor that *60 Minutes* had paid for the interview, which Hersh denied.)

Midway through the second season, Wallace made news with an

interview with Eldridge Cleaver, at the time a fugitive from justice and, as a leader of the Black Panther Party, which advocated the violent overthrow of the U.S. government, one of the most controversial figures in American radical politics. Cleaver had been arrested a year earlier in a police shoot-out at Panther headquarters in Oakland, California, and later charged with assault with intent to kill; he fled the country to avoid a trial. In the winter of 1970 he was living in exile in Algeria when Wallace (who had contacts in the black community from an interview years earlier with Malcolm X) reached him by phone and asked for an interview. After some delicate negotiations (Cleaver first asked for money, then settled for a tape recorder pedal to aid in the transcription of tapes for his forthcoming memoir), Wallace left for Algeria on New Year's Day, 1970.

The interview itself made up only a few minutes of the story about the Panthers, but garnered headlines nevertheless:

WALLACE: When the American people hear that you want to shoot your way into the United States Senate, take off the head of a senator—

CLEAVER: Into the White House and take off the head of Richard Nixon, you see.

WALLACE: What does that mean? This is rhetoric?

CLEAVER: This is not rhetoric.

After the story aired, Wallace knew exactly what it meant when he saw the headlines in newspapers around the country, and when the Justice Department subpoenaed notes and outtakes from the interview. It meant *60 Minutes* had finally arrived.

Chapter 5

Mr. Hewitt's War

In spite of the increasingly positive critical reception, the ratings remained just as bad in the second season. *Marcus Welby, M.D.* was an instant monster hit for ABC, the number one show on television, whereas *60 Minutes* ranked 92nd out of 103 any prime-time series and stayed alive only because of its low cost to CBS. The fact that it was on just twice a month also meant its ratings didn't drag on the network's overall numbers, which were bolstered by top 10 shows like *M*A*S*H* and *All in the Family*.

But the show's future didn't get any brighter when in November 1970, two months into the show's third season, Harry Reasoner announced to Hewitt that he was jumping to the fledgling ABC News, where he would finally get to anchor the evening newscast every night of the week. As Reasoner had been fond of saying, Walter Cronkite was showing no inclination toward walking in front of a speeding truck.

Reasoner could have remained with *60 Minutes*, of course, but the idea of cohosting a low-rated prime-time show that ran every other week, when it wasn't being preempted, lacked sufficient appeal for a man accustomed to the fame that came from anchoring a nightly network newscast, not to mention the better hours and lighter workload. While Wallace was happy with his newfound berth as Hewitt's hatchet man, Reasoner rankled at the notion that this might be the end of the line for him. CBS News management continued to think of him as lazy, and he knew there wasn't much chance of advancement, whereas the opportunity to anchor the evening news on ABC represented a step forward, as well as more money for less effort. His decision to leave *60 Minutes* turned out to be surprisingly effortless.

The first call Hewitt made after getting Reasoner's resignation was to Charles Kuralt.

By the fall of 1970, the talented CBS News correspondent had become a household name with a series of oddball reports he'd been doing for the Cronkite show called "On the Road," in which Kuralt and a cameraman would pile into a Volkswagen bus and drive across the United States in search of stories. Kuralt began his "On the Road" reports in the fall of 1967 from Vermont and New Hampshire, where he kicked things off with an elegy to fall foliage. ("To drive along a Vermont country road in this season is to be dazzled by the shower of lemon and scarlet and gold that washes across your windshield.") Within months, Kuralt had found himself a permanent assignment and a huge following among viewers. His deep, distinctive voice and affable personality appealed to an audience in search of comfort in the midst of an unpopular war in Southeast Asia and student unrest at home—and to a producer like Hewitt who needed a new big-name anchor for his struggling Tuesday night show. But Kuralt had no interest in giving up his gig, going into its fourth year; besides, he had his own issues with Hewitt's style. He hated Hewitt's propensity to cut things short, believing his limited attention span would be the ruin of ruminative stories of the sort Kuralt wrote.

After Kuralt refused Hewitt, the next candidate was Morley Safer, then the London bureau chief of CBS News, an erudite Canadian who'd made a considerable name for himself reporting from such foreign battlegrounds as Vietnam, Nigeria, and Northern Ireland. Safer grew up in Toronto, where his father owned an upholstery business. In 1951, he was hired as a reporter on the Woodstock, Ontario, *Sentinel-Review*. From there he made his way to a job with the Canadian Broadcasting Company, where at first he was more producer than correspondent. He wrote copy for the nightly newscast before being switched to a show called *CBC Newsmagazine,* which bore a vague resemblance to the format later perfected by *60 Minutes* (a point that still rankles Safer in less charitable moments). Later, he moved to London and covered the 1956 Israel-Egypt war for Canadian television.

For several years he reported from Africa and Europe until he was hired away by CBS News in 1964 by Fred Friendly, who made him the number two correspondent in London and sent him almost immediately to the growing conflict in Vietnam. In October 1965, Safer and two CBS cameramen were shot down in a helicopter 280 miles north of Saigon. In 1966, the *New York Times* reported that the assistant secretary of defense had written to Friendly objecting to a Safer story—one that showed U.S. Marines burning a South Vietnamese village at Cam Ne.

On November 12, 1970, Bill Leonard called Safer in Paris, where he was covering the funeral of French president Charles de Gaulle, to offer him the *60 Minutes* job. "Shit, can you call back in a year?" was Safer's response. He had a new baby daughter born the previous April, and the family had just moved into a newly renovated house in London. The 39-year-old foreign correspondent, a dandyish dresser with a taste for the finer things, rather liked his London life—which included the ownership of an antique Rolls Royce—and wasn't sure he wanted to give it up for such a long-odds gamble. He got CBS's assurance that if *60 Minutes* got canceled, he could have his old job back. Safer spent just one night in that London house before accepting the job on *60 Minutes* and moving to New York.

By this time, Wallace had firmly established his reputation as maniacally competitive; his aggressive and often flamboyant approach to the show meshed seamlessly with Hewitt's. He, too, loved the spotlight—Reasoner's fame had gotten in his way, and once he was gone

Wallace saw no further obstacles to becoming the lead correspondent of *60 Minutes*. He and Safer had met only once before—in London, when Wallace and his wife went to the theater one night with Safer and his wife, Jane—and he'd come away thinking that Safer wasn't going to be a threat. Safer's position as newcomer would allow Wallace to exercise his muscle as senior partner, and become the most famous face on *60 Minutes*.

Safer, of course, had other ideas. The competition began immediately, resulting in fierce fighting over ideas, producers, and position on the broadcast and raging battles between the two men, with hallway screaming matches, of the "Fuck you!" "No, fuck you!" variety, alternating with extended periods of angry silence. Both men still readily acknowledge their history of battles, though describe each other now as friendlier adversaries, if not friends. "We went a couple of years without speaking," Wallace says. "It was unpleasant," agrees Safer. Hewitt merely shrugs at the memory of those days, perhaps recalling his own steady diet of raging conflicts with both men.

On March 16, 1971, Safer and his producer Joseph Wershba (a distinguished alumnus of the Murrow era, who had produced the famous *See It Now* broadcast about Senator Joseph McCarthy) delivered the first major *60 Minutes* investigation of government corruption: "What Really Happened at the Gulf of Tonkin?" On August 4, 1964, a reported attack on two U.S. destroyers, the *Maddox* and *Turner Joy,* was used to justify the first bombing of North Vietnam. Their report, six years after the fact, raised doubts about the attack, strongly suggesting that the Pentagon may have altered facts about the events. The piece would earn *60 Minutes* its first Emmy award in the fall of 1971.

In April 1971, Wallace and Hewitt traveled to the LBJ Ranch for an interview with the former president, a conversation in which Wallace had been forbidden to ask Johnson about Vietnam, only to have Johnson bring it up himself and make headlines.

JOHNSON: Throughout our history our public has been prone to attach presidents' names to the international difficulties. You will recall the War of 1812 was branded as Mr. Madison's War, and the Mexican War was Mr. Polk's War, and the Civil War or War Between the States was Mr. Lincoln's War, and World War I was Mr. Wilson's War, and World War II was Mr. Roosevelt's War, and Korea was Mr. Truman's War, and President Kennedy was spared that cruel action because his period was known as Mr. McNamara's War. And then it became Mr. Johnson's War, and now they refer to it as Mr. Nixon's War in talking about getting out. I think it is very cruel to have that burden placed upon a president because he is trying to follow a course that he devotedly believes is in the best interest of his nation. And if those presidents hadn't stood up for what was right during those periods, we wouldn't have this country what it is today.

After three seasons on Tuesday nights, CBS programmers moved *60 Minutes* to Sunday at 6:00 P.M. CBS News president Richard Salant, among many others, fought the switch, believing that the network wanted to dump its best prime-time news offering into the "ghetto" of Sunday afternoons. Public affairs programming always took that slot. While it didn't compete with hit prime-time shows on other networks, it suffered from its position following professional football on most Sundays in the fall—meaning frequent last-minute preemptions of the broadcast and an erosion of an audience it had worked so hard to find.

In any case, a regular Sunday night slot meant doubling the number of pieces, doubling the workload—and doubling the potential for loud, angry conflict. Within one year of Safer's arrival, the atmosphere at *60 Minutes* had transformed from the leisurely pace of a biweekly production to the frenzy of a weekly circus. The intense rivalry emerging between Safer and Wallace cost the *60 Minutes* crew much of the collegiality that marked the show's earliest days. They were working harder than ever on a broadcast that still hadn't found its footing, and the result was a toxic and exhausting environment—mitigated somewhat by the exhilaration of creating something that existed nowhere else on television. Most weeks, the producers and correspondents worked late on Saturday night to get their stories ready for a Sunday broadcast; in a few rare instances, the show went on live. As hard as it became, no one minded the long hours and many seemed to thrive on the constant battles. The yelling had begun in earnest. This was Mr. Hewitt's War.

The cacophony at *60 Minutes* stemmed from Hewitt's own long-standing love of loudness. He had long been notorious for barking orders, shouting at underlings and intimidating colleagues with his famously foul language. While it seemed fitting for a nightly news show with the attendant deadlines and tensions, its constant presence on the set of a weekly newsmagazine seemed less a matter of necessity than of habit; it was simply how Hewitt communicated and always had. And sometimes it merely reflected his unbridled and unmatched enthusiasms.

"Come here and fucking look at this!" he would scream after screening a piece for the first time, walking the halls to gather every producer, secretary, and correspondent he could find to get them to see what was so amazing. It remained a relatively small staff, and it didn't take much to cram everyone into the screening room to see the latest cut of a piece. In spite of the bluster, Hewitt's democratic quality endeared him to his staff; he was always reaching out to anyone for an opinion or at least a sign of approval.

But he could also scream louder and longer than anyone on the floor and was viewed less as a mediator than a catalyst for conflict among the correspondents and producers. Everybody loved to pepper their conversations with obscenities, and the words "Fuck you!" could often be heard in the hallways. Just as often, Wallace or Hewitt would walk out of a conversation or screening as a way of making a point to the other. Hewitt, in particular, was also known as a man capable of apology, but it could take a while to arrive.

The yelling was only a small component in a system of story development and production that was unique in television. While most other news shows followed the top-down edicts of an executive producer, *60 Minutes* content came from the reporters and correspondents. Each producer's responsibility was to develop ideas appropriate to his own correspondent, then make a case for the story, first to the correspondent and then to Hewitt via the Blue Sheet, the term for a written proposal. Once the Blue Sheet was approved, that would give the correspondent the exclusive right to the story.

Of course, this prompted producers to "Blue Sheet" story ideas that seemed far-fetched at the time—producers liked to cite "An Interview With God" as the classic wishful Blue Sheet—but nevertheless would lock in the assignment. At that point, the two correspondents might find themselves in Hewitt's office, yelling obscenities at each other over rights to the story. Eventually, one would storm out in anger, slam his office door shut, and stop speaking to the other—sometimes for days and weeks, if not months.

But the unlimited freedom to develop stories and the chaotic, competitive nature of the *60 Minutes* shop also led to a level of creativity unheard of elsewhere in television news.

Around the time the show moved to Sunday night in the fall of 1971, a young former reporter for *Time* magazine named Barry Lando was working a dead-end assignment on the *CBS Weekend News*. He'd been brought on as assistant manager of the CBS Midwest bureau in Chicago, just in time for the 1968 Democratic Convention and its historic aftermath, not to mention the ghetto riots and campus uprisings of that period. His work in Chicago earned him a transfer to New York. Full of energy and ambition, Lando devoted his spare time to writing memos to Don Hewitt at *60 Minutes*, pushing ideas and stories. He made the impolitic move of fighting Mike Wallace over turf rights to a story in Vietnam and discovered that Wallace had the kind of supreme authority he lacked—and craved.

At the start of the show's fourth season, Hewitt called Lando with an offer to join a new "breaking news" team the show was forming to

better cover last-minute stories. He and Phil Scheffler, a Hewitt protégé from the Douglas Edwards days, would be charged with racing
around the world in search of fresh footage and unique angles on that
day's news events. A challenge, Lando thought, but reason enough to
grab the chance to work at the network's hottest news show.

Lando and Scheffler spent weeks trying to work out the logistics
of the plan before finally abandoning it as unrealistic; given the constraints of current technology, there was no way to get film ready for air
with enough time left to prepare good stories. The biggest breaking-
news story of the day was in Vietnam. How would they ever be able
to cover it better than the reporters on the scene?

But Lando was now a part of *60 Minutes*, and Wallace saw his arrival as another chance to sharpen the focus on investigative journalism. By then the crack team of producers ranged from young, energetic men like Lando to older, seasoned producers like Scheffler (who
began at CBS as Hewitt's copyboy in 1951) and Wershba. Wallace
wanted them to chase stories that would keep shocking people and
earn the loyalty of an audience grown cynical about government and
power.

Right away, Lando got an assignment taken straight from the pages
of the alternative press—a provocative article in *The Washington
Monthly* about government officials and legislators sending their kids
to ritzy Washington private schools while supporting government-
enforced busing policies. The result was a celebrated piece that contained what may have been the first truly magical moment in the
history of *60 Minutes*.

Lando and Wallace went to the district's elite schools, including
Georgetown Day School and St. Alban's School for Boys, and discovered that the parent rosters included liberals like Supreme Court Justice Thurgood Marshall and Senator Edward Kennedy, as well as such
commentators as the *New York Times* Tom Wicker and the *Washington Post*'s editor Ben Bradlee. With Wallace as his front man, Lando

tried to shame the liberals who refused to comment on camera. Standing in front of the Senate Office Building, Wallace told viewers: "We asked Senator Kennedy to talk to us, but he declined."

The magic arrived as Lando, Wallace, and a film crew stood near Capitol Hill where Wallace was interviewing Walter Fauntroy, the black liberal congressman who represented the District of Columbia in Congress, and whose child attended Georgetown Day School. In a bit of pure serendipity, just as Fauntroy was defending his position, a group of anti-busing picketers walked by, including a white woman with an anti-busing placard who walked directly behind Fauntroy. "Mike!" Lando hissed at his correspondent. "Look over there!"

Wallace saw the woman and waved her over. What followed went directly into the piece, this way:

WALLACE: As we were talking, nearby about a hundred and fifty representatives of anti-busing groups from across the country were protesting in front of the Supreme Court. After their protest, a group of the ladies from Texas and Michigan walked past the Capitol, where Congressman Fauntroy and I were talking.

FAUNTROY: Going to have to—

WALLACE: May I interrupt you for just a second. Ladies, would you come over here for just a second? We had no idea that you were coming. This is Congressman Fauntroy from the District of Columbia, and we're talking about the very subject of busing at this instant. Now, is it because you are—obviously you're hardly going to suggest that you're racists—is it because it's race or is it education that you're against forced busing?

WOMEN: Education.

WOMAN: The children cannot get an education on a bus all day long. I don't care how you spell it or write it, they cannot do it.

FAUNTROY: The assumption is that your children will suffer because of the quality of education that is achieved through busing. And we are definitely at odds at that point.

At which point, Wallace tried to ask the women a question about the need for busing to accomplish the goals of integration. But they still had questions of their own.

WOMAN: May I ask you a question? Where do their children go to school? Private schools or public schools? Eliot Richardson, where does his kids go to school? Kennedy, where does his kids go to school?

FAUNTROY: Yes, the answer is, I believe, that all of them have their children in private schools—

WOMAN: Well, let's get them out—

WOMAN: And get us all on this socialistic trend, all on the same level.

FAUNTROY: I have my child in a private school. Let me finish—

WOMAN: Then you're discriminating against me because my child's in a public school that's integrated. . . .

WOMAN: Now, you are our leaders and we ask you as our leaders to provide an example. If you truly believe that a child may get a quality education in a racially balanced school, we think that you should step forward and say, "Here is my child, and I want to put him in a racially balanced school." That's all we ask.

When the piece, entitled "Not to My Kid, You Don't," aired on November 14, 1971, Fauntroy accused *60 Minutes* of setting him up. But Lando knew better. He'd gotten a perfect illustration, on his very first piece for the show, of the kind of alchemy that seemed to descend upon *60 Minutes* in its pursuit of stories.

Much of the creative chemistry was fostered by the absence of discernible rules. Lando and his fellow producers loved the freedom and latitude that came with no meetings, no memos, and few, if any, real policies. That may be what prompted Lando, less than two months after the Washington piece aired, to deliver a boundary-stretching piece to Hewitt on amnesty for Vietnam draft resisters. This would be the first in-depth look American TV would take at the fate of the young men who'd moved to Canada on principle and now wanted to come home—with no legal consequences.

The interviews he got were candid and provocative, but the story's first cut came in at 35 minutes—more than twice the length of a typical *60 Minutes* piece. After screening it, he returned to the editing room to search for five minutes to cut. But those five minutes couldn't be found, and Hewitt—not bound by any particular rules about length—agreed to run it as it was. Thus Lando's second story was another in classic Hewitt form, a dramatic collection of interviews that together told the story of these embittered afterthoughts to the Vietnam nightmare, including this extraordinary emotional conversation between Wallace and Gertrude Duff, the mother of a deserter seeking amnesty.

WALLACE: What do you say, what is your feeling about the, I suppose, the millions of Americans who are saying to themselves at this moment, "Look, they turned their back on this country, they turned their back on their duty. Let them stay up there and rot." Mrs. Duff?

MRS. DUFF: That's a tough question because that's the way I felt, but if nothing else comes of this, I think my son has caused us to open our minds a little bit, which on—I think was pretty closed on this issue. Red, white, and blue, that's me, that's what I've always been. . . . But basically, the way our son feels, basically, it's the same as we feel. But it's a whole new different way of looking at things and doing things. Sometimes I look at him and I think he has more moxie than I would ever have had at that age. I know at that age I was—always had dreams. I dreamed of great things, but I never really carried them through. But I think he has a dream, an idea, and I think he's doing something about it.

WALLACE: And to the mothers and fathers of the kids who fought and some of them were wounded and some of them died, what do you say to them?

MRS. DUFF: Oh, I put myself in their place and it's—

At that moment, Wallace had signaled to the cameraman to stop filming. It was clear to everyone at the interview that Mrs. Duff was about to start crying. What was less apparent was that legendary tough-guy Mike Wallace—the father of two sons, one now deceased—was also on the verge of tears. It turned out there was only so much Wallace's black hat could hide.

Chapter 6

Is There a Question in There Somewhere?

Up until the fall of 1972, *60 Minutes* used its investigative muscle to champion the point of view of the little guy—the man with the beer and the Barcalounger who lived in Hewitt's head. Exposés, profiles, and investigations were all geared toward protecting those without the clout of a network news division. There were no sacred cows. But ultimately, how could that square with Hewitt's need to be a player—to be inside the power structure? As the successful and prominent executive producer of a prime-time series entering its fifth season, Hewitt wrestled increasingly with this dilemma, trying to strike a balance between his personal desire for acceptance by those richer and more powerful and his professional commitment to tough journalism.

The Nixon administration quickly crystallized this conflict—for Hewitt and for Wallace, who continued to admire the man who'd only a few years earlier offered him a job in the White House. By late 1972, when the rest of the news media had begun to cover the Watergate scandal as an ongoing story, their ambivalence was starting to show.

60 Minutes had never directed its editorial efforts toward aggressive coverage of Nixon. Wallace had scored an early coup in getting

Vice President-elect Spiro Agnew to sit for an interview in January 1969, before his inauguration—and the result was a gentle chat. (Agnew memorably used the occasion to predict that after the first year of the Nixon presidency, he would prove so crucial to the workings of government that "it's going to be very difficult for the people who are attempting to cast me in the role of the Neanderthal man to continue to think that way.") On May 26, 1970, 24-year-old Tricia Nixon took Wallace and Reasoner on an embarrassingly sycophantic tour of the White House's private quarters. (When Wallace gently probed as to whether the cigars in a White House humidor might be Cuban, Tricia replied: "No, I don't think they're Cuban cigars because Fidel Castro hasn't been here on a state visit for a long time.") On October 13, *60 Minutes* delivered a less than devastating profile of Henry Kissinger, Nixon's national security adviser and the architect of his Southeast Asian bombing strategy.

On November 24, Wallace finally managed to at least touch on a small bit of controversy, with an edgy profile of embattled Interior Secretary Walter Hickel, who had famously written a letter to the president urging him to become more responsive to student protesters. But then the episode of February 2, 1971, returned to the softball treatment with an inside account of the preparations for a White House state dinner. A year later, on February 13, 1972, viewers were treated to a tour of Air Force One. Clearly, if there was one American institution that didn't panic when *60 Minutes* called, it was the White House.

It wasn't until April 2, 1972, that even a hint of federal government scandal turned up on *60 Minutes*. Dita Beard, a lobbyist for International Telephone & Telegraph, had been linked to a memorandum that implied a connection between the company's contribution to the 1972 Republican Convention and the settlement of three antitrust cases with the company. Wallace had known Beard from his days as a political reporter, and almost a week after testifying to a Senate subcommittee from her Denver hospital bed, Beard consented to slip out to meet secretly with Wallace. A two-column headline on page 75 of the next day's *New York Times*—"Mrs. Beard Defies Her Doctors to Give an Interview to CBS"—revealed the growing stature of the show, at least as measured by its ability to generate headlines.

With the unfolding of the Watergate scandal, and the stories that swirled around Nixon during the fifth season of *60 Minutes*, the basic contradiction of Hewitt's character became more pronounced even as his show became more successful. The straddle became more painful and awkward: the rest of the media was going toe-to-toe with the establishment just as Hewitt was becoming so much a part of it.

The show worked best when it shined its spotlight on human-scale corruption—as Wallace demonstrated on February 4, 1973, with a chilling expose of Lieutenant Colonel Anthony Herbert, a Vietnam War veteran and hero who had charged his commanding officers with covering up war crimes.

Herbert had claimed for years that he was removed from his command because of his efforts to call attention to the crimes. Those charges had gotten considerable play in the news media, where many reporters had found fame by reporting on wartime atrocities. However, dogged investigation by Wallace's producer Barry Lando discovered that Herbert's claims could not be verified, particularly some of those in *Soldier,* a book he'd written recounting his Vietnam experiences.

This led to one of the great theatrical stunts in the early years of *60 Minutes,* in which Wallace, in the middle of his interview with Herbert, announced that a fellow officer who'd served in Vietnam, Major Jim Grimshaw, was waiting in the next room ready to refute Herbert's account. Wallace, looking serious if not gloomy, brought no theatrics whatsoever to the interview, the substance of the moment offering plenty.

HERBERT: Bring him in.
WALLACE: Fine. . . .
HERBERT: Good. And ask him the same questions.
WALLACE: You can ask him whatever questions you want to. Here he is right now. (*Grimshaw enters.*)

HERBERT: Hello, Jim.

GRIMSHAW: Hi. How are you doing?

HERBERT: Very fine.

WALLACE: Jim, have you heard what's been going on between the Colonel and me?

GRIMSHAW: Yes.

HERBERT: Okay . . .

WALLACE: Have you read the book? Have you read the book?

GRIMSHAW: Yes, I have read the book.

WALLACE: Do you think it's accurate, by and large?

GRIMSHAW: Well, before the incidents—we have to talk about the incidents that I'm personally involved in.

WALLACE: All right. Sure.

GRIMSHAW: So now we're talking about three incidents when you get right down to it.

WALLACE: And you've told me—

GRIMSHAW: I'm telling you two-thirds, then, are not true.

It was a stunning television moment, the kind of journalism *60 Minutes* was best at—exposing cons pulled on the news media and, by extension, the American public. The story made more headlines after Herbert decided to sue *60 Minutes* for libel, in a case that went all the way to the Supreme Court. Ultimately the court ruled in 1979 that Herbert, as a public figure, had the right to examine the internal motivations—the state of mind—of the journalists who had sought to ruin his reputation. The case became a landmark of libel law. In years to come, some believed it contributed to a pall cast over investigative journalists. In 1986, a federal appeals court threw out Herbert's suit, saying he had no grounds for his libel claims against Lando, Wallace, and CBS.

The show's first Watergate-related piece showed up on May 20, 1973, shortly after print reporters Bob Woodward and Carl Bernstein collected their Pulitzer Prize for reporting on the Watergate break-in and cover-up for the *Washington Post*. Called "Teapot Dome," this "explainer" piece reviewed the scandal that had rocked the administration of President Warren Harding, in the early 1920s—meaning it as a kind of precursor of current events.

At around the same time, Hewitt had fired the hugely entertaining Nicholas von Hoffman as a *60 Minutes* commentator. Von Hoffman, an unabashedly outspoken liberal, described Nixon one week as "a dead mouse on the kitchen floor that everyone was afraid to touch and throw in the garbage." Whatever Hewitt's politics might have been, any visitor to his office knew how much he treasured the moments spent inside the greatest office of them all: the Oval Office. His walls were plastered with pictures of Hewitt standing alongside several American presidents, including Truman, Eisenhower, and Kennedy.

In the absence of fresh reporting by Safer and Wallace, the investigative strengths of *60 Minutes* were largely not in evidence during the Watergate period. Instead, the show found its Watergate voice during a June 1973 Wallace interview with John Ehrlichman, Nixon's former chief domestic adviser, shortly after Nixon fired him and chief of staff H. R. Haldeman, his hand forced by numerous disclosures concerning their role in the Watergate cover-up. Wallace had pursued both men for interviews. Ehrlichman was the first to agree, a decision he would come to regret.

Like most public villains who appear on *60 Minutes*, Ehrlichman believed he had a better shot at redemption if he "chatted" in America's living rooms than if his remarks were on the printed page. This turned out to be naive. It was in the Ehrlichman interview (which aired on June 29, 1973, in the midst of the Senate Watergate Committee hearings) that Hewitt and Wallace made most effective and memorable use of the tight close-up camera technique first used on Wallace's old *Night Beat*. Every bead of sweat on Ehrlichman's face was visible—this was enough to make even the most innocent of men appear nervous and guilty—and Wallace peppered him relentlessly with tough questions about the break-in and its aftermath.

WALLACE: You sent some pretty sloppy guys to do that high security work.

EHRLICHMAN: Well—

WALLACE: Agreed?

EHRLICHMAN: I certainly—can't disagree with that in terms of
that—that break-in business. There's no way to—to condone
that.

And later:

WALLACE: Did you see Senator Weicker enumerate a list of the
illegal or unconstitutional or unethical acts committed by
various persons, either in the White House or employed by
officials of the White House?

EHRLICHMAN: No, I didn't.

WALLACE: Let me read them—a list of acts committed by people
in the White House or employed by people in the White House
or employed by people in the Cabinet, you know what I'm saying: Breaking and entering. Wiretapping. Conspiracy to foster
prostitution. Conspiracy to commit kidnapping. Destruction of
government documents. Forgery of State Department documents and campaign letters. Secret slush funds. Laundering
money in Mexico. Payoffs to silence witnesses. Perjury. Plans
to audit tax returns for political retaliation. Theft of psychiatric
records. Spying by undercover agents. Bogus opinion polls.
Plans to firebomb a building. Conspiracy to obstruct justice.
And all of this by the law-and-order administration of Richard
Nixon.

EHRLICHMAN: Is there a question in there somewhere?

* * *

Despite high-profile stories and better-than-average critical reception,
the show continued to bottom out in the ratings. One day in the spring
of 1973, a recently hired *60 Minutes* producer named Harry Moses

(brought in by Hewitt and Wallace on the basis of a freelance piece
they'd seen) took advantage of the free-for-all atmosphere by pitching
a story based on a single word: pimps. Moses, a wiry young man with
an inventive mind and an acute TV sense, had no particular idea what
he wanted to say about them, or where he would find them, or whether
there was anything to report about them at all. Nevertheless, all he had
to do was nail Hewitt in a hallway. "Hey, Don," Moses said to Hewitt one
morning on the way to the bathroom, "how about a story about pimps?"

"Kid, that sounds great, let's do it," Hewitt replied. That was all
it took for Moses to devote the next several weeks to the seamy world
of prostitution. Operating without supervision or limits, Moses then
had the latitude to craft the story any way he wanted. The result,
which aired on Friday, August 31, 1973, was energetic and just a little wild, more like something from a counterculture 1960s newspaper
than a 1970s network news show. In fact, *60 Minutes* had been influ-
enced as much by contemporary print media as by anything else then
on national television. While *Life* magazine was Hewitt's stated model,
more often the show resembled the weekly city publications that
became popular across the country in the late 1960s. The show's fas-
cination with rip-offs and restaurants, drugs and sex, echoed the
alternative press, or even *New York Magazine,* at that moment a hot
new weekly under the leadership of its own innovative editor, Clay
Felker. Even Safer's writing bore the imprint of the new journalism
(with a bit of the dandy Englishman thrown in) as it dove straight into
its dicey subject.

SAFER: Pimp! The dictionary's not certain of the origin of the
word, but that's not important. Everyone knows what it means.
It used to be that pimps were part of the sleazy underground
of every big city. But today they've come out in the open. They
get interviewed in the slick magazines. Their customized cars
("pimpmobiles") and their foppish clothes make fashion news.
Almost all pimps are black. They give themselves names like
Hollywood, Silky, Dandy and Snake. Who are they? How do

they get women to prostitute themselves? *60 Minutes* looked into the world of the pimp—the man who would be nothing without his woman.

Moments later, Safer interviews Silky:

SAFER: This is Silky, who describes himself as having a Ph.D. in pimping. He claims to earn as much as the president: $200,000 a year. He wears a $5,000 watch and a $4,500 ring. Pimps are nothing if they're not conspicuous consumers. *(To Silky)* You know, the word "pimp" has a certain pejorative sound. It's a nasty word. Does it bother you?

SILKY: To whom?

SAFER: To many people. To myself, for example.

SILKY: Not—not to an individual who's dedicated their life to it.

SAFER: You talk about it almost as though it's a very special calling.

SILKY: Well, that's just what I feel.

SAFER: Describe a typical day—a typical day in your life. How does it start?

SILKY: I wake up, decide whether to go out, or decide whether to go back to sleep.

SAFER: That's it?

SILKY: That's typical.

SAFER: That's all you do all day?

SILKY: Practically. . . .

SAFER: Would you rather be doing something other than what you're doing?

SILKY: Not necessarily. Really, I wouldn't rather do anything but lay in the bed and pimp.

* * *

While most network TV shows rested during the summer, *60 Minutes* charged forward with stories, taking advantage of every chunk of airtime it could get. The summer of 1973—with the Senate Watergate

Committee hearings drawing huge audiences to their sets on a daily basis—provided a perfect opportunity.

In July, Mike Wallace took a break from covering Watergate to return to the pop-culture beat, interviewing literary bad boy Norman Mailer on the occasion of his new biography of Marilyn Monroe, who died of a drug overdose in 1962. (Wallace and Mailer had met on *Night Beat* in 1957 for an interview in which Mailer had declared that then-President Eisenhower was "a bit of a woman.") Mailer had later given Wallace's career a boost by sitting for an interview on *Night Beat* in November 1960, the day after the author famously stabbed his wife. Their ongoing relationship gave Wallace license to probe into Mailer's psyche and point of view on the actress, for a piece *60 Minutes* called "Monroe, Mailer and the Fast Buck."

> WALLACE: You don't believe she was murdered, though, really. Down bottom . . .
>
> MAILER: If you ask me to give a handicapper's estimate of what it was, I'd say it was ten to one it was an accidental suicide. Ten to one.
>
> WALLACE: At least.
>
> MAILER: But I would not—I could not ignore the possibility of murder.
>
> WALLACE: And do you believe Bobby Kennedy was there, had been with her that night?
>
> MAILER: It's possible.
>
> WALLACE: I'm asking you again.
>
> MAILER: I don't know.
>
> WALLACE: Handicap it.
>
> MAILER: I'd say it's even money.

*　　　*　　　*

Five seasons in, the correspondents made it look easy. Wallace and Safer were rapidly becoming well known—though perhaps not as much as Hewitt wanted—for the way their personalities and approaches shaped the stories they told. Stories always included long shots of the correspondent in conversation with his subject, even though in those days only one camera was used—meaning the cameraman had to shoot reverse angles later to incorporate the correspondent. Still, it was impossible to imagine a *60 Minutes* interview without Mike or Morley nodding or shaking his head. Unlike most TV reporters, they were allowed—indeed, encouraged—to promote the notion with viewers that they were the primary reporters of their stories, gathering the information and telling it as though they'd devoted weeks of their life to each *60 Minutes* segment.

It wasn't true, of course.

By 1973 there were at least a dozen full-time *60 Minutes* producers who traveled the world to report stories on behalf of the high-profile correspondents. Since Wallace and Safer were each responsible for upwards of 25 stories a year, in some cases they had only a few days to contribute to the production of a piece. The producer not only did all the background reporting; he also sometimes wrote the script (especially for Wallace) and typically supervised the editing. Many story ideas were generated by producers, too—leaving the correspondents to function, in some cases, as on-camera performers, reading from a script or a prepared list of questions.

Nevertheless, when the piece aired, it was always Wallace or Safer front and center. The only credit given to the producer was his name imprinted on the opening "book" that gave the story its title, and functioned as a backdrop to the studio opening that preceded each story.

Which is why, shortly after the Herbert piece aired in February 1973, a group of producers, led in part by Lando, asked for a meeting with Hewitt and the correspondents to debate the issue. It was a stormy meeting. In the Herbert story, Wallace in his studio introduction had given Lando additional credit for his reporting; some producers felt that kind of credit belonged on more pieces, arguing that for the show to continue to represent itself as a bastion of truth and integrity, it needed to clearly reveal its own inner workings to its viewers. It was fundamentally dishonest, they said, for Wallace and Safer to imply, by omission, that they'd done the reporting for a piece when in fact they usually had not.

"The show is a soap opera about people pretending to be reporters," Lando angrily said to his bosses.

"People are tuning in for Mike and Morley," Hewitt heatedly told the producers who gathered in the show's screening room. "They don't watch for Barry and Joe and Bob. If we tell them how it's done, it destroys what makes the show special, that it's the adventures of these two reporters." Besides, said Hewitt, none of the show's producers had the skill to appear on camera, whereas the correspondents could do a producer's job just as well if they only had the time.

The producers fought back with the only argument in their arsenal—that to falsely represent the process was to engage in exactly the kind of duplicity the show shredded its interview targets for. They understood Hewitt's argument, of course; they just didn't agree with it.

Having little choice, the behind-the-scenes reporters accepted the reality that the adventures of Mike and Morley would continue without modification, though not without a bad aftertaste in the mouths of some of the show's finest producers.

Chapter 7

Actually, It Was
Oscar Katz's Idea

By the 1970s, Hewitt was on his second marriage; he and Mary Weaver
had gotten a Mexican divorce in early 1963. In June of that year he'd
married Frankie Teague Childers, a fellow divorcée who had been public relations adviser to the U.S. delegation to the United Nations, and
staff director of the Senate Committee on Juvenile Delinquency. Frankie
Hewitt was president of the Ford's Theater Society in Washington, D.C.,
and spent a good deal of time traveling between the two cities. Hewitt's
three children from his first marriage—Jeffrey, Steven, and Jilian—
were now in their twenties; he and Frankie had a daughter of their
own, Lisa, born in 1967.

From the earliest days, Hewitt was known around CBS as something
of a ladies' man. He had a flirtatious, old-world nature, and he thought
nothing of turning his charms on a female coworker, no matter where
she ranked in the chain of command. In an occupation heavily pop-
ulated by straight-laced men in business suits, Hewitt—with his loud,
plaid jackets and turtleneck sweaters, bushy hair and toothy smile—
stood out from the crowd.

Which is how it came to pass that Hewitt found himself in London one day in November of 1973, making a pass at a beautiful, blonde former *Washington Post* reporter named Sally Quinn.

In a moment of ratings-induced weakness, Richard Salant had agreed the previous winter to hire the stylish writer to cohost the *CBS Morning News* with veteran newsman Hughes Rudd. It proved to be an ill-fated venture, and Quinn was savaged from all corners of the media establishment. Aaron Latham—coincidentally, dating the beautiful, blonde CBS Washington correspondent Lesley Stahl at the time— did a hatchet job on Quinn, insinuating that she'd used her looks to get ahead. CBS was anxiously looking for any way possible to defuse the situation.

One idea was to send Quinn to London in November for the wedding of Princess Anne to Captain Mark Phillips, a high-profile assignment that would pair her with the producing talents of Hewitt, who had years of experience with special-events coverage, and with managing difficult talent.

Hewitt was already in London when Quinn arrived, and he greeted her at the airport with a hug and a kiss. The two had met several times before, and Quinn knew his wife from Washington social circles. She also knew about his reputation as a flirt, but never expected it to affect their working relationship—at least not until five minutes into their car ride into London from the airport. (The details of this episode come directly from Quinn's account in her 1975 memoir of her CBS experiences, *We're Going to Make You a Star*.)

"God, we're going to have fun," Hewitt told Quinn. "London is such a great place to have an affair."

"Oh, Don," Quinn replied. "I couldn't think of anything nicer if I weren't already in love with somebody else." Quinn was referring to her boyfriend, Ben Bradlee, the editor of the *Washington Post*.

"Yeah," Hewitt countered, "but he's there and I'm here."

"Yes, but he's here with me in spirit."

"Oh, don't give me that shit," Hewitt said, then proposed dinner that night at a romantic London restaurant named San Lorenzo. Quinn used the dinner to explain to Hewitt her desire to remain calm and focused on this trip, after the tension she'd been experiencing in New York; Hewitt told her that "getting it" would help solve her problems. The back-and-forth continued between them; Hewitt became "very aggressive," Quinn wrote, as the night wore on. "The whole thing was almost obscene." Finally, in a moment of exasperation, he gave up the fight.

"Well, if you won't sleep with me," Hewitt told Quinn, "I'll sleep with Barbara Walters."

In a 1991 *Rolling Stone* article about *60 Minutes,* Mark Hertsgaard reported that "according to numerous past and present staffers, male and female, various forms of sexual harassment of female employees have been a routine part of office life since the show's beginning." One woman told Hertsgaard of an encounter with Hewitt that took place "before his current marriage," which was in 1979. Finding herself alone with Hewitt, she recalled him asking her "weird" questions about her personal life. "Before she knew it," Hertsgaard reported, "he had grabbed her and started to kiss her. With great strength, he grasped both her forearms right below her elbows and 'rammed me up against the wall—bang!—and pinned me there. I couldn't get away from him no matter how hard I tried. I was shaking. I remember he had stuck his tongue down my throat.'"

According to a 1998 *Salon* interview with Hertsgaard, the woman also told the reporter (though it was cut from the published article) that Hewitt followed her into a stairwell, where she finally escaped Hewitt's clutches by "kicking him in the balls," only to encounter him again the next evening at a formal gala. She was wearing a backless gown. Suddenly she felt someone running his fingers up and down her bare back, and turned to discover Hewitt. "Don't be scared," Hewitt reportedly told her. "I just think you're a very attractive girl."

Hewitt denied all the allegations—"Absolutely untrue!" he told Hertsgaard—and, according to Hertsgaard, went to *Rolling Stone* publisher Jann Wenner to try to kill the piece. (Hewitt then denied to Hertsgaard that he had spoken with Wenner.) Hertsgaard told *Salon* that Wenner later confirmed that he had spoken with Hewitt and apologized to the journalist for having done so. Hertsgaard said the story then sat at *Rolling Stone* for almost a year, until word of a *Wall Street Journal* story on Hewitt pushed the magazine to publish its scoop in a truncated form.

As for Wallace, Hertsgaard reported only that the correspondent had frequently patted women's behinds and snapped their bras. "Mike was very good at it," one female staffer said. "He could do it with one hand. He'd sneak up behind you and suddenly—zing!—you're sagging out all over and he's giggling his way up the hall." Wallace both admitted his behavior to Hertsgaard and apologized for it. "I have done that," Wallace readily conceded in the 1991 article, and added that he hadn't snapped a bra in over a decade. "I guess to a certain degree it's generational, to a certain degree it's high spirits."

"I would find it very upsetting," Don Hewitt told *Rolling Stone* in 1991, "if there is a problem of sexual harrassment at *60 Minutes*, and I would make every effort to have that person removed from the premises, because it is morally abhorrent behavior and illegal."

In 1997—at a time when women had been awakened to the issue of sexual harassment in the workplace, and empowered by Anita Hill confronting future Supreme Court Justice Clarence Thomas on national television—Hewitt, now 74 years old, was himself again accused of incidents of sexual harassment, this time by a female former *60 Minutes* editor, in a case that eventually reached the top corporate levels of CBS.

The woman, then in her thirties, claimed she had been subjected to harassment by Hewitt while working at *60 Minutes*. The woman reportedly left *CBS News* after being unable to get a transfer from *60 Minutes* to another show and went to work at another network.

At the time of her return to full-time employment at *CBS News* in 1994, the woman reportedly told human resources personnel about the incidents but didn't file a complaint with CBS against Hewitt until 1997. The woman later hired an attorney, which raised the possibility of a lawsuit. Such a suit would have brought immediate media attention to her claims and caused considerable embarrassment for Hewitt, one of *CBS News*'s most valuable assets. In February 1998, despite the network's official denial of the woman's charges, CBS settled with her for a mid six-figure amount. The woman continues to work for *CBS News* as a producer.

Ironically, just as her settlement was being negotiated, both *60 Minutes* and the country were immersed in parsing allegations of sexual harassment against President Clinton; in March 1998, *60 Minutes* got a huge ratings bump from an Ed Bradley interview with Kathleen Willey, who was among Clinton's most prominent accusers.

Meanwhile, back in the 1970s, *60 Minutes* was working on a piece that was, perhaps, the first of its kind: an investigation of the news media by the news media. This proved to be an exposé that would reach to the highest ranks of modern TV journalism, the anchor desk of the *CBS Evening News* and the most trusted man in America, Walter Cronkite.

While the print media was mostly digging through government documents looking for the next big Watergate scandal—hoping for the kind of cachet that had attached itself to Bob Woodward and Carl Bernstein after their Pulitzers and movie deal—*60 Minutes* (and in particular the ambitious producers working for Mike Wallace) was developing an early form of what would become a staple of the broadcast in the years to come: the investigative story with a "gotcha!" component. In taking on the media itself, Wallace was wagging his finger at the men and women who were busy becoming heroes to the rest of the nation, holding them to the same standards they were applying to others. He and Barry Lando appeared to relish putting the spotlight on reporters and editors who'd been given meals, plane trips, hotel rooms, and gifts in an unspoken—but understood—quid pro quo for favorable coverage.

Wallace also seemed to get a kick out of the surprise attack. He loved the drama of springing an unexpected question or fact on an interview subject, allowing the camera to capture the discomfort that usually followed.

That emerged in an interview with Paul Poorman, managing editor of the *Detroit News,* who had himself conducted a study about the junket problem for an industry group. Wallace got Poorman to denounce journalists taking freebies from corporations, only to follow up with a megadose of his own hypocrisy:

POORMAN: I—I think that this whole issue is greeted with tightly controlled apathy on the part of many newspapermen. But it— there is a growing concern.

WALLACE: Your paper has outlawed all gifts, right?

POORMAN: Uh-huh.

WALLACE: Okay. What about discount prices for the press, your reporters and yourself, from automobile manufacturers?

POORMAN: Yeah, that—

WALLACE: Is that out?

POORMAN: That's out, and—

At that moment, everything came to a halt—the cameraman turned to Lando and informed him that he'd run out of film and had to put a new roll into the camera before Wallace could proceed. Wallace seized the moment and turned to Lando. "Do I have to ask this question?" he asked. "Is it fair?"

Lando had seen this before—Wallace's occasional reluctance to surprise the subject with damning information. It wasn't that Wallace was afraid to drop a bomb into the interview; he knew that's what viewers wanted from him. He just wanted to be sure he was justified in doing so. Quickly, Lando persuaded Wallace that it was a legitimate line of inquiry, and by the time the cameraman had reloaded, so had Wallace.

WALLACE: Now, I understand from somebody on your own paper that you got a new car, and that you yourself fairly recently saved several hundred dollars on the purchase of a new car—

POORMAN: Yeah, three years ago.

WALLACE: Okay, three years ago—and got a discount.

POORMAN: Got a discount of several hundred dollars. I think that is wrong to do. I think it's just something that shouldn't be done, and I won't do it again and no one on my staff will.

WALLACE: Well, I understand that some people on your staff still do, still get discounts—

POORMAN: It's possible. It's a firing offense, and—and they know that.

Elsewhere in the piece, Wallace and Lando tackled even bigger targets, like NBC's highly successful *Today Show,* and nailed them just as effectively. "When NBC's *Today Show* spent a week in Romania and one in Ireland, air fares and hotel bills were picked up by the Irish, the Romanians, and Pan American Airways," Wallace reported. "When *Today* travels overseas, all the expenses over and above their normal budget are paid for by the host country."

Lando's reporting turned up a list of top TV and print reporters who'd gotten gifts from corporations, a list that included Walter Cronkite. Perhaps as a courtesy to their colleague, the *60 Minutes* piece that aired on January 20, 1974, didn't include details of Cronkite's behavior, merely listing him among the guilty parties.

The piece also examined the corporate corrupters themselves, including Wallace and Lando's own employer, CBS. Their camera captured Win Fanning, a TV critic for the *Pittsburgh Post-Gazette,* as he opened an envelope from CBS—given to him during a press junket in New York City—with two $10 bills provided by CBS to cover "incidentals." After the story ran, a CBS spokesman conceded to the *New York Times* that the practice of giving cash "looked bad," but defended the practice as the best means of covering small expenses. "I don't want to talk about that," was Cronkite's irritated response to the *Times* when asked about the piece. A CBS News spokesman described Cronkite's behavior as "a personal thing" that didn't relate to his activities as anchorman.

* * *

In 1974, the Watergate stories still trickled in, and *60 Minutes* was still trying to cover the biggest story of its six-year life without doing much beyond big interviews. Despite its feverish commitment to tough, sweeping journalism elsewhere, for Watergate the show continued to depend mostly on one-on-one chats with scandal-related figures by Mike Wallace, balanced occasionally by Safer's human interest reporting. The fact was that nobody was digging—and the *60 Minutes* Watergate log looks limited now in contrast with the journalistic enterprise found elsewhere in those tense final days of the Nixon administration.

On January 27, 1974, Wallace sat down with Egil "Bud" Krogh, a former Ehrlichman aide serving a prison term for his role in the burglary of the office of Daniel Ellsberg's psychiatrist. (Ellsberg, a longstanding enemy of the Nixon administration, was the former Kissinger aide responsible for leaking the Pentagon Papers to the *New York Times* and the *Washington Post*.) On April 7, 1974, Safer returned to an Indiana town he'd visited in July 1973 for an update on "Listening to Nixon Country." Donald Segretti, Nixon's infamous dirty trickster, appeared for an interview on April 28, 1974. On May 5, two profiles—of Father John McLaughlin, the deputy assistant to the president, and David Frye, a noted Nixon impressionist and comedian—took a quirky, beside-the-point view of the Watergate story. Wallace then scored the first TV sit-down interview with Charles Colson, a former White House aide and recent born-again Christian, in a piece called "Come to Christ" that ran on May 26, 1974. On June 16, "A Tale of Two Inmates" contrasted the experiences in Allenwood prison of two high-profile inmates: Egil "Bud" Krogh and former New Jersey congressman Cornelius Gallagher.

Eventually, *60 Minutes* started working a different angle to get big Watergate stories. To score its biggest Watergate scoops yet, *60 Minutes* used a technique unavailable to most reporters: it persuaded CBS to pay a news source $15,000.

"The Man Who Wouldn't Talk . . . Talks" might have also been called "The Network That Wouldn't Pay . . . Pays." Coming almost a year to the day after Wallace's story about junkets for journalists, it demonstrated the awkward flip side to the issue of networks and rules. In this instance, the network agreed not only to pay an interview subject but also to allow him to dictate the terms of the interview's content. (In the current edition of the CBS News rulebook, the network continues to offer a loophole for news sources who insist on controlled interviews: "While not encouraged, an agreement to exclude a question or area of questioning may occasionally be granted." As for paying an interview subject, the rules state simply, "Interviewees may not be paid for appearances in CBS News broadcasts.") The interview at issue was an unrevealing talk with G. Gordon Liddy, one of the original Watergate burglars. Liddy—who had established up front that he would say nothing of substance about Watergate, adding to the mystery of why CBS paid anything at all for it, let alone $15,000—was less inclined to offer facts than opinions, albeit entertaining ones.

WALLACE: What's your opinion of John Dean?
LIDDY: I think, in all fairness to the man, you'd have to put him right up there with Judas Iscariot.
WALLACE: Judas Iscariot? In other words, he betrayed Christ? Christ being Richard Nixon?
LIDDY: No, he being a betrayer of a person in high position.
WALLACE: And what do you think his motive was?
LIDDY: To save his ass.

Liddy called Nixon "a very sick man," but whenever Wallace asked a probing question he replied dryly, "substantive area—no comment." Still, the interview easily generated enough press for *60 Minutes* to justify the expenditure. In Wallace's memoir, *Close Encounters,* he says that CBS "made no secret" of the payment to Liddy, but the fact of it appears nowhere in the piece itself as broadcast. The evident success of their "investment" emboldened the powers that be at CBS to keep the checkbook handy. Sure enough, only a few weeks later, a better interview—with a higher price tag—came along.

In retrospect, it's stunning that CBS News agreed to it, but after a jury convicted H. R. "Bob" Haldeman in January 1975 of perjury, conspiracy, and obstruction of justice, the network paid the disgraced official $100,000 for an interview with Mike Wallace. As a bonus, the producers would be granted access to some home movies Haldeman had shot during his White House years. While Wallace now freely admits to a $100,000 payment, at the time the figure of $25,000 was being leaked to the media.

The news of the CBS News–Haldeman deal prompted self-righteous protest from other journalists and networks. "We would not pay Haldeman or anyone else for a news interview," William Sheehan, president of ABC News, sniffed to a reporter. In his regular op-ed column in the *New York Times*, James Reston blasted the move: "Isn't this a dangerous precedent? Isn't it buying, not a property, like memoirs, but buying news? If CBS will pay this kind of money for Mr. Haldeman, won't other big shots or notorious characters demand their price? . . . The practice blurs the line between entertainment and information— a line CBS itself has tried hard to keep straight and clear in the past."

In the interview, Haldeman slickly portrayed himself as an innocent victim caught in the media crossfire. "CBS News—and the public— were had," complained a *New York Times* editorial. The home movies, perhaps unsurprisingly, turned out to be boring.

These days Hewitt tries to distance himself from the Haldeman interviews by claiming that they were not aired on *60 Minutes*. That turns out to be technically true, but it's a distinction perhaps lost on viewers and media critics. When asked if they aired during the *60 Minutes* time slot, he says, definitively, "No." But in fact the interview aired as a CBS News production on two successive Sunday nights in March 1975 in the *60 Minutes* time slot—and with the star correspondent of *60 Minutes* asking the questions—though it won't turn up on any "Best of *60 Minutes*" compilations.

Three seasons after *60 Minutes* was moved to Sunday nights, the show continued to be a ratings disaster. Fortunately, CBS didn't care.

For one thing, its flagging Nielsen numbers didn't count against the network's overall ratings, because its 6:00 P.M. time slot fell outside of prime time. Plus it was cheap: it still cost less than $100,000 to produce an episode—fictional shows could cost at least twice that, if not more—and that made it a profitable enterprise, even at the bottom of the ratings. *60 Minutes* had also proven itself a consistent news-making machine and an editorial success. Hewitt's concept worked, and the other networks were toying with the notion of similar news-magazines to compete with the *60 Minutes* formula.

In the spring of 1975, the men who ran CBS's programming department—led by CBS president Robert Wood—were considering their options for the fall schedule. The network was riding high with the success of its iconic comedy lineup; Emmy winners *All in the Family* and *The Mary Tyler Moore Show* gave CBS not only TV's top-rated comedies but also bragging rights to having developed some bona fide cultural landmarks.

But hanging over all three major networks was the so-called access rule mandated by the Federal Communications Commission in 1971, which allowed the networks to program only three hours a night of prime time, giving up the fourth hour to local stations in the top 50 markets. The networks had been fighting it for years; now, the legal battle was nearing an end, and the networks had lost. The FCC allowed only one exception to its rule: on Sunday night, a network could keep the fourth hour for documentaries, public affairs programs, or children's shows. That prompted NBC to move its highly rated *Wonderful World of Disney* to the Sunday night at 7 slot. ABC put its own children's show, *Swiss Family Robinson,* up against Disney.

CBS had no existing children's show to shove into the slot, so they developed a family series, *Three for the Road,* that they hoped to pass off as children's programming, exempt from the new regulations. It starred Alex Rocco as Pete Karras, a widower who takes his two sons, Vincent Van Patten and Leif Garrett, with him on his travels as a photographer. But more than 40 local CBS affiliates showed the good taste to turn it down; not surprisingly, they preferred to carry their own local public affairs programming instead. Local stations were frustrated; NBC and ABC affiliates had pushed their local offerings back to Sunday night at 6, but that option wasn't available to the CBS outlets—the Sunday 6:00 P.M. time slot belonged to *60 Minutes*.

And so by November—with *Three for the Road* being the lowest-rated show on television—CBS development executives realized they needed a new plan for Sunday nights. Then an obscure CBS programming executive named Oscar Katz came up with perhaps the most financially rewarding idea ever hatched in the history of television programming.

Katz, a vice president of CBS, had been an executive at Desilu Productions, the company behind the CBS classic *I Love Lucy*. It occurred to him that perhaps the answer to CBS's Sunday night problems could already be found on the current CBS Sunday night schedule: What if the network were to simply shift *60 Minutes* from 6:00 P.M. to 7:00 P.M.? Katz reasoned that it would fulfill the network's obligations under the access rule and would also let the local stations use the 6:00 P.M. slot for their own public affairs programming.

CBS announced that on December 7, 1975, *60 Minutes* would move to Sunday nights at 7:00 P.M. As a result, his show would no longer face automatic cancellation each fall when CBS broadcast NFL football on Sunday afternoons. That meant an uninterrupted weekly schedule, less chance of being preempted, an increased appetite for stories—and the immediate necessity of adding a third correspondent to help handle the load. Fortunately an obvious choice loomed—an old Hewitt protégé, now a handsome network news star, famous and charismatic enough to threaten Wallace and Safer and make *60 Minutes* a more competitive shop than ever before.

Chapter 8

In the Line of Fire

Few careers compare with the awe-inspiring trajectory of Dan Rather, a handsome Houston lad from modest circumstances who in 1950 got himself into Sam Houston State Teachers College. A series of small-market jobs led him to the Houston CBS television affiliate. In 1961, Hurricane Carla blew through Texas and the reporter chained himself to a tree. In 1962, Rather was hired by CBS News and sent to New Orleans to head up the bureau there. He reported to Don Hewitt.

In November 1963, Rather flew to Dallas to help run the coverage of President Kennedy's trip. His aggressive street-level reporting from Dallas on the Kennedy assassination and its aftermath (and the fortunate decision not to deck Abraham Zapruder and walk off with the film) earned him a promotion to the White House beat in 1964. In 1965, CBS News asked Rather to run the prestigious London bureau; he went, but quickly realized the big story was in Vietnam. After a year's worth of combat coverage he returned to the White House and became a familiar, authoritative face on the *CBS Evening News*.

Dan Rather, a star in the making, had an uncanny ability to bring attention to himself. In the summer of 1968, he was beaten and shoved by a security detail on the floor of the Democratic National Convention in Chicago, in full view of CBS cameras that broadcast it live. "I think we've got a bunch of thugs in here," said anchorman Walter Cronkite as he narrated the events from his broadcast booth. The incident earned Rather new status at CBS as a victim of unwarranted attack. (The assault would turn out to be just the first in a series of weird physical confrontations over the course of his career, including a celebrated and bizarre mugging on a New York street in 1986 by a man muttering, "What's the frequency, Kenneth?" and a fight with an erratic Chicago cab driver in 1980.) He covered the Nixon presidential campaign that fall (sitting in for Mike Wallace, who had left to cohost *60 Minutes*), then returned to the White House after the election. Although Rather's name came up as a replacement for Reasoner in 1970, he was passed over in favor of dark horse Morley Safer.

Staying at the White House turned out to be yet another brilliant career move. Rather quickly distinguished himself as the president's most relentless antagonist in the White House press corps. In 1971, before the break-in had even occurred, Nixon operative John Ehrlichman targeted Rather for removal in a breakfast meeting with Salant. Once the *Washington Post* broke the Watergate story, Rather began to take on the president in ways that earned him even more scrutiny from the White House and the public.

Their first notable face-off came in August 1973, when Rather began a news conference question this way: "Mr. President, I want to state this question with due respect to your office, but also as directly as—"

"That would be unusual," Nixon interrupted Rather.

At another news conference, one question from Rather—about Nixon's state of mind concerning calls for impeachment—prompted the president to reply, "Well, I'm glad we don't take the vote of this room, let me say."

But their most memorable showdown took place in March 1974, when Nixon came to address a meeting of the National Association of Broadcasters in Rather's hometown of Houston. It was all very civilized, as the president genially fielded softballs from the audience and White House correspondents for CBS, NBC, and ABC. Toward the end, Rather introduced himself to ask a Watergate question, and his name prompted both cheers and boos from the crowd. "Are you running for something?" Nixon asked Rather.

"No sir, Mr. President," Rather replied. "Are you?"

That brief interchange was an immediate transforming moment for Rather. Which was interesting, in part, because in retrospect his response to Nixon makes very little sense. What did Rather mean, exactly? It's hard to believe that Rather's mind immediately leapt to the metaphoric notion of Nixon "running" to keep his office in the face of impeachment. Still, Rather's willingness to repeatedly take on the president so directly evidenced his doggedness as a reporter—a characteristic of his personality that Rather has never tempered. (Almost a quarter-century after becoming the anchor of *60 Minutes*, Rather continues to compete. His scramble for a wartime interview with Saddam Hussein in 2003 was only one recent example. CBS insiders have speculated that the reason there are no other star reporters at CBS News is that Rather can't stand the idea of competition.)

An increasingly annoyed White House wanted Rather out, and CBS wasn't going to fight the feds. A compromise was reached (after Rather entertained offers from NBC and ABC) that put him in charge of *CBS Reports,* the now-creaky documentary unit begun by Edward R. Murrow and Fred Friendly, less than a month after Nixon resigned as president. He was also given the anchor desk at the weekend broadcasts of the *CBS Evening News*. Rather wasn't happy. He'd been shuffled off to a part of CBS News so removed from the action that it wasn't even in the same building as Walter Cronkite—and seemingly for political reasons that made little sense. Hell, his new offices didn't even have hot water. It wasn't long before he found himself fantasizing about a position on Hewitt's *60 Minutes*. Wallace signed on to the plan—he loved the idea of vying with a formidable opponent like Rather and proving himself the more capable reporter. Safer never liked Rather much, but in any case, by the time it was settled that *60 Minutes* would be televised every week starting in December 1975, Rather's future on the program was set.

At 7:00 P.M. on Sunday, December 7, 1975—with Dan Rather officially on board as the show's third correspondent—the new season began with a piece by Wallace called "Secret Service Agent # 9," about a man few Americans had heard of until he appeared on *60 Minutes*. His name was Clint Hill, and he was a broken man.

Hill had been part of the Secret Service detail that protected President Kennedy during his visit to Dallas on November 22, 1963. He was the agent who climbed onto the president's limousine moments after the first shot was fired. Hewitt had heard rumblings about Hill and speculated that he might have a good story to tell. Producer Paul Loewenwarter reached him by phone and sensed that the former agent was feeling guilty over the way events had played out in Dallas that day. There was certainly enough potential, Loewenwarter thought, to justify renting a suite at the Madison Hotel in Washington and flying down with Wallace to interview Hill.

But for the first hour or so of conversation, Hill seemed oddly stiff and ill at ease; his answers were weak and unemotional. Wallace was bored and annoyed, his eyes rolling to the ceiling as Hill droned on. Finally, he motioned to the cameraman to stop filming.

"This is just pabulum," Wallace told Hill. "You're not telling us anything. This is just not of interest."

Hill looked back, stunned, as Wallace continued in a manner he often used to get reluctant subjects to talk.

"You've got a story to tell," Wallace went on. "You were part of this major event, part of history. And you're just not telling us how you feel about it." He stopped speaking and motioned to the cameraman to start up again. Wallace then asked the ashen Hill—now retired— to review publicly, for the first time, his feelings about the Kennedy assassination.

WALLACE: Can I take you back to November 22 in 1963? You were on the fender of the Secret Service car right behind President Kennedy's car. At the first shot, you ran forward and jumped on the back of the president's car—in less than two seconds—pulling Mrs. Kennedy down into her seat, protecting her. First of all, she was out on the trunk of that car—

HILL: She was out of the back seat of that car. Not on the trunk of that car.

WALLACE: Well, she was—she had—she had climbed out of the back, and she was on the way back, right?

HILL: And because of the fact that her husband's—part of his—her husband's head had been shot off and gone off to the street.

WALLACE: She wasn't—she wasn't trying to climb out of the car? She was—

HILL: No, she was simply trying to reach that head. Part of the head.

WALLACE: To bring it back?

HILL: That's the only thing—

The former agent, so impassive only minutes before, burst into tears at that moment, the camera in characteristic tight close-up on his face. Wallace allowed him to pull himself together for a moment. Hill, gripping a cigarette in his fingers, smoked it down to the butt as Wallace continued:

WALLACE: Was there anything that the Secret Service or that Clint Hill could have done to keep [the assassination] from happening?

HILL: Clint Hill, yes.

WALLACE: "Clint Hill, yes"? What do you mean?

HILL: If [I] had reacted about five-tenths of a second faster, or maybe a second faster, I wouldn't be here today.

WALLACE: You mean, you would have gotten there and you would have taken the shot?

HILL: The third shot, yes, sir.

WALLACE: And that would have been all right with you?

HILL: That would have been fine with me.

WALLACE: But you couldn't. You got there in—in less than two seconds, Clint. You—you couldn't have gotten there— You don't— you surely don't have any sense of guilt about that?

HILL: Yes, I certainly do. I have a great deal of guilt about that. Had I turned in a different direction, I'd have made it. It's my fault.

WALLACE: Oh, no one has ever suggested that for an instant.

HILL: I—

WALLACE: What you did was show great bravery and great presence of mind. What was on the citation that was given to you for your work on November 22, 1963?

HILL: I don't care about that, Mike.

WALLACE *(reading)*: "Extraordinary courage and heroic effort in the face of maximum danger."

HILL: Mike, I don't care about that. If I had reacted just a little bit quicker—and I could have, I guess. And I'll live with that to my grave.

Hill's consuming grief delivered *60 Minutes* a classic water-cooler story, one that cemented 57-year-old Mike Wallace's reputation as the most deft and probing interviewer of his time. In addition, after a long series of hard-headed sessions with major social and political figures, Wallace's Clint Hill conversation revealed a sensitive side to the reporter that many had never seen before. "Secret Service Agent #9" also stood perfectly for what *60 Minutes* produced so well—the visual intersection of news and narrative. In fact, the emotional turmoil of Clint Hill later became the back story for the Clint Eastwood character in *In the Line of Fire,* the 1995 thriller with John Malkovich as the would-be presidential assassin who preys on an agent's dark secret.

When it worked the way it was supposed to, as in "Secret Service Agent #9," *60 Minutes* gave viewers small, beautifully crafted movies with fully developed story arcs—what Hewitt called "packaged reality." And just as Hewitt, the Hildy wannabe, once imagined bridging the worlds of news and show business, the producer of a *60 Minutes* piece now functioned less like a journalist and more like a movie director.

In December 1975, a 33-year-old North Carolina journalist named Patrick O'Keefe placed a call to Lewis Lapham, the editor of *Harper's* magazine. O'Keefe had done the occasional story for Lapham, nothing extraordinary. He was an ambitious young man, not too thrilled to be teaching journalism at the University of North Carolina at Greensboro, where the likelihood of stumbling on stories worthy of a *Harper's* assignment was not all that high. O'Keefe decided to call Lapham on this particular day because of a recent phone call to the university from a man identifying himself as Chuck Medlin. It seemed that Medlin wanted to write a book but needed help; hence his call to the school, searching for a writer to help him tell his rather dramatic and commercial story. Medlin—a scowling low-life who had the uncanny ability to strike mortal fear into just about everyone—claimed to know the location of missing Teamster's Union president Jimmy Hoffa, who had disappeared the previous July in what most Americans logically assumed was a case of murder. Medlin also said he knew who killed Hoffa.

O'Keefe met with Medlin, who passed along some colorful details of meeting the Hoffa killer in prison not so long ago. Afterward O'Keefe quickly called Lapham and pitched the story. Normally considered an erudite intellectual with little taste for the sensational, Lapham liked the idea enough to advance O'Keefe $700 to fly himself and Medlin to New York.

The next day, Lapham met Medlin in person and immediately realized the gangster would be better suited to Don Hewitt's show, so he called Hewitt to recommend that he meet with O'Keefe. Hewitt, of course, was thrilled—the prospect of breaking the Hoffa case was irresistible. Hewitt immediately gathered his senior staff—including Safer (who later claimed that it was his misfortune to have worked late that day) and producer Joe Wershba—in his office for a meeting with

O'Keefe and Medlin to discuss the story, and the possibility of paying them for the biggest potential exclusive in *60 Minutes* history.

"How do you know where the body is?" Hewitt asked Medlin, according to a 1978 *Rolling Stone* account. Medlin told the *60 Minutes* boss that he had shoved a .38 down someone's throat and "got him to tell."

A palpable sense of terror enveloped the room. "I have a beautiful .357 Magnum underneath my bed," Medlin told Hewitt and his nervous producers.

"What is it about you that makes people accept your warning that you'll do something to them?" Hewitt asked. Medlin immediately kicked his leg out, right near Hewitt's head. "Well, that's a good way to show your authority," was Hewitt's response.

Medlin looked around the room at the assembled, trembling group. "I'd like a beer," he snapped.

"I'd have to send out for it. We don't have it in the cafeteria," a secretary whispered, according to a later *New York Times* report.

"Send out," Hewitt said urgently. "Send out!"

Medlin explained to the group that he was a hired killer, and at various points he threatened to kill people who were irritating him. By the end of the meeting, Hewitt had agreed to pay O'Keefe $10,000 in cash—a consultant's fee that would ensure his and Medlin's help in retrieving the missing body of Jimmy Hoffa.

After the meeting, Hewitt called Dick Salant to get his approval for the expenditure. Salant said okay, and Hewitt told Wershba to go to Salant's office to pick up the money.

When Wershba entered the office, the CBS News executive had $10,000 in cash waiting on his desk.

"Are we doing the right thing?" Salant asked Wershba as he counted out the money.

"No, we don't know whether this guy is crazy," Wershba replied. "We're not doing the right thing."

But both men knew there was no refusing Hewitt. His show's ratings were finally starting to climb, and there was no doubt in anyone's mind that if Medlin somehow turned out to be right, it would be the scoop of the year, if not the decade.

Wershba brought the money back to the *60 Minutes* offices, where Medlin and O'Keefe were waiting. Before they left for Florida—to be joined shortly by Hewitt, Safer, and Wershba—Medlin agreed to sit down with Safer for an on-camera interview. During that conversation, Medlin matter-of-factly laid out the story of Hoffa's disappearance for the wide-eyed Safer and Hewitt.

SAFER: Where is Jimmy Hoffa?

MEDLIN: Key West.

SAFER: Where precisely?

MEDLIN: Smith Shoal Light . . . that's where Hoffa is. It's a rock pile.

SAFER: Dead?

MEDLIN: Dead. . . .

SAFER: Just lying there in the water?

MEDLIN: No, he's in cement. . . .

SAFER: How was he killed?

MEDLIN: He was stabbed on a goddamn boat. . . .

SAFER: Will you show us where Jimmy Hoffa is buried?

MEDLIN: I said I would. If I say I will, I will.

After the interview, Medlin convinced O'Keefe to let him hold the cash; the two men left together that night for Florida.

By the time Safer, Hewitt, and Wershba got to Florida, Medlin had gone missing, along with the $10,000.

That, of course, didn't deter Hewitt from hiring a boat and going to the location Medlin described, in search of Hoffa. They found nothing, of course. When they got back to the hotel, Hewitt suggested to Wershba that he tell the story of the rip-off to Martin Waldron, a reporter from the *New York Times*, who they'd noticed was staying at the same hotel. The next day, the debacle appeared on the front page of the *Times* under the headline, "Hoffa Tipster Gone; CBS Is Out

$10,000." It embarrassed most of those associated with the incident—but not Hewitt, of course, whose show business instincts told him that there's no such thing as bad publicity. To him, it was just a $10,000 bet that hadn't paid off.

Back at the office, *60 Minutes* producer Paul Loewenwarter was placing calls to his sources at the Environmental Protection Agency in Washington about a potential story. Lately, however, he'd been getting a rather odd response to such calls. Rather than answer his questions about a specific story he was working on, they'd ask him questions about ideas he had for future stories about the agency. Finally Loewenwarter asked his sources why they were so interested. "Well, you see," one source confessed, "if you tell us now what you're going to be investigating next, that way we can go to our bosses and get some changes implemented by saying, 'If we don't do something soon, then *60 Minutes* is going to do a piece.' It saves a lot of time in the long run, plus the embarrassment of being exposed on *60 Minutes*."

At the time, Loewenwarter was working on Dan Rather's first real piece for *60 Minutes*, about workers at a small Allied Chemical plant in Virginia where pollution resulting from the manufacture of Kepone (a pesticide most commonly used overseas) was allegedly causing brain damage among workers. Rather and Loewenwarter had traveled to the town of Roswell, Virginia, with *60 Minutes* cameraman Billy Wagner to talk with plant workers. In some cases, their exposure to Kepone had reportedly caused tremors, twitches, and other uncontrollable movements resulting from brain damage caused by pesticide inhalation.

One worker, J. O. Rogers, had been hospitalized five times with nervous tremors. In Rather's conversation with Rogers, he'd found that one test to determine the extent of brain damage was for a subject to drive in a bolt with a screwdriver. With Rather and Loewenwarter looking on, Rogers tried to perform the test for the CBS camera.

Wagner, the cameraman, zoomed in on Rogers's hand as he took the screwdriver. For approximately 45 seconds—an eternity in television time—the camera focused on the trembling hand as the man tried, repeatedly and unsuccessfully, to insert the head of the screw-driver into the bolt. Finally, he gave up. It was a powerful visual image, stronger than any words Rather might have said, and vividly conveyed the damage done by this dangerous poison. Loewenwarter had done his research well, having found Rogers and numerous other victims, as well as a "smoking gun"—clear evidence that Allied Chemical scientists had ignored knowledge available to them that might have prevented the exposure. But he needed Rather, who knew as well as anyone how to deliver a knockout blow.

Rather went on to describe other victims—including one man who had, as Rather put it, "37,000 times more Kepone in his liver than is permitted in a public sewer"—before moving on to Loewenwarter's evidence, presented in a direct confrontation on camera with the man Allied Chemical had represented as the nation's leading expert on the dangers of Kepone: William Moore, a chemist and chemical engineer and the director of research for Allied's agricultural division. Sitting opposite Moore, Rather turned on the heat as powerfully as he had done on Richard Nixon two years earlier:

RATHER: My problem—and I want to be candid with you—is what we have here, in no small way, is a who-done-it. I want to ask you, Mr. Moore, whether you've seen any of these materials, which were put out by Allied Chemical, studies sponsored by Allied Chemical. We have three of these blue books. Right on the cover: "Kepone Compound 1189, Allied Chemical, General Chemical Division." Now, this was published in July 1961. Are you familiar with these materials? This . . .

MOORE: No.

RATHER: Never seen those?

MOORE: Never seen them.

RATHER: Right in the summary, very top: "The characteristic effect of this compound is the development of DDT-like tremors, the severity of which depends upon dosage level and duration of exposure." Quote, unquote—from the first sentence of the summary. You didn't know about this?

MOORE: No, no.

RATHER: Mr. Moore, let me read you something that Allied Chemical gave to us this afternoon. Now, this is a direct quote from an Allied Chemical spokesman. We went to Allied Chemical, asked: Who is the nation's expert on Kepone? And the Allied Chemical spokesman said, quote, "The nation's expert in the manufacture of Kepone, totally knowledgeable about the hazards of the product and the safeguards necessary to produce it, is Mr. Moore."

MOORE: Well, that's an interesting comment.

RATHER: Is that true?

MOORE: Well, certainly not.

RATHER: I'm a reporter, and this leaves me at a loss. Allied Chemical, which is a big outfit with a lot of experience in this, says you're the nation's leading expert.

MOORE *(laughs)*: Well, I certainly know the chemistry of Kepone. I—

RATHER: Totally knowledgeable about the hazards of the product and the safeguards necessary to produce it?

MOORE: I would say, no, I haven't seen those data.

When the piece, "Warning—May Be Fatal," aired on December 14, 1975, it brought nationwide attention to the matter and helped lead to 153 indictments and a $13 million fine against Allied Chemical. The story had appeared almost two weeks earlier as a page one exclusive in the *Wall Street Journal,* demonstrating to Hewitt yet again the power of television to adapt and dramatize a story for maximum impact. It was exactly the way he'd envisioned it more than a quarter of a century ago. TV was where Hildy Johnson belonged.

Chapter 9

The Thousand-Pound Pencil

Lucy Spiegel, a young researcher for *60 Minutes*, didn't consider that she might one day be viewed as a television news pioneer on the day in early 1976 when a CBS camera began following her around for what would become a classic Mike Wallace story on fake IDs. The idea was straightforward enough: demonstrate how easy it had become not only to fraudulently obtain passports, drivers' licenses, and voter registration cards but also to use them to commit felonies. In fact, the subject had been suggested to Wallace by Frances Knight, head of the U.S. Passport Office, who was increasingly alarmed by the number of identity-fraud scams.

What made Spiegel's journey historic was the storytelling technique involved. By filming her movements through the various layers of bureaucracy, then following up with question-and-answer confrontations by Wallace and producer Barry Lando, *60 Minutes* laid out the story with a new level of realism. Wallace and Lando—aided by Spiegel—conveyed how frighteningly easy it was to become someone else in America, no questions asked.

Speigel began her odyssey at the Municipal Building in Washington, D.C., where she applied for a replacement birth certificate—for a child who had died two decades earlier. Lando had supplied her with the name of the dead child, along with just enough facts to convince an unsuspecting clerk.

Lando had arranged for Wallace to interview the head of the office, John Crandall. The plan was to set up the camera in the front of the office, so that when Spiegel arrived to apply for her certificate, the CBS camera could zoom in on her without arousing suspicion that she was there undercover. After Spiegel went in, Wallace commenced to grill Crandall on what she was doing:

> WALLACE: I asked Mr. Crandall if it might not be possible that the woman in the checkered shirt, whom we were filming, was an imposter, applying for the certificate of a person who had actually died years ago.
>
> JOHN CRANDALL: We would have no way of knowing. That's right. . . .
>
> WALLACE: So what you have here is a legal document that this woman can use—for whatever purposes.
>
> CRANDALL: For whatever purpose. To claim estates, to inherit money, to get passports, to get unemployment. For almost anything.
>
> WALLACE: And if she were an imposter—I'm sure she's not, but if she were an imposter—she could use it for fraudulent purposes?
>
> CRANDALL: Yes, she certainly could.
>
> WALLACE: To rip off whatever she wanted to rip off?
>
> CRANDALL: I think I better ask her if she's going to.

Crandall then approached Spiegel and asked her, with the camera rolling—but without the *60 Minutes* crew disclosing its relationship with Spiegel—whether she was an imposter. She denied it; that settled that. Armed with her new birth certificate, Spiegel got a Maryland identification card (equivalent to a driver's license) as Wallace,

Lando, and the camera followed in her wake. After that she proceeded to apply for an all-important Social Security number. Again, with the cameras rolling, under the guise of a general story about identification, they caught this piece of film:

SOCIAL SECURITY CLERK: Do you have proof of age with you?
SPIEGEL: I have my birth certificate.
SOCIAL SECURITY CLERK: May I see it, please? All right, thank you very much. You should be receiving this within six weeks.

The group left the Social Security office and headed for the state welfare office, where Spiegel applied for food stamps; in doing so under an assumed name, she was breaking the law—perhaps the first crime ever committed in front of a television camera by a representative of a major American news organization. Next, she went to get a driver's license, a crucial step in the building of a false identity; a license would permit her to cash checks. The learner's permit was easily obtainable by mail; the license would arrive a few days later. (The *60 Minutes* piece never quite explained how Spiegel got around the exams required for a driver's license, a shortcut that probably went unnoticed on television.)

Next came a passport, the toughest form of identification to get. Speigel simply went to her local post office in Bethesda (again with CBS cameras right behind); within two weeks, her passport came in the mail.

Now the fun began. Spiegel opened a checking account at a Maryland bank, then took her new checks to a Washington, D.C., camera shop, where she admired a camera in the window. Going inside, with Wallace, Lando, and the CBS camera in full view of the shop's employees, she told the merchant she wanted to buy it.

CAMERA SHOP MERCHANT: The price is $95, and there's a $4.75 tax.
SPIEGEL: Okay.
MERCHANT: $99.75.

SPIEGEL: All right.
MERCHANT: You pay by check, right?
LUCY: Right.
MERCHANT: Okay.

When Spiegel had finished writing the phony check, Wallace stepped up to the counter to speak to the sales clerk.

WALLACE: As far as you're concerned, this lady is okay?
MERCHANT: Yes.
WALLACE: You're sure?
MERCHANT: I'm quite sure.

Speigel went on to fraudulently buy $636.30 worth of camera merchandise, even though she had far less in her checking account than that. Next stop—the Eastern Airlines ticket office, where she bought a one-way ticket to Mexico City leaving that night. Once again, she emerged successful. Afterward, Mike Wallace stepped up to the counter, microphone in hand:

WALLACE: I wonder if I can ask you some questions?
AIRLINE AGENT: Sure.
WALLACE: First of all, forgive me, this young woman could simply go to Mexico and disappear from sight, and Eastern Airlines would be out 170-odd dollars.
AIRLINE AGENT: That's right. Well, I'm quite satisfied that she is okay. I mean—
WALLACE: Why?
AIRLINE AGENT: Well, I just have that feeling. After all, I have been in the business twenty-eight years. I should know a little about accepting checks.

The "Fake IDs" segment proved more than just how easy it was to forge an identity; it also demonstrated that *60 Minutes* wasn't reluctant to bend the rules of journalism to make its point. Surely it said in a rule book somewhere that CBS News reporters were expressly prohibited from committing felonies in pursuit of a story. But was there any other way, really, to make the point of this one? At the time Lando and Wallace didn't think so, although Lando recently expressed some regret about the techniques used on this piece. "We never really considered what the effect would be on a person's life, by putting them on national television and making them look foolish," Lando says. "We probably cost some innocent people their jobs, who were just doing what they were supposed to do." But back then, Lando embraced the latitude *60 Minutes* gave him to get the story, and Wallace—well, Wallace just loved the camera, and he knew precisely how to use it for maximum effect. His pointed post-scam interviews put his instincts as a showman on full display, and once the story aired, the response only fueled his desire to flaunt his on-air persona.

Wallace may have been recognized as the show's most aggressive muckraker, but all three correspondents heatedly vied for airtime with pieces designed to use the show as an instrument for self-promotion and headline grabbing—a way of doing well by doing good. Wallace and Rather weren't the only ones changing laws and getting indictments; Safer's January 5, 1975, story about gun purchases made in South Carolina—"Have Gun, Will Travel"—resulted in a new handgun law.

In news accounts about *60 Minutes* Hewitt had taken to referring to his correspondents as his "tigers." And, yes, there were news accounts at last; by 1976 the mainstream media coverage was steadily increasing, and the reviews were predominantly positive. But nothing mattered so much to Hewitt and his staff as having their exploits chronicled in the *New York Times* and, better yet, praised. They usually had the support of their hometown paper; but when they didn't, it hit them harder than any other critique imaginable.

In the fall of 1975, consumer advocate Ralph Nader tipped off producer Harry Moses about a young, disillusioned project manager for the

Nuclear Regulatory Commission named Robert Pollard. It had been Pollard's job to assess the safety of various power plants around the country, and he'd become convinced that some plants were unsafe—unsafe enough that his failure to get them shut down had made him deeply frustrated, and thus a potentially explosive central character for a *60 Minutes* piece. In Pollard, Moses sensed he'd found exactly the right person to dramatize a vitally important (but potentially dull) story. With Pollard's help, Moses studied nuclear power safety for three months, until one day he stumbled on the hook he needed.

Pollard had been rambling about not being able to convince his bosses of the meltdown threat at several nuclear power plants, including Indian Point Three power plant up the Hudson River from New York City. "I want to resign," Pollard told Moses. "I want to make a big impact."

"You want to make a big impact, Bob?" Moses responded. "Resign on the air!"

While he realized this might be hard to engineer for maximum effect on a show that wasn't broadcast live, Moses nevertheless believed it was the perfect way to deliver a devastating blow to the federal agency responsible for regulating nuclear power. He envisioned a dramatic sequence in which Pollard would tender his resignation, and his bosses—with Mike Wallace and camera close at hand—would scramble and no doubt lie to counter their righteous employee's explosive allegations. It would make great television.

But for the piece to work the way he wanted it to, they'd have to get the head of the Nuclear Regulatory Commission—William Anders, a former astronaut—to appear on camera with Wallace without knowing of Pollard's plan.

The delicate task of securing Anders's cooperation was assigned to Ellen Collyer, a *60 Minutes* associate producer, who placed a call to Anders's public relations consultant to arrange an interview. What Collyer didn't know was that her 45-minute conversation with the consultant was tape-recorded. (This wasn't illegal in New York State.) A subsequent account of the conversation in the *New York Times* reported that "Anders would agree to come on the program to explain the agency's role in nuclear safety; however, he did not want to get involved in a debate, either direct or simulated through film-editing techniques."

"Who the hell else is going to be on the program?" the Anders spokesman demanded, then backed off: "But you don't know either, do you?"

"At this moment, no," Collyer said.

In fact, Collyer (along with Wallace and Moses) knew full well that Pollard would appear on the program. They fully intended the piece to be a debate over the safety issues raised by Pollard and had every intention of cross-examining Anders on his performance and that of his agency. It was going to be a classic Wallace "gotcha!"

The piece "How Safe Is Safe?" aired on February 8, 1976, three years before the accident at the Three Mile Island nuclear power plant; it served as one more example of the show's prescience. But it also demonstrated the ways in which television journalism can sometimes telegraph ideas in simplistic ways to make a point and offered a vivid glimpse into an essential difference between print and television reporting. For a *60 Minutes* producer, it was not only necessary to tell the story; it was also important to create drama, and quickly.

First, Wallace introduced Pollard—not just as an expert but as an utterly sympathetic expert, backed up by shots of the 35-year-old former Navy man with his wife and two young sons. Wallace then moved to the heart of the matter, with a megadose of embellishment for dramatic effect.

WALLACE: This is the nuclear power plant Bob Pollard worries about—Indian Point Number Three, up the Hudson River from New York City. When it goes into operation (if it goes into operation), it'll furnish 900,000 kilowatts of energy to New York City and Westchester County. But Bob Pollard says it does not meet today's NRC safety regulations. *(To Pollard)* Give me the bottom line. Indian Point is 45 minutes from my home. I have a right to know whether that plant is going to be safe when and if it goes into operation.

POLLARD: In my opinion, it—it will be just a matter of luck if Indian Point doesn't sometime during its life have a major accident.

Several minutes later, Wallace interviewed Anders, and quickly launched a missile into the conversation:

WALLACE: Have you ever heard of a fellow by the name of Bob Pollard, Mr. Anders?

ANDERS: The name does not jump to my memory.

WALLACE: Bob Pollard is one of your project managers, and he resigned today. Reason he resigned was, he is not sure about the safety of your program.

ANDERS: Bob Pollard has never tried to contact me or any of the members of the commission. I never even heard of Bob Pollard before.

After some additional discussion about plant safety issues, the tension began to ratchet up a few notches, with Anders placing an on-camera phone call to Ben Rusche, the director of the Office of Nuclear Regulation for the NRC, to find out more about Pollard.

BEN RUSCHE: Well, Mr. Chairman, I am not aware, or was not aware, of Mr. Pollard's disturbance, nor his likelihood to resign, or any indication of this. . . . I have had him at meetings in my office for a couple of times. Of course, I don't—I don't know the gentleman that well. I would have guessed that that sort of fitness report would have been an appropriate fitness report.

WALLACE: Appropriate?

RUSCHE: Yes. We have in our interactions, of course, recognized that he has a specific, what shall I say, has given very specific and acute attention to a number of the fine points of rules and regulations which appear to give him some internal problems.

At this point in the interview, Anders became uncomfortable, knowing that Pollard—this man he did not know—was being criticized, in the presence of Mike Wallace on *60 Minutes*, for precisely the sort of nit-picking that can be seen to save lives.

ANDERS: Well—well, that—that certainly is what people are being paid to do.

RUSCHE: Sure.

ANDERS: And keeping in mind, of course, that we're—that your conversation, in case I didn't get it across to you, is being recorded—

RUSCHE: Yes.

Anders clearly understood, by then, what was happening—but too late to keep the viewer from seeing what *60 Minutes* wanted them to, a government bureaucrat criticizing the courageous behavior of the story's designated hero, fearless young Bob Pollard.

Not everyone thought this was such great television. Foremost among the skeptics was John J. O'Connor, the *New York Times* TV critic who had been a champion of the show since arriving at the paper in 1971 from the *Wall Street Journal*. His doubts deepened once he had been given access to the transcribed conversation between the *60 Minutes* researcher and the public relations consultant to the NRC's Anders. The consultant had expressed concern that his client might be unwittingly dragged into the very kind of debate over safety that the piece ultimately became.

Before writing his critique, O'Connor visited *60 Minutes* to get its side of the story. When he was ushered into Wallace's office, O'Connor recalled, he was greeted by Hewitt and Wallace, who both proceeded to yell at him about his plan to publish a critical column. But the hard-nosed style that was so effective around the office and against the bad guys failed to dissuade the critic. He returned to his desk and filed a harshly critical commentary on *60 Minutes* and its methods.

"How, then, does a TV newsman convince a potential target of an investigation to expose himself, perhaps unflatteringly, before a camera?" O'Connor wrote in a lengthy essay for the Sunday paper's "Arts and Leisure" section. "One way, it seems to me, borders dangerously on what could be interpreted as false pretenses and entrapment." After laying out a compelling case for entrapment of Anders by *60 Minutes*, O'Connor did due diligence by printing the show's responses, which argued that by telling Anders that the topic of that segment was "the safety of nuclear reactors," they'd given him sufficient and fair notice. It was a powerful essay, but it had little impact compared to the *60 Minutes* piece itself, which reached a far larger audience.

Hewitt's response in the *Times* to O'Connor's argument couldn't have been more explicit: "Anyone who submits to an interview on television is fair game for anything." He later added, "Within his field of expertise." This echoed an earlier description of the medium's power by Wallace, its foremost manipulator. "Television," Wallace once said, "is a thousand-pound pencil."

Chapter 10

Too Much Profit

Behind the one-way mirror were CBS cameraman Walter Dumbrow and producer Barry Lando; inside the closet was Mike Wallace. And in the front room of the ramshackle storefront on Chicago's Morse Avenue, *60 Minutes* had set up shop with the local Better Government Association. The mission: to catch laboratories in the act of setting up Medicaid kickback arrangements by using an ersatz "medical clinic" staffed by two BGA investigators. A Senate subcommittee was already investigating clinical labs that paid money to doctors and medical clinics to get their business, in return for the lucrative reimbursements from Medicaid for blood and urine tests. And some doctors had reported that labs were even offering to pay their rent and overhead in return for their Medicaid testing.

But *60 Minutes* wanted to document this for itself—and Lando decided the best way to do so was by using a hidden camera, something never before done by a TV news organization. It was a sort of entrapment, to be sure, yet it was all within the confines of Illinois law and all done for the benefit of a viewer whose eyes might glaze over at the thought of a story about Medicaid fraud.

It was January 1976, and the show was just beginning to show signs of ratings strength. Now more than ever, the goal of Hewitt, Wallace, and everyone else at *60 Minutes* was to get the audience to come back every week. Lando loved to use Wallace as the surrogate for an outraged public—and to milk the dramatic effect of his presence for everything it was worth. But Wallace wasn't sold on the Medicaid scam story right away. When he landed in Chicago to begin the final phase of the reporting, he huddled with Lando. "Are we sure this is a crime?" he asked.

Lando, having spent the better part of two months reporting the story without the cameras in the room, was able to lay out for his correspondent the laws being violated, the millions of dollars involved, and the potential result of exposing the fraud on *60 Minutes*.

Wallace was convinced.

The next day, with BGA personnel Doug Longhini and Geraldene Delaney behind a desk in the seedy office (and Wallace, Lando, and Dumbrow safely out of sight), the clinic was officially "opened" and a parade of visitors from numerous labs began. Longhini and Delaney were careful to never indicate that they wanted kickbacks in return for lab referrals. Of the 11 labs that came, 9 made kickback proposals in front of the *60 Minutes* camera. Several were invited back for a second meeting; at that time, Wallace was ready to make his move. Dumbrow's camera recorded the conversation as Wallace narrated.

WALLACE: First to arrive—two men who said they were the owners of North Side Clinical Labs. North Side's Medicaid business has rocketed from $28,000 a year in 1974 to almost $1 million a year by 1975, an increase of 3000 percent in one year's time. As we said, Illinois law prohibits secretly recording a person, so we taped only one side of the discussion—just the questions of the BGA investigators, who this time included Pat Riordan playing the role of the clinic doctor. Standing behind the wall in the back, I could hear what was going on in the front office.

Part of the North Side Lab offer was that if the Medicaid business the clinic sent them amounted to more than $1000 a week,
they would return 50 percent of that money to the clinic by
leasing a small space in the back.

RIORDAN: So I could get $500 a week?

WALLACE: In other words, by renting a few square feet in the clinic
hallway to the lab, the clinic could earn from that small space
alone more than four times the rent of the entire clinic.

RIORDAN: We'd be getting in rent for that hallway $2000?

At which point Wallace opened the door to the closet where he'd
been hiding and walked into the room, holding a microphone.

WALLACE: Pardon me just a second, fellows.

Wallace explained that he was "recording for broadcast," though
he failed to give his name or mention that he was with *60 Minutes*—
none of which was required by law but might have been of interest
to the parties being exposed to Dumbrow and his camera. What followed was what Wallace described as "a pretty frank discussion" about
kickbacks, in which the visitors more or less admitted to wrongdoing
in front of the *60 Minutes* camera. Emboldened, Wallace and his team
kept going, and the encounters kept getting more interesting. Wallace
continued to tell people only that he was "recording for broadcast."
It wasn't until his final grand entrance—after hearing yet another
promise of kickbacks from "Mr. E—— of DJ Laboratories"—that
someone reacted to him as something other than an odd intrusion.

WALLACE: I want to interrupt, if I can. I'm recording this for broadcast, and I just heard you say that you will give back 25 percent
in a kickback, 25 percent on a rebate. Is that correct, Mr. E——?

LAB REPRESENTATIVE: Well—wait a minute. You look familiar
to me.

Wallace didn't respond by identifying himself. Instead, he simply reminded the gentleman that he was "recording for broadcast," at which point Dumbrow left his hiding spot to film the goings-on.

WALLACE: Mr. E——, tell me something. How much in the way of kickbacks and rebates do you get involved with, and why?
LAB REPRESENTATIVE: I—I don't give—I don't give kickbacks.
WALLACE: You just—I heard you right in here. You offered 25 percent in a rebate to these two gentlemen, to this new clinic.
LAB REPRESENTATIVE: Well, I—I didn't mean it that way.
RIORDAN: What was the 25 percent in reference to?
LAB REPRESENTATIVE: I think I better not say anything now.

Later, Wallace, Lando, and Dumbrow went to the office of DJ Labs to investigate further. After they'd spent time asking questions of one of the lab's owners, its attorney stepped in front of the *60 Minutes* camera, jostling it. What followed on screen was the appearance of a camera being moved about, with the back of the lawyer's head filling the frame.

UNIDENTIFIED LAWYER: Sir, you have no right to be here. I ask you to leave. . . . Don't touch me. . . . You're interrupting a business and—
WALLACE: No, no, no—
UNIDENTIFIED LAWYER: I'm sorry, sir, you have no right—Don't touch me, and don't you dare take my picture without permission!

Once again—and while adhering to the letter of the law—Wallace and Lando had pushed the form into a new narrative direction. "The Clinic on Morse Avenue" aired on February 15, 1976, using a style of storytelling more akin to movies than to a news program—which was precisely why *60 Minutes* was attracting more viewers than ever, suggesting to Hewitt and his team that their formula might have caught on at last.

By June, the show was established in its Sunday-at-7 time slot as a perfect counterpoint to the family programming offered by the other networks—*The Wonderful World of Disney* on NBC and *Swiss Family Robinson* on ABC—attracting more than 23 million viewers who had few alternatives in the no-cable universe of network television. The show had acquired a polish and style that reflected its seven years on the air and the now-considerable experience of its correspondents and producers.

The team of Wallace, Safer, and Rather had a potent effect on viewers; the three men quickly became stars in their own right. When Rather went out on the road to report stories, producers noticed a Redford-like following for the correspondent among starstruck locals. He was the show's glamour boy, while Safer and Wallace added weight and wisdom. By that fall they'd been scrutinized in *The New Yorker* and on the front page of the *Wall Street Journal*. The *Journal* headline ("'Sixty Minutes' Mixes News and Show Biz to Provoke and Amuse") went right to the heart of Hewitt's philosophy, and the piece quoted Hewitt as saying, "We try to present and package reality as attractively as Hollywood packages fiction."

The success of the show was finally prompting others to find fault with the *60 Minutes* formula. By this time, O'Connor of the *New York Times* had become a voluble critic of the show he'd once championed. In the *Wall Street Journal* article he spoke of a "seeming anxiety to construct production values for a 'hot' story," which he said raised "unfortunate but legitimate questions" about the journalism on *60 Minutes*. Charges of "managed news" came from prominent (and bruised) targets such as Charles Luce, the head of Consolidated Edison, whose power plant had been the target of Wallace's piece about the disillusioned Pollard. The article in the *Wall Street Journal* also marked the first of many times in Wallace's career in which he suggested the possibility of burnout at his job. "I'm tired," he told the *Journal*. "I can't keep this pace up much longer."

But the criticisms paled by contrast to the financial bonanza created by the show's success. A *New York Times* story reported that rates for a 30-second commercial on *60 Minutes* leapt from $12,500 in the early 1970s to a top price of $50,000—equivalent to the cost of a commercial on a hit CBS series like *Barnaby Jones*. One CBS News producer recalled hearing Richard Salant, the president of CBS News, tell correspondent Eric Sevareid that because of the financial success of *60 Minutes*, he could no longer represent the news division as a money-losing entity: "There's just too much profit."

Meanwhile, the roaring success of *60 Minutes* gave Hewitt unprecedented clout for the producer of a news show. He'd gone from a pariah of the news division, a decade earlier, to its hottest star. To capitalize on the success of *60 Minutes*, CBS News executives approached Hewitt in 1976 with a plan for another newsmagazine, to be called *Who's Who*. They'd recruited CBS News producer John Sharnik (who had worked with Rather at *CBS Reports*) and, with his and Rather's input, they had come up with a weekly series that would focus more on personalities than stories. They auditioned several women as cohosts—including Jessica Savitch of NBC—before settling on Washington writer Barbara Howar, who'd recently published a gossipy bestseller, *Laughing All The Way*.

Just as *60 Minutes* had been based on *Life* magazine, this show would use Time Inc.'s new baby, *People,* as its creative model. With its slick stories on show-biz entertainers balanced against human interest stories of personal crisis, *People* had cleverly tapped into the pop culture obsession of a society recuperating from the social upheavals of the previous decade. Cover stories on celebrities like Joe Namath and Burt Reynolds and Dolly Parton made *People* a guilty pleasure for millions, and CBS was determined to do the same with *Who's Who*—though with a stronger, *60 Minutes*-style emphasis that included cultural icons like author Lillian Hellman and conductor Leopold Stokowski. Hewitt would be involved in overseeing the production. Howar and Rather were to concentrate on the celebrities, while Charles Kuralt, contributing a weekly essay, would handle the human interest angle.

The hour-long show premiered on Tuesday, January 4, 1977, at 8:00 P.M.—up against two of ABC's biggest hit comedies, *Laverne and Shirley* and *Happy Days*. Hewitt was on another suicide mission, not unlike the one he narrowly survived in the late 1960s, against *Marcus Welby, M.D.* Despite surprisingly decent reviews (John Leonard, of the *New York Times*, called it, ironically, "more like the late, lamented *Life*" than its actual *People* magazine model) the show was quickly canceled, with a 29 share—a ratings achievement that today would make it the biggest hit on television. One effect of the show, it turned out, was to anger the *60 Minutes* correspondents, who resented Hewitt's involvement elsewhere. Wallace, notably, raged against Hewitt for failing to spend more time in the *60 Minutes* office.

Now that Hewitt had gotten a taste of success, his long-held passion for money and power clicked into high gear. He wasn't subtle about wanting an ownership position in a show he produced.

"I want Norman Lear money," he was fond of saying, in reference to the enormous financial windfall afforded the producer of another CBS hit series, *All in the Family,* after it was sold into syndication. Instead he got Hewitt money, which was by then in the hundreds of thousands of dollars—a lot for a TV news producer, but nothing compared to the titans of industry he most admired.

In 1977, Hewitt's cravings for money and power led him to Patsy's Restaurant on West 56th Street with ABC's flamboyant entertainment chief, Fred Silverman. Hewitt had known Silverman from his days as a programmer for CBS. Silverman was working to improve the ratings of ABC's new show, *Good Morning America,* which was up against the hugely successful *Today Show* on NBC. Silverman wondered if perhaps he could convince Hewitt to leave *60 Minutes* to run this shaky enterprise.

"Sure," Hewitt said over a plate of Patsy's pasta, "on one condition. I get to own half the show."

According to Hewitt, Silverman considered the proposal seriously enough to take it back to ABC and weigh the economics, but eventually reported back to Hewitt that such an arrangement would be prohibitively expensive. (In 2004 Hewitt suggested that he would be at least $1 billion richer today had that deal gone through.)

By then, other networks were scrambling to imitate the formula that had given CBS its windfall. NBC had previously launched a magazine show called *Weekend,* which aired once a month in the Saturday-at-11:30 P.M. time slot, alternating with *Saturday Night Live,* then a burgeoning pop-culture phenomenon. But unlike *SNL, Weekend* never took off.

In the spring of 1978, at the behest of ABC News president Roone Arledge, ABC launched its own newsmagazine show, *20/20,* which seemed to be trying hard to resemble *60 Minutes,* at least in ratings. As cohosts the network picked former *Esquire* magazine editor Harold Hayes and Australian critic Robert Hughes. ABC let them loose on would-be "gotcha!" investigations, such as one by Geraldo Rivera (a young, confrontational ABC News hotshot who appeared to be modeling his career after Mike Wallace) into how racing greyhounds were being given jack rabbits to use as bait for training purposes. After one episode, Arledge realized the mistake in direction—"I hated the show," he told the press—and quickly replaced Hughes and Hayes with the amiable former *Today Show* host Hugh Downs. Despite ABC's protests that it wasn't imitating *60 Minutes,* its story selection and approach didn't differ that significantly; much as *60 Minutes* had begun in 1968 with Mike Wallace's report on the bioterrorist threat, *20/20* kicked off with a sensational two-part report on nuclear terror.

Hewitt was not out of line to covet millions; in the spring of 1976, ABC's Arledge had ponied up $1 million a year to lure Barbara Walters away from NBC to coanchor the evening newscast with Harry Reasoner—making her the first seven-figure player in the news business and raising the bar for everyone else. Hewitt and his correspondents, already feeling the heady thrill of high ratings, sensed the possibility of similar riches in their future.

But the first person to feel the impact of the Walters bonanza was Harry Reasoner, who suddenly found himself cohosting an evening newscast he'd previously called his own. By early 1978, he'd started talking with CBS about a possible return, and in May, Reasoner announced he would resign from ABC to produce documentaries at CBS. By that time the *60 Minutes* slate was full; Rather, Safer, and Wallace dominated the show, and Reasoner was forced to take an office at the fading *CBS Reports* documentary unit while he bided his time for an open slot.

Once it came that winter, Reasoner realized that *60 Minutes* was not the show he'd left behind. Gone was the rapport that existed between Wallace and himself, replaced by a level of intense rivalry and competition that didn't sit well with Reasoner's laconic style. The three marquee correspondents fought bitterly over everything—stories, producers, and Hewitt—and long stretches of silence were commonplace. The battle for producers had become a regular cause for closed-door meetings, in which the best of the bunch were horse-traded for lesser lights. Wallace didn't mind his reputation as the most wildly competitive of the group; if anything he nurtured it by grabbing the best producers and stories for himself whenever and however he could. And story ideas—supposedly protected by the "blue sheet" system devised in the show's infancy—were now fair game,

From all this backstage skullduggery there emerged one agreeable new element: the return of Andy Rooney to CBS and *60 Minutes*. Rooney had left the network shortly after Reasoner, for a job at PBS's *The Great American Dream Machine*. Later he joined his old pal at ABC, and now that Reasoner had returned to CBS, it made sense for Rooney to come back, too. This time the show would make more use of Rooney's growing gifts as an on-air personality. Hewitt had always wanted more humor and commentary on *60 Minutes*. At one point he even thought about having Rooney write a cartoon strip for the show; the notion of Rooney's wry wit as a weekly insert seemed a logical idea. And so, on a slow Sunday in July 1978, "Three Minutes or So With Andy Rooney" made its first appearance on *60 Minutes*, filling in for the "Point-Counterpoint" feature. Rooney devoted that first segment to driver safety over the July Fourth weekend—spotlighting the odd, counterintuitive fact that more people died in the four days after that weekend than during it.

ROONEY: This suggests two things. One, no matter what we do, whether we're climbing ladders or driving cars, a lot of people die doing it. And second, considering the number of people driving somewhere over the Fourth, the chances are that, car for car, it's one of the safest weekends of the year to be going someplace.

The camera returned to two grinning correspondents.

RATHER: I'm Dan Rather.
WALLACE: I'm Mike Wallace. We'll be back next week with another edition of *60 Minutes*.

Thus another *60 Minutes* tradition was born.

From all that on-camera smiling, it no doubt appeared to audiences that *60 Minutes* was the sort of place where everybody got along and went out for dinner after work and hung out in the hallways trading stories about the weekend. But even with critical success and ratings always on the rise, it remained a rancorous headquarters, with everyone going in separate directions. Rather stayed out of the line of fire by indulging his longstanding love of travel; he often disappeared for days at a time, having little contact with Hewitt or other executives. Wallace was on the road just as much, and when time permitted he preferred to relax at his vacation home on Martha's Vineyard. Safer, the cosmopolitan urban dweller, used his spare time to paint, read, and soak up high culture and good wine. Hewitt, now divorced from his second wife, Frankie, had started dating former *Washington Post* reporter Marilyn Berger; Mike Wallace had fixed them up. ("Just what I need, a journalist," Hewitt cracked when Wallace told him about this attractive reporter he thought Hewitt should date.) He now owned a weekend home in Bridgehampton, where he relished his access to the power brokers who spent their spare time relaxing on the lush confines of the Long Island Sound. The last thing any of these men wanted to do was toast the fruits of their labor together.

On Sunday, November 26, 1978, *60 Minutes* became the highest-rated show on television for the first time in its 10-year history. *All in the Family* and *Alice,* the two shows that followed it on CBS on Sunday nights, ranked second and third in the ratings, respectively. This also marked the first time in the history of television that a regularly scheduled nonfiction program ranked number one—and would have been cause for celebration anywhere else in television except *60 Minutes,* where everyone was too busy battling for the lead position on next week's show.

Chapter 11

Did You See That Great Piece on *60 Minutes?*

Av Westin could have been Don Hewitt. Much like Hewitt, Westin was something of a *wunderkind* producer at CBS News in the 1950s and 1960s, only to find himself in the 1970s in the position of many other middle-aged news producers—without a show to call his own. Unlike many, Westin was honest enough to admit that he'd had one good idea fewer in his life than Don Hewitt, and thus resigned himself to a less exalted fate. A good-natured guy with prodigious producing talents, Westin continued to make his mark in broadcasting, first as a producer in public television in the early 1970s and eventually back in network news as executive producer of ABC's *World News Tonight*. In August 1979, as Hewitt's show continued to beat the competition, Westin was appointed by ABC News as vice president to, among other things, oversee the overhaul of the troubled *20/20*.

But Westin—nothing if not practical—told his colleagues at ABC News that Hewitt had something going for him that they could never hope to have with their show, or any other newsmagazine they might develop: a protected time slot. Perhaps if ABC or NBC had dared to dabble in a Sunday night newsmagazine back when *60 Minutes* first moved to the 7:00 P.M. slot, they might have had a chance. Now it was too late—*60 Minutes* owned that hour, and no one else would ever get it back.

That wasn't the only explanation Westin offered for the success of *60 Minutes*. His thoughtful insight into the show's mammoth ratings was as dead-on accurate as it was depressing to news purists.

"The thing about *60 Minutes*," Westin later recalled telling his bosses, "is that people start the weekend off feeling very noble about themselves. They think, 'I'm going to finish that book,' or, 'I'm going to go to a museum,' or 'Maybe I'll paint a picture.' But by Sunday night, most Americans, weary from the workweek, haven't bothered to do much of anything to tax their brains. So then along comes *60 Minutes*, and it's at 7:00 on Sunday night, and it's a chance to do something a little constructive—maybe to learn something, or see something interesting, or watch something other than a ballgame or a movie. And since *60 Minutes* tells stories in such an interesting way, it's not a painful experience. Then, when they get to work the next morning, they have something to talk about at the water cooler. They can say, 'Did you see that great piece on *60 Minutes* last night?' And it makes them feel a little better about themselves."

That, Westin explained, is why *60 Minutes* worked—and why no matter what he or anyone else did to compete, they were bound to end up just a little less successful than Hewitt and his tigers.

Harry Reasoner negotiated his return to *60 Minutes* in January 1979 at the height of its ratings and earning power.

By then *60 Minutes* had become the network's only consistently top-rated broadcast; according to a *New York Times* calculation, the show was able to charge $215,000 for each minute of commercials, but it cost less than $200,000 a week to produce. With six minutes of paid commercial time per hour, one estimate put the show's profit for the 1979–1980 season at $25 million.

Soon after he came back, Reasoner observed to colleagues that

Hewitt hadn't calmed down—an understatement, as always, from the mild-mannered Reasoner. In May 1979, Hewitt was married for the third time, to Marilyn Berger—Wallace's matchmaking had paid off. Reflecting Hewitt's highly developed champagne tastes, the couple were wed on *La Belle Simone,* a yacht owned by Levittown tycoon Bill Levitt and his wife, Simone. Soon afterward, with the new Mrs. Hewitt flirtatiously leading the way, he managed to ingratiate himself on a Hamptons street corner with CBS owner William Paley, who had a house near Hewitt's. Paley unhesitatingly befriended the creator of one of his network's newest and biggest sources of profit. (The Hewitts remained close friends with Paley for years afterward; Hewitt proudly repeats that he and his wife were present in the hospital when Paley died in 1991.) By then Hewitt was 57 years old, but he had enough energy to devote his usual long hours to the show and still find time to court the rich and famous—the club he'd always longed to join.

Reasoner's colleagues, who were knocking out upward of 30 stories a year, seemed similarly vigorous. All three had become famous— more so than Hewitt—and the show's success gave the correspondents wide leverage to continue their headline-earning investigations. It also opened doors to celebrities who had never talked on television before. Stars knew they'd get fair treatment from the show, as well as a kind of gravitas not afforded elsewhere. And the timing continued to be impeccable—not just the timing of the stories but the correspondents themselves, whose instincts for being at the right place at the right time remained unparalleled.

On January 14, 1979, the show aired Morley Safer's interview with Katharine Hepburn, the legendary—and legendarily reclusive— actress, who had granted Safer a session after meeting producer Jim Jackson and him in London, for reasons Safer could only surmise. Maybe she loved *60 Minutes,* he thought.

Nevertheless, Safer almost botched the interview. Hepburn had warned him that if he arrived at her East Side townhouse even one minute after the scheduled 12:00 noon interview, she would cancel it and send the camera crew home.

On the day of the interview, Safer got into a cab with what he thought would be plenty of time to get there. But by 11:50, he was still caught in traffic; at 11:55, he still hadn't reached her front door. With seconds to spare, Safer realized he had no other option; he jumped out of the cab blocks away and raced all the way to her house, arriving breathless and terrified at her front door at precisely 11:59.

"Mr. Safer," Hepburn said as she answered the door herself, "you are a very lucky young man."

Safer's luck continued once the interview got underway, as he explored the eccentricities of the idiosyncratic actress.

HEPBURN: I won't go to a restaurant now.

SAFER: You don't go out to restaurants?

HEPBURN: I don't go out to restaurants because they charge $60 a meal, and I can serve you here anytime you want to come. You give me $60 and I'll give you dinner.

SAFER: Are you a bit of a—how should I say this—

HEPBURN: Tight.

SAFER: Tight?

HEPBURN: No, I'm not tight, I just don't like injustice . . .

SAFER: If you hadn't been an actress, what would you have been?

HEPBURN: I never thought. I would have tormented some man, I suppose, and had about eight children. And tormented them.

After the interview, and out of view of the CBS cameras, Hepburn took Safer on a tour of her home's private quarters, including the part of the house where she'd lived with Spencer Tracy.

Not to be outdone, of course, Mike Wallace swooped down in late April with a breaking-news interview of his own. Just as Wallace was about to interview Johnny Carson, the elusive host of NBC's *Tonight Show*—after months of negotiations—newspapers around the country bannered the news that Carson might be leaving the show because of a contract dispute with Fred Silverman, the head of the network. Wallace was able to capitalize brilliantly on the interview and do what

60 Minutes had come to do best: get noticed. Guests had become so familiar with the show's routine that they knew precisely how to handle interviews. A master like Carson clearly relished the chance to cross comic swords with Wallace.

> WALLACE: Is there anything you'd like to say to Mr. Silverman?
> CARSON: I hope when this show is seen that you're still with NBC.
> *(Laughs)* I'm as cruel as you are.
> WALLACE: Is it a—is it a fact—
> CARSON: What—what—what—is what a fact?
> WALLACE: Is it a fact that in the middle—
> CARSON: Boy, you're getting warmed up now, aren't you?
> WALLACE: Yeah. Is it—
> CARSON: Takes you a while, but, boy, when that cruel streak starts to come up, you're murder.

For all the scoops and quotes and exposés and headlines, the success of each story always came back to what made Hewitt happy: great characters and human drama. And sometimes the best of these came in the form of pieces about unknowns, men and women who earned a showcase on *60 Minutes* for their achievements, not their failures or their fame. Which is what led Morley Safer, in the fall of 1979, to the memorable story of a Chicago schoolteacher named Marva Collins, who had started the West Side Preparatory School in 1975, an alternative school for inner-city kids. Collins was an extraordinary but largely unrecognized character doing something groundbreaking and important; Safer's spotlight on her would earn her unimagined fame and financial support. (The story also marked probably the first appearance of what would become a staple of television news—the profile of the inspirational inner-city teacher. In the years to come, would-be Marva Collinses showed up with regularity on every newsmagazine and evening news program.)

The Collins story also reminded viewers—and Hewitt as well—of Safer's singular talent among the *60 Minutes* crew. While Wallace soared with his interviews, and Rather scored with his dogged determination, Safer brought to certain stories a unique voice that reflected his personal gifts as a writer. Despite a team of talented producers, no one could ever mistake Safer's words for anybody else's. Safer claims to have written the first draft of every story he did for *60 Minutes* until approximately 1999, when at last, he says, he entrusted the task to producers. The Collins story was a perfect example of Safer's poetry:

> SAFER: You have it all here on West Adams Street, all the familiar big-city blight: the forever broken windows, the burned-out flats, the disemboweled abandoned cars—all that look and smell that even a crystal afternoon cannot change. And up the street or around the corner, you have a school that, for whatever reason, does not teach, and children who, for whatever reason, do not learn—castaways to that ever-growing legion of unskilled black teenaged unemployed. And then you have 3819 West Adams, just another tired-looking house with a blank face staring out at a mean street. But come on in 3819, come on in and take a look. And what you find on the inside could not be more different from what you see on the outside. Come on in and take a look: alert and challenged children being pushed way beyond the boundaries most school systems set.

Without flowery language or far-reaching metaphor, Safer could set a scene with words that created as much a mood as any picture, and with subjects like Collins, he was giving distinction to *60 Minutes* as something more than just a muckraking institution out for headlines.

At a few minutes after midnight on October 21, 1978, Jane Curtin and Dan Aykroyd turned to each other on the "Weekend Update" segment of *Saturday Night Live* and began a sketch called "Point-Counterpoint." Savvy viewers recognized it perhaps as an arcane reference to the *60 Minutes* segment of the same name, in which Shana Alexander and

James J. Kilpatrick had been trading barbs for years. Curtin led with a strong opinion, but the memory of it pales next to what followed, when Aykroyd looked dryly into the camera and intoned, "Jane, you ignorant slut."

Among other things, that night marked the beginning of the end for "Point-Counterpoint" on *60 Minutes*. Hewitt later claimed that the feature—which had begun in the early 1970s with Nicholas Von Hoffman and had grown into a regular (and, at times, tedious) closer to the show—had already run its course when *Saturday Night Live* skewered it. It is true that the parody segment lasted through the end of the current *SNL* season, which repeated the "Jane, you ignorant slut" joke several more times before Aykroyd and Curtin left the cast in the spring of 1979. And it is also true that a few months after that (in September 1979) it was announced that Alexander was quitting her position on *60 Minutes* after a fight with Hewitt over salary. She claimed in the *New York Times* that Hewitt refused to raise her weekly $600 fee for appearing on television's top-rated show. Hewitt countered that Alexander had demanded a raise to $1,500 a week. "I never disagreed with Shana and her strong support of the proposition that men and women should get equal pay for equal work," Hewitt told the *Times*, "but when she demanded two and a half times what Jack [Kilpatrick] received, I had to say no." Alexander denied having asked for that much, and insisted she sought a raise for Kirkpatrick as well. It was a chance for Hewitt to simultaneously get rid of Alexander and make himself look like the wronged party.

In the fall of 1979, with the show now so totally in the spotlight (what greater badge of status as a cultural icon could there be than to be regularly parodied on *Saturday Night Live*?) Hewitt knew he had the leverage to expand and deepen his territory more than ever before. It didn't hurt that his old friend Bill Leonard—who more than anyone else at CBS News was responsible for getting *60 Minutes* on the air back in 1968—was about to replace Dick Salant. Hewitt was ready to add yet another correspondent to the mix. It wasn't enough to have Reasoner back; he wanted someone young, fresh, and different to enliven the mix. He was ready to cast another star, and this time he didn't need any advice about who to pick. The perfect performer for *60 Minutes* was already working at CBS News, and Hewitt couldn't wait to hire him; he had to hurry, though, because the man he had in mind had a tendency to get bored and restless.

In 1971, just as *60 Minutes* was moving to Sunday nights, Ed Bradley moved to Paris, leaving behind a perfectly respectable job as a reporter for WCBS News radio in New York. It was just the kind of move you'd expect from Bradley, who cared far more about being happy than being famous. He loved music, especially jazz. He probably loved music more than journalism, which is how he ended up hanging around Paris without a job or an income for quite a while, hanging out in smoky bars and enjoying the moment with the kind of calm and contentment a man like Hewitt would never understand. But eventually, of course, the money ran out, and—Paris being an expensive city for an impoverished and unemployed 29-year-old—Bradley wandered into the CBS radio office in Paris to see if they might need a stringer. He didn't want a full-time job, though—just enough work to pay the bills and stay as long as possible. And somehow, as had always been the case for Bradley, things worked out better than he expected. It wasn't long before he landed on television for CBS; eventually the news division asked him to go to Vietnam as a contract assignment reporter, at a salary of $20,000 a year. He wasn't thrilled about the money—it was half what he'd been making in radio—but he took it anyway, and it turned out to be a canny career move. Bradley covered Vietnam, Cambodia, and Laos before CBS brought him to Washington in 1974.

The move proved frustrating. Bradley didn't like being the new guy in the Washington bureau, getting lousy assignments that no one else wanted, so he took a month off from work and went to Canada to ski; afterward he drove across Canada to Windsor and then to Detroit, to visit his father. Along the way he formulated a plan for what came next: Go back and give this your best shot. Don't put any time frame on it. If it's not working, you'll know it's not working. And be careful with your money. You'll still be on contract (to CBS News), you'll have to ride out the contract. Then you can quit CBS News forever.

A fortuitously timed return trip to Cambodia in the winter of 1975 rendered all that moot. The Khmer Rouge had started their annual dry-season offensive, and many said that this time they would at last succeed in toppling the American-supported government led by President Lon Nol. Bradley jumped on Pan Am Flight 1 from New York to Southeast Asia and arrived in the midst of chaos and breaking news stories everywhere he looked. In February, Bradley was on hand to report the successful overthrow of the government of Cambodia, followed in April by the fall of Saigon—and was evacuated from both places by military helicopter. For 24 eventful hours, Bradley was the only TV journalist on the scene to gather first-person reports of the Saigon evacuation.

Bradley returned to the United States a network news star and quickly advanced to the front of the line for plum Washington assignments. He began the 1976 presidential campaign covering Democratic Senator Birch Bayh of Indiana and finished as a reporter on the Jimmy Carter campaign. It was during that campaign that he made the acquaintance of *Rolling Stone* reporter Hunter S. Thompson, who invited Bradley to come with him to cover the Florida primary. He turned that assignment into a job covering the Carter White House for the next two years, and his acquaintance with Thompson became a lifelong friendship.

But even at the pinnacle of broadcasting, Bradley grew restless. It seemed a part of his nature to want to escape the confinement of a full-time job; no matter how golden the handcuffs, he still felt imprisoned by the demands of deadlines. By 1978 he had gotten himself transferred to a job held only three years earlier by Dan Rather—chief correspondent for *CBS Reports*. It was an escape to the world of hour-long documentaries and the freedom he'd been wanting for so long.

It was a good gig for Bradley. He relished the chance to do documentaries on subjects of his own choosing, and over most of the next two years, his broadcasts earned him attention as both a thoughtful journalist and a smooth-talking on-air personality. Even by the late

1970s, black reporters remained a small minority in television news, and in blunt Q-ratings terms, even fewer were in the same league as Ed Bradley. His handsome face and perfectly modulated voice made him a natural, and an obvious choice for job openings. It was around this time that Bradley got married, briefly, to Rita Coolidge's sister, Priscilla; he'd been married once before, in the early 1960s.

Thrilled with his new job, Bradley did hours on the boat people in Cambodia, the Three Mile Island nuclear disaster, the Central Intelligence Agency, and a two-hour show on the impact of *Brown v. Board of Education*. But eventually Bradley started to notice that CBS wasn't giving the show any more time slots; he soon had his eye on the door yet again, this time looking across the street from his office at CBS News—where the staff of *60 Minutes* had set up shop in a nondescript office building that housed a car dealership on the ground floor.

A year earlier, in July 1978, Walter Cronkite had gone to the office of newly appointed CBS News president Bill Leonard and dropped a bit of unexpected—and unwelcome—news on the new boss.

"Is there anything I can do for you?" Leonard asked his biggest star performer. "Is everything all right?"

"Well . . . well, Bill, actually, there's one little thing," Cronkite said.

"Go right ahead, Walter." Leonard already knew that whatever it was, it wasn't going to be little.

"Well," Cronkite said, "I want to give up the *Evening News*." After registering the shock on Leonard's face and explaining how the weight of the show had become unbearable after nearly two decades as anchorman, Cronkite had concluded, "I'd be a damn fool not to quit while I'm ahead." It was a decision Cronkite would live to regret, particularly once CBS News froze him out of a future on-air role in network news coverage. (Now 87 years old, he most recently hosted a political special for MTV.)

Cronkite's contract kept him in the job until his sixty-fifth birthday in 1981, but Leonard understood that he needed to move quickly and decisively to find a successor. One crucial reason: Leonard wasn't the only news president in town shopping for an anchor. With Reasoner's departure from ABC and the debacle of the Barbara Walters pairing, Roone Arledge was looking for someone with well-established credibility to be the new face of ABC News, and he was obviously willing to pay for it. Just about everyone in the business knew the face he had in mind: Dan Rather's.

Until just recently, CBS insiders had voiced a decided preference for Washington correspondent Roger Mudd as Cronkite's successor; had Arledge not started waving a lot of money around, Mudd might have gotten the job. But Arledge, who suspected that the promise of a bigger paycheck might entice Rather to leave *60 Minutes* (where he earned $300,000 a year) and CBS for the chance to anchor his own nightly newscast, put a $2.2 million annual salary on the table, prompting a heated round of negotiations between CBS and ABC through Rather's tough-talking agent, Richard Leibner.

The price was not insignificant—$22 million over 10 years and the eventual loss of Roger Mudd—but Leonard finally paid it on the morning of February 18, 1980, at which point Dan Rather prepared to leave *60 Minutes* for the seat behind the most trusted desk in America.

Hewitt, ever the pragmatist, didn't devote much time to bemoaning the loss of his star, having already picked Ed Bradley to take his place. Besides, he knew that in a few months—well before Rather was set to bolt—*60 Minutes* would air a piece that would likely be remembered, far more than any single nightly newscast could, as a defining moment in the history of the show and of Rather's career.

Chapter 12

I Never Saw the Knife

Gunga Dan was born on the night of April 6, 1980. To the single-minded Dan Rather, the image of the correspondent swaddled in a blanket and a knit cap and being smuggled into war-torn Afghanistan was intended to give this difficult and complicated story a human dimension for Americans unconcerned about a small country under attack. But in typical Rather fashion, "Inside Afghanistan" quickly became more about Rather than about the horrors he was reporting, whether by accident or by design.

It all began in late December 1979, two days after the Soviet Union invaded Afghanistan. Soon after Christmas, Rather went into Hewitt's office—they were the only two people left at *60 Minutes* that night, by Rather's account in *The Camera Always Blinks Twice*—and proposed going to Afghanistan to report on the war. "Forget it," Hewitt said, making it perfectly clear to Rather that he wasn't all that interested in Afghanistan.

"Come on," Hewitt told his reporter. "It's New Year's. Go home. Enjoy the holidays."

But Rather pressed repeatedly to go, despite the huge expense and great difficulty involved. In January he dispatched his producer Andrew Lack to Pakistan to find intermediaries who might take them across the border. In late February, shortly after signing his contract to take over the *Evening News*, he traveled to Pakistan to meet up with Lack and begin their journey into the heart of war. Because of the story's exorbitant cost—estimated at twice the $45,000 budgeted for a typical *60 Minutes* story—they decided not to let CBS management in on their plans. Rather, Lack, and a camera crew entered Afghanistan the only way possible—under cover, on foot, and dressed in native garb. Almost immediately the story they hoped they'd find revealed itself: the Soviets were indeed using napalm and gas to kill innocent civilians in a brutal war effort. The story, gruesome and dramatic, was everything Rather could wish for.

But by any standard of reporting, it was a difficult one to get. At times, the crew had no option but to sleep together in a single room or on the roadside, often for just a few hours. They'd walk, then rest for 10 minutes of every hour; after six hours of walking they would stop to sleep for four hours. At all times, one of them remained awake to keep watch. Every so often, Lack and Rather would take a sip from a flask of Kentucky whiskey Rather had brought along. They walked through rice paddies and past old opium poppy fields in a perilous search for witnesses to the atrocities alleged against the Soviets. They crossed the Kabul River by holding onto flotation devices fashioned from the inflated bellies of dead cows and water buffalo. Some of the crew contracted dysentery; gradually their food supplies dwindled to nothing.

Toward the end of the trip, as Rather and his producer realized they would need some additional shots for cutaways, Rather suggested he outfit himself with a turban. One of their guides put a turban on Dan's head to ready him for a shot, until Lack got a good look at him and vetoed the idea—"afraid I would make an ass of myself," Rather later recalled.

Lack—a talented producer who had been rescued from an advertising job in 1976 to work on *Who's Who*—took the raw footage from the trip and turned the experience into a compelling story, with Rather and the CBS cameras as the eyes and ears of the Western world. But running throughout the piece was an awareness that perhaps this method of reporting would prove suspect to a cynical American audience—hence this somewhat defensive introduction read by Mike Wallace and written by Hewitt himself. From the beginning of the show in 1968 through his retirement in June 2004, Hewitt claims to have written every opening "tease" for *60 Minutes*—the brief introductions that lead into the show itself and highlight its most dramatic elements.

WALLACE: If you want to know what's going on in Afghanistan, there's only one way: you go in yourself. And there's only one way for an American to do that: make contact with a rebel group just over the border in Pakistan, disguise yourself as a native, and let the rebels smuggle you into their country. That's exactly what Dan Rather did to cover the war Afghan rebels like these are waging in their country against the Soviet invaders. The number of refugees from that war is staggering. Rather says the roads leading out of the country are choked with them. But then you leave the roads and start up into the mountains. Somewhere up in these hills, there's a ridge looking down on a Soviet emplacement. It'll be dark by the time you get there, and you'll be out of breath from the climb. But up on that ridge, Dan Rather found the war he came to cover. Through an interpreter, Rather interviewed a white-bearded guerrilla fighter known as Yassini—who lived, as Rather said, "on the run, moving from mountain hideouts through tiny villages of straw and mud huts to the opium fields that often provide him and his men cover from the Russian aircraft that circle continuously." Yassini stood in for all the witnesses Rather and Lack had met and interviewed.

RATHER *(to the interpreter)*: Has he seen any napalm?

NABY *(interpreter for Yassini)*: Yes. You mean the one that throws down fire on us?

RATHER: Yes.

NABY: Yes. They also use gas, yes . . .

RATHER *(to a doctor with Yassini)*: He's absolutely sure it was some sort of gas?

NABY: He says what I can be sure of is that there was a smell, and then when—when that happened, we were all unconscious for about half an hour.

The piece contained many such stirring interviews, and dramatic news—news perhaps even to the American government, which was ill-informed about the events inside Afghanistan. But the extent to which Rather himself dominated the images of "Inside Afghanistan" was unprecedented, even for a program designed to showcase the further adventures of Mike, Morley, Harry, and Dan. The reaction was nothing like he'd hoped it would be.

Tom Shales, the *Washington Post* TV critic, eviscerated the piece and Rather in his day-after review, with the memorable moniker "Gunga Dan" contained in the review's headline and the following lead:

Your assignment, Dan, should you agree to accept it, is to penetrate the Afghanistan border, gain the confidence of resistance fighters there, let your beard grow a few days, wear a funny hat, and file a story for *60 Minutes* that will have Roone Arledge absolutely chartreuse with envy. . . .

We may never know precisely how dauntless Don Hewitt, producer of *60 Minutes*, and daring Dan Rather, crown prince of network news, plotted the slightly sensational Afghanistan war repost seen on CBS last night. But the result was in the best and worst ways typical of the program and its enterprise: punchy, crunchy, highly dramatic, and essentially uninformative.

Except that, yes, we knew something about the war against the invading Soviet troops before *60 Minutes*, but, and this is important, did we know how the war was affecting Dan Rather?

The *Post* critic went on to describe Rather's outfit as something out of *Dr. Zhivago*. "Vanessa Redgrave wearing the same outfit would have been welcomed at any chic party in Europe," Shales wrote. "Somehow one got the feeling that this was not so much Dan Rather as Stuart Whitman playing Dan Rather. Or Dan Rather playing Stuart Whitman playing Dan Rather. Perhaps it's all part of the New Reality." Shales concluded by wondering "whether Murrow is smiling down approvingly or spinning in his grave."

Murrow might also have been a bit skeptical in the summer of 1980, when for the first time Hewitt and CBS dared to rerun old segments of *60 Minutes* instead of producing new ones. The notion of news as something with rerun value was yet another pioneering Hewitt idea and, as usual, one that sparked controversy. CBS justified it as a practical development, giving the producers and correspondents a chance to take time off. "They're like good racehorses," Hewitt explained, giving his tiger metaphor a brief break. "They just have to be rested."

As was often the case, Hewitt's old nemesis Fred Friendly surfaced in high dudgeon over the idea. "These are important, complicated times," Friendly told Tony Schwartz in the *New York Times*. "How can the highest-rated and best news show on television put on a rerun of an interview with Johnny Carson, or a story about panhandling, when there is so much going on in the world?" When Schwartz pointed out to Friendly that his own *CBS Reports* had run repeats during the early 1960s, Friendly replied, "I don't hold myself up as a model of virtue," adding that "I would hope we've made some progress in twenty years." One area in which there had apparently been no progress during that same 20 years was in the relationship between Friendly and Hewitt.

It was a van, ordinary in all respects and unlikely to be noticed by anyone, unless you were looking at it carefully enough to have your curiosity piqued by the drapes over the back windows, and colored gel over the sides. On the roof of the van was a sign that said Emergency Service, and it was hoped (by *60 Minutes* cameraman Wade Bingham and producer Marion Goldin) that would be enough to keep the police from disturbing the journalists inside, who were there on a mission: to photograph a Los Angeles physician as he walked from a parking lot to the clinic where he worked. The physician in question was being investigated for Medicaid fraud—which, in light of the success of the 1976 "Clinic on Morse Avenue" piece, made him perfect fodder for a team working for Mike Wallace. It was Bingham's job to shoot film without the doctor realizing it, as part of an October 1979 exposé undertaken in a manner *60 Minutes* had practically invented—the hidden-camera investigation.

With the ascent of Wallace wannabe Geraldo Rivera on ABC's *20/20*, the hidden camera and "Mike jumping out of closets" (as Morley Safer referred to the technique) wasn't quite as fresh as it had been three years earlier. But Bingham, who had become something of an expert in such matters, continued to strive for fresh angles and techniques, hiding cameras in all manner of containers. He'd used large women's pocketbooks, schoolbags, and suitcases, all of which had to be soundproofed to obscure the noise a film camera made when it was turned on. Plus Bingham would typically have to cut a hole in the side of the bag, big enough for the lens to poke through. Despite his experience, it was still a shady new world for Bingham, who'd come to *60 Minutes* after a distinguished career shooting stories all over the world for CBS, from Pakistan to Hawaii to Tokyo. He'd been brought back to New York by no less a figure than Edward R. Murrow and later shot film for Hewitt on documentaries that included that famous hour with Frank Sinatra in 1965.

The "gotcha!" technique had been refined by Wallace, his producers, and cameramen since the Medicaid kickback piece. In May 1977, an investigation into child pornography had taken producer Barry Lando and cameraman Larry Travis undercover into a Los Angeles pornography store, acting like customers in search of kiddie porn. Examining movies being sold under the counter, Travis (his camera buried inside a shoulder bag) filmed this exchange:

CLERK: This is Lulu. Beautiful.
LANDO: How old is she?

CLERK: Thirteen.

LANDO: Thirteen?

CLERK: Uh-huh.

It was juicy stuff, even though Travis had been forced to go outside every so often and reload his small hand-held camera, which couldn't hold more than 30 seconds of film.

By 1979 the technology had advanced to the point where Bingham could shoot extensively to get the shot he wanted. And by the time "Edward Rubin, M.D." aired on October 21, 1979, how-we-got-that-picture had become the story; Wallace seemed almost as interested in telling the viewers about the subterfuge as he was in explaining the allegations against the doctor: complicated charges, including the possibility that he'd received cash payments from patients as well as reimbursements from MediCal (the California version of Medicaid) and that he was getting back part of the fees for x-rays and other tests he'd ordered. Wallace did a series of interviews with Rubin's detractors, then set up shop in front of Rubin's clinic, with this narration over the footage shot by Bingham.

WALLACE: This is Dr. Edward Rubin. He ignored our letters and telephone calls requesting an interview. Nonetheless, we did manage to photograph the silent Dr. Rubin coming to work.

Cut to a shot of Wallace approaching the doctor with a microphone in his hand:

WALLACE: Dr. Rubin, I wonder if I could talk to you for just a moment, sir. Dr. Rubin?

Rubin ignored Wallace. Thus what in a newspaper story would have been a simple sentence—"Dr. Rubin declined to comment"—had become the most compelling visual aspect of the story. Rubin's encounter with the dogged Wallace would be what viewers remembered

and talked about the next day—as opposed to, say, the heinous crime
of Medicaid fraud.

But for all of Wallace's success, some careful observers were worried that
his work might be slipping. The swelling ranks of Wallace imitators was
contributing to a sense that his style of journalism, once fresh and original, was in danger of becoming predictable. Hewitt was among those
determined to ensure that Wallace remained in a class by himself—
understanding better than anyone the correspondent's unique role in
the success of *60 Minutes*.

Which is what led Hewitt to find himself one day in the spring of
1980 in conversation with Ira Rosen's mother.

Rosen was then a 26-year-old producer for Channel 9, a local New
York television station, where he had his own weekly newsmagazine
show modeled after *60 Minutes*. He'd been a journalist from his late
teens in Pontiac, Michigan, where he covered the Mafia and sports for
the local paper, but he'd taken a liking to television, particularly the
style of journalism in vogue at CBS with correspondents like Wallace.
He'd even done his own modified versions of the pieces he admired, including a story about secret films at the Pentagon with its own "gotcha!"
elements.

One day that spring, a *60 Minutes* projectionist ran into Hewitt in
the company cafeteria. "I saw this piece last night on Channel 9," he
said. "It was just the kind of piece Mike Wallace used to do." Incensed
that anyone believed Wallace had stopped doing great stories, Hewitt
tore back to his office to find out exactly who'd done this reportedly
brilliant segment. He got a copy of the tape, then tracked down Rosen's
home number—and reached Rosen's mother.

"I'm sorry, Mr. Hewitt," Rosen's mother told him, "but Ira already
has a job," and hung up on him. That sealed it for Hewitt—he would
make it his mission to wrestle Rosen free from the clutches of Channel 9. In a span of weeks Rosen went from local television to *60 Minutes*, where he produced for Mike Wallace. In 1989, after nine years
at the show, Rosen left to become a senior producer for ABC's *Prime*

Time Live, where he introduced hidden-camera and other *60 Minutes* investigative techniques to the show, cohosted by *60 Minutes* alumna Diane Sawyer. Then, in the spring of 2004—in the wake of a *Prime Time* shakeup—Rosen returned to *60 Minutes* as a producer for Steve Kroft.

But despite Hewitt's passion for the ambush interview, confrontational journalism, and "gotcha!" stories that gave the show its juice, there remained within him some uncertainty over their continued use. Perhaps for that reason, the show began its 1981 season with an unusual hour devoted exclusively to an examination of itself. Jeff Greenfield, a CBS News media critic, was brought in to moderate a panel that included Ellen Goodman of the *Boston Globe* and Herbert Schmertz, vice president of Mobil Oil, who'd often been outspoken in his criticism of the news business. The general conclusion of the panel was that the techniques used by *60 Minutes* posed serious fairness questions. Discussing the Wallace-Lando "Fake ID" story from 1975, Goodman observed: "You're saying in pursuit of deceit, deceit is okay. What happens if this becomes pervasive?"

Hewitt found himself in full self-criticism mode—a radical departure from his typical attack posture. He conceded that the ambush approach was "a technique that has been abused" and promised that it would be used less often in the future. "It's like trying to get a man to testify against himself," Hewitt reluctantly admitted, caught in his own "gotcha!" moment.

In June 1981, in preparation for the upcoming season, the support staff of *60 Minutes* was handed a Herculean logistical challenge: to get the entire cast of *60 Minutes* in New York at the same time to pose for a picture. As the number one show on television, *60 Minutes* needed a fresh group portrait to send out each season; chances were, newspapers and magazines would print it on the covers of their Sunday television guides, and it would be used frequently in advertising and corporate promotion. It was a corporate imperative and a matter of maintaining stardom—which is why everyone had taken time from their frantic travel schedules to gather in a New York photographer's studio to pose yet again.

The regularity of the photo shoot also had something to do with the dizzying (at least by *60 Minutes* standards) changes in the cast in recent years. First Mike and Harry, then Mike and Morley, then Mike and Morley and Dan, then Harry again . . . it was getting a little hard for viewers to recall who exactly was on *60 Minutes* from season to season. A new snapshot always helped.

This year, the picture would include, for the first time, its newest correspondent, Ed Bradley, hired to replace Dan Rather. Bradley, about to turn 40, stood slightly in awe of the men he was about to pose with—Mike Wallace, 63; Morley Safer, 49; and Reasoner, 58, were among the most prized on-air talents at CBS News. It was a heady experience to stand in such distinguished company; these guys, after all, had helped lead *60 Minutes* from the depths of ratings hell to the top of the mountain. They'd also become, in the process, the biggest stars of the news business. Even for a supremely confident man like Bradley, there was something electric, something truly memorable about a moment like this in a career.

The photographer took one last look at the three reporters and said, "Smile!" At that precise moment, Wallace leaned down into hissing distance of Bradley's ear.

"You know, if this show goes into the dumper," Wallace whispered to his new colleague, "they're going to blame it on you."

Bradley was able to hide his shock as he and Wallace smiled together for the camera. The picture came out perfectly, preserving for Bradley a quintessential moment that would serve as a portent of the dangers ahead at *60 Minutes*. Moreover, it was a permanent reminder to Bradley to watch his back at all times.

Almost immediately, Bradley had to contend with Wallace's hypercompetitive instincts, which first flared in a pitched battle over the services of a valued producer, Steve Glauber, who had joined Wallace's unit to replace the departing Marion Goldin.

When Bradley learned that Glauber had been poached from his

staff, he immediately stomped into Hewitt's office and demanded a reason. It was never Bradley's style to be cowed by management. "Hey, I don't have a voice in this?" he asked. "It happens like that?"

"It's for the good of the show," Hewitt explained.

"No, no, no," Bradley replied, his anger rising. "I don't accept that. This producer is working for me, and you're just going to take him away without asking me about it? Bullshit. So who do I appeal to at the next highest level?"

The next day a CBS News vice president came to *60 Minutes* for a tense meeting with Hewitt, Wallace, Bradley, and Phil Scheffler, who had recently replaced Palmer Williams as the senior producer of the show.

"We think that it's for the good of the show," explained the CBS executive, "because Marion's gone, that Steve go to Mike."

Bradley looked around the room at his new colleagues and realized he had no hope of salvaging the situation.

"You know, this was all decided before I got in here," Bradley said with resignation. "No matter what I said, this was going to happen." At which point he turned to face Wallace directly.

"I never saw the knife," Bradley whispered to Wallace. "It won't happen again."

The producer issue was particularly important to Bradley; for all his gifts, he'd never been known as a particularly energetic writer for television, and he knew it. Often he depended entirely on his producers to deliver camera-ready copy to him; he preferred a constant travel schedule and endless reporting to the idea of sitting alone in his office writing a script. In the fall of 1981 he went on air with memorable stories about the Irish Republican Army and a profile of the philosopher-journalist I. F. Stone. And within just two months he'd delivered one of the most memorable pieces ever aired on *60 Minutes*—a heart-wrenching profile of the singer Lena Horne, a piece that demonstrated Bradley's interview gifts and the show's own continued appetite for definitive interviews with cultural icons. In it, he got Horne to confess—with tears streaming down her cheeks—the pain she felt at growing up as a light-skinned black woman who could pass for white. Horne also talked with Bradley about her passion for sex in a way that appeared to be thinly disguised flirtation.

> HORNE: If a lady treats other people as she'd like to be treated, then she's allowed to go and roll in the grass if she wants to.
> BRADLEY: Even if she's 64?
> HORNE: Even if she's 64. Particularly then!

It was as refreshingly honest an answer as had been given on *60 Minutes*, and Hewitt's longstanding affection for the Horne piece perhaps had something to do with Horne's energetic attitude toward age and sex, which bore a significant resemblance to his own.

Chapter 13

Watermelon and Tacos

With Reasoner back at *60 Minutes* and Bradley on the team, all looked right to the outside world. The show had never been better than in 1981. Stories on homelessness, surrogate mothers, chemical dumping, and the murder of Malcolm X were balanced by trenchant profiles of journalist Tom Wolfe, architect Paolo Soleri, Russian poet Joseph Brodsky, and tennis star Martina Navratilova. Hewitt's formula had effectively killed off the competition on other networks. The show was earning an estimated $70 million a year in profit, and Hewitt and his tigers had become major television celebrities.

Behind the scenes, however, the atmosphere remained toxic. There was rarely a time at *60 Minutes* when everyone was speaking to each other; at any given moment, at least two correspondents (Wallace and Safer, Safer and Rather, Wallace and Bradley) were embroiled in a conflict serious enough to warrant the silent treatment. With *60 Minutes* still hovering around the number one spot in the Nielsens and consistently in the top 10, the show's success spurred the correspondents to battle for supremacy in the eyes of Hewitt as well as the public. Nobody backed off. Nobody gave in.

While Wallace, Safer, Reasoner, and Bradley all had gentlemanly aspects to their character, at times they all got caught up in the competitiveness that was also essential to Wallace's nature. Though he could also be a seductive and charismatic leader, his producers contended he could also be something of a bully. Most of them say in his defense that it was always about the work, but late-night calls from Wallace to criticize their performance or demand more of their time left them drained. It wasn't uncommon for even the most loyal Wallace producer to defect to another correspondent's team for a year, seeking a respite from the grind. Paul Loewenwarter, who had worked steadily and without complaint for Wallace since the show's earliest days, took time off from him at one point to "recharge his batteries," as he put it, before returning later. "Wallace is Wallace," Loewenwarter explained, echoing the conflict felt by so many who were captivated by the correspondent's magnetic aura but feared his lacerating criticism. Wallace had no tolerance for anything but the best and often picked apart his producers' work with the same kind of abusive and obscene language that had become commonplace in the show's screenings and hallways.

Wallace, to his credit, didn't deny his difficult manner. When long-time producer Norman Gorin was in the hospital recovering from major surgery, Wallace sent a cactus to him with a note that read, "From your prickly friend." To which Gorin replied: "Nice try, but adding the suffix doesn't change a thing."

Despite his courtly demeanor, Safer often found himself drawn into battle. His relationship with Rather had always been rocky, going all the way back to conflicts from their days in Vietnam together. There had also been a period of silence between Safer and Reasoner over minor issues that somehow exploded into larger ones. He screamed back in screenings when Hewitt yelled at him, and later kicked himself for stooping to his boss's level. That said, Safer appreciated the way Hewitt could quickly forget his anger. Often, five minutes after an expletive-laden diatribe, Hewitt would wander into Safer's office and sit down for a jaw, as though nothing had happened. Often he even apologized.

Safer's issues with Wallace went deeper than with the others. In the early days of *60 Minutes,* the two men had spent at least two years not speaking to each other, and the wounds from that schism took a while to heal. They were cordial to one another, but at heart their relationship had no hope of becoming anything more; in fact, Safer kept an old 1968 campaign button that read "To Hell With Wallace" on his office wall. Their conflicts ranged from control of producers—a matter of supreme importance to Wallace—to ownership of story ideas.

Everyone was always in some kind of battle with Hewitt, whose ego had been further inflated by the show's continued triumph. His screening room persona as the American Everyman gave him a platform to attack his correspondents and their pieces on a regular basis. While they often conceded that their boss was a "genius" at editing pieces in a screening room, they were just as likely to label him an idiot savant out of earshot. The more famous they became, the less likely any of them were to tolerate Hewitt's critiques of their work.

It was hard for anyone to find fault with the piece Harry Reasoner delivered on the night of November 15, 1981, "The Best Movie Ever Made?" If ever the main character of a *60 Minutes* story was the correspondent telling it, this was it—an elegiac examination by Reasoner of *Casablanca,* undertaken for no reason whatsoever, except that Reasoner happened to love the film. Producer Drew Phillips dutifully came up with a few news pegs for the piece: it turned out, for instance, that replicas of Rick's Cafe were opening up everywhere, and a recent showing of the movie in Pittsburgh pulled in a crowd of 1,200. Here and there, Phillips and Reasoner interviewed moviegoers about the experience of seeing it or found trivia concerning the production. But mostly the piece existed to allow Reasoner to rhapsodize about a movie that touched him like no other. Intercutting what was essentially an essay by Reasoner with clips from the movie itself, it gave viewers a rare glimpse into the psyche of a man they knew only through television.

REASONER: Our romantic minds are a hodgepodge, storage rooms full of objects meaningless in themselves except as they serve as props to bring back a song or a smile or a remembered line. . . .

Phillips had arranged for the props from *Casablanca* to be used in the piece, including the legendary piano at which Dooley Wilson, as Sam, played "As Time Goes By."

REASONER: Bogart liked music, too. Although as every student of trivia knows, he never said, "Play it again, Sam." By the time he said what he did say, most of the bourbon in the bottle was gone.

More clips, more comments, and then this poetic summation of the story:

REASONER: If in a standard movie boy meets girl, boy loses girl, boy gets girl, this was boy gets girl, boy loses girl, boy gets girl back, boy gives up girl for humanity's sake. That's better than *Gone With the Wind,* when he gave her up out of ennui. . . . There is great power in the ending, too, possibly because almost up to the moment it was filmed and up to the moment an audience sees it for the first time, nobody knew what the ending was going to be. Rick gets everybody together at the airport, and keeps Claude Rains in line with a gun in the now-famous trench coat.

Another clip from the movie followed, then this snippet from Reasoner's interview with Ingrid Bergman.

BERGMAN: Now, we were going to shoot two ends: one that I stayed on the ground with Humphrey Bogart, and my husband would be so understanding and so generous that he would say good-bye—*(laughs)*—and leave alone; or I would go with my husband, feel my duty, and Humphrey Bogart would be alone in the fog. And we shot that scene first. Cut, and everybody said that's it, we don't have to shoot the other end, because we cannot get anything better than this. But they didn't know until they saw it.

REASONER: To tidy things up, Rick shoots the Nazi major, and Claude Rains gets the opportunity to take advantage of the film's most dramatic pause. . . . And that leads to what sure has become the most familiar exit line in movie history.

At which point the necessary clip played—"Louie," Rains says to Bogart, "I think this is the beginning of a beautiful friendship"— followed by Reasoner's own classic ending, a glimpse of him at his most eloquent and touching.

REASONER: I don't suppose then or now young men wind up for good with the young women with whom they first saw *Casablanca*. I didn't. The story seems to lead to bittersweet endings in real life, too. But you never forget who you first saw it with. I wonder if she remembers. If she does, here's looking at you, kid.

*   *   *

In 1981, *60 Minutes* represented a rare bright spot on the CBS News balance sheet. Dan Rather's arrival as anchorman on the *CBS Evening News* translated into an immediate ratings drop for that broadcast, and the network continued to struggle with its morning show, now well behind both the *Today* show and *Good Morning America*.

The network had trouble on another front, too: the burgeoning success of afternoon talk shows, in particular Phil Donahue's popular 4:00 P.M. weekday series. In a desperate effort to compete, CBS News convinced the men of *60 Minutes*—Mike, Morley, Ed, and Harry—to appear on *Up to the Minute*. It ripped off various aspects of the Sunday night show, including the large stopwatch that appeared behind the correspondents. They took turns each week hosting the show, which featured audience participation led by that week's guest correspondent. The show would deal each day with a variety of topics aimed at women, such as "Aggressive Women: Turn On or Turn Off?" and included parenting commentary from Bob Keeshan, otherwise known as Captain Kangaroo—who'd been given this slot in return for donating a half-hour of his morning time to the news division.

But by November, after just two months on the air, *Up to the Minute* was canceled, its ratings even lower than the previous occupant of the time slot—reruns of *One Day at a Time*. As it turned out, the *60 Minutes* stars were no guarantee of ratings outside their protected Sunday nighttime slot, to which they happily retreated.

Success was beginning to take its toll on the *60 Minutes* team. The worst of it came in the form of increasing media scrutiny, mostly focused on Mike Wallace—still the show's biggest star and thus its most obvious target.

In January 1982, the *Los Angeles Times* revealed that Wallace—the correspondent who most loved catching people unawares with a camera—had himself been taped surreptitiously, with embarrassing results. It happened the previous March, when Wallace was interviewing a bank executive in San Diego for a story about lien contracts, in which customers unwittingly put their houses up as collateral for loans to buy amenities like air conditioners and carpeting. Minorities in particular were losing their homes in foreclosures by unscrupulous lenders. It was a well-intentioned piece, but while doing the San Diego interview, Wallace let slip a politically incorrect wisecrack that was recorded on tape.

"I wonder why they sign those contracts without reading them," remarked someone in the room with Wallace, according to a record provided by the bank, which later claimed it had gotten Wallace's permission to videotape the interview. (Wallace insisted the remarks were made during a break in the interview, while a *60 Minutes* cameraman was reloading his camera, having run out of film.)

"They're probably too busy eating their watermelon and tacos," Wallace replied.

Wallace didn't deny the remark to the *Los Angeles Times*, but told reporter Nancy Skelton for her page-one story on January 10, 1982: "Look, I happen to have a penchant for obscenity and for jokes." The next day in the *New York Times*, Wallace claimed the comment was "off the record" and was made to elicit "latent racist" views from the interview subject. "In hindsight," Wallace said, "it's conceivable that I made a mistake."

The *Los Angeles Times* reported that Wallace asked the bank to erase the comment from its tape. In the *New York Times* account of the incident, Hewitt defended Wallace and claimed that the correspondent had thought better of his request after having made it. "Mike called the bank back," Hewitt said, "and said forget it, that if they eliminated any part of the tape it could be misconstrued, and he didn't want that to happen." Ever the master of spin, Hewitt pointed out the irony that Wallace's piece was designed to help minorities. "Like almost everyone else in America, Mike sometimes indulges himself in ethnic humor," Hewitt said. "It has been my experience that the people with the least bias sometimes tend to do that."

But as Wallace would have been the first to admit, the comment was completely in character for the blunt and outspoken correspondent. Despite Hewitt's protestations on Wallace's behalf, the news that his biggest star had been caught saying something inappropriate on tape seemed like the only irony worth noting.

Only a few days later came the airing of "The Uncounted Enemy: A Vietnam Deception," a *CBS Reports* documentary produced by George Crile, with Wallace narrating. It wasn't done under the auspices of *60 Minutes,* and Crile, who had done most of the reporting himself, had brought Wallace into the project mainly for his interviewing talents.

When the 90-minute documentary aired at 9:30 P.M. on Saturday, January 23, 1982, it created an immediate firestorm for Wallace, Crile, and CBS News itself and only deepened the correspondent's despondency over the recent downturn in his reputation.

The documentary charged that in the period before the 1968 Tet offensive, American intelligence had altered estimates of Viet Cong troop strength to bolster the government's position that it was winning the war. It specifically accused General William C. Westmoreland, the commander of U.S. forces in Vietnam from 1964 to 1968, of having conspired to misrepresent the size and strength of Viet Cong guerrilla forces in order to curry favor for the war effort, which was going badly. But even though Westmoreland and other top officials sat willingly for interviews, Westmoreland was quick to deny the charges; in a news conference several days later, he called the documentary "a vicious, scurrilous, and premeditated attack on my character and personal integrity." CBS responded that Westmoreland's charges were "totally unfounded." The news media largely sided with CBS News; editorials and reviews regarded the documentary as a powerful exposé of military manipulation.

There were exceptions, though. In a May 1982 article entitled "Anatomy of a Smear," two reporters for *TV Guide* charged CBS with its own distortion of facts to fit its thesis. The article specifically accused the producers of having "rehearsed" an interview, contrary to network rules and then edited out points of view that didn't agree with that of the documentary. While the magazine took pains to note it wasn't challenging the essential truth of the Crile-Wallace documentary, it still managed, by use of the loaded word "smear," to taint what had been considered a first-rate reporting job.

What made matters even worse for Wallace was the reaction of CBS News, now under new management. Bill Leonard, the executive who'd been responsible for getting *60 Minutes* on the air to begin with, had been overthrown in favor of Van Gordon Sauter, a bearded dynamo from the Midwest who (at least to the old-timers at CBS, of which there were many) seemed more concerned with the superficial aspects of news—sets, graphics, and the like—than with the serious business of news gathering. Rather than coming to its defense, Sauter immediately commissioned an inquiry into the charges against the documentary, creating what Wallace felt was an atmosphere of uncertainty about it.

The network assigned Burton Benjamin, a former CBS documentary producer and now a senior executive producer of CBS News, to look into the accusations. In July, after reviewing Benjamin's report, Sauter issued an eight-page memo that sharply criticized aspects of the documentary—and implied that Wallace had not been active enough in the reporting, creating a disconnect that should be avoided in "projects of a complex and controversial nature."

It may not have been the reaction Westmoreland wanted—he called the report a "whitewash"—but in true military fashion he sensed division in the ranks and moved to exploit it. In September, Westmoreland filed a $120 million libel suit against CBS; among those named in the lawsuit were Sauter, Crile, and Wallace. It would be a long, ugly, and expensive legal fight.

By 1983, after 15 years on the air—with 5 of them spent among the top 10 shows—it wasn't uncommon for those involved in *60 Minutes* to take brief breaks from looking forward by patting themselves on the back. They had done a tenth anniversary show, and now a fifteenth. Mike Wallace was hard at work on an autobiography (with Rather collaborator and CBS News historian Gary Paul Gates) to be called *Close Encounters*; Hewitt had a memoir in the works, too—to be called *Minute by Minute,* with the modest subtitle, *The Best Show on TV Becomes the Best Book on TV.* May 1983 marked Wallace's sixty-fifth birthday—particularly notable in that CBS would make what appeared to be its first exemption to its mandatory retirement age by allowing him to sign another contract. Hewitt, a few years later, would be its second. (This was no mere technicality: Eric Sevareid and Charles Collingwood, two CBS stars of earlier vintage, had been forced to retire at age 65.) Of course, as Wallace was the first to note, the decision had only to do with economics, since it would have been a reckless business decision to break up the *60 Minutes* team at the top of its game. The show ranked number one for the season, and was regularly watched by 40 percent of the television audience. *60 Minutes* had devoted 1.4 million minutes to nearly 1,500 stories, and Wallace the workhorse had done nearly 500 of them. His contract earned him more than $1 million a year, and soon afterward Hewitt would join him at the seven-figure mark—an unheard-of sum for a news producer never seen by the audience at home.

March 1968: Mike Wallace and Harry Reasoner in an early promotional photo for *60 Minutes*. The opening look of the show changed before it debuted, but the logo itself has stayed roughly the same, as has Wallace's hair.

1969: The Tag Heuer stopwatch replaced a Minerva in 1969 to become the show's most visible symbol until the late 1970s, when it was sent to the Smithsonian Institution and replaced by an Arista stopwatch. The watches worked pretty well, except when they fell down during filming, or when a fly landed on the face.

August 29, 1977: Hewitt and Wallace conferred frequently with Palmer Williams, Hewitt's longtime second-in-command. Williams was often referred to as the conscience of *60 Minutes* and was responsible for much of the show's early look and content. He retired from CBS in 1981 and died in 1996.

December 13, 1968: Reasoner and Wallace pretend to have a meeting in Don Hewitt's office. In reality, there were never any meetings at *60 Minutes,* except maybe in the men's room.

December 7, 1975: In the Madison Hotel in Washington, D.C., Wallace interviews former Secret Service agent Clint Hill and his wife, Gwen, about his guilt over having failed to save President Kennedy's life in November 1963. Hill didn't open up until Wallace, frustrated, ordered the camera turned off and accused him of delivering "pabulum."

July 13, 1973: Wallace interviews Norman Mailer on the release of *Marilyn*. In the interview, Mailer bets "even money" that Bobby Kennedy was in Marilyn Monroe's hotel room on the night of her suicide.

January 14, 1979: Morley Safer ended up getting along well with Katharine Hepburn, but only after racing on foot through midtown Manhattan to get to her East Side town house on time for their scheduled noon interview. Hepburn had warned that if Safer were a minute late, she'd cancel the session. He arrived, out of breath, at 11:59 A.M.

March 21, 1976: Dan Rather interviewing Robert Redford for an early piece. Producers out on the road with Rather often noted that the correspondent himself received Redford-like treatment from adoring fans.

December 1975–June 1981: Rather, Safer, and Wallace, the team that led *60 Minutes* from last place in the ratings to become the number one show on television.

April 6, 1980: "Gunga Dan" was born in a celebrated trek through Afghanistan by Dan Rather, for a story intended to expose Russian infiltration; the segment instead focused the media's attention on the theatrics of Rather, who was about to leave *60 Minutes* to replace Walter Cronkite as anchorman of the *CBS Evening News*.

June 10, 1981: The first group portrait of Hewitt's "tigers," post-Rather. Moments before this picture was taken, Wallace whispered into new-arrival Bradley's ear: "You know, if this show goes into the dumper, they're going to blame it on you."

September 1984: One of a series of promotional shots taken of Diane Sawyer after her arrival at *60 Minutes*. It didn't take long before she shifted her image from Sixties Stenographer to Glamorous Blonde TV Goddess.

April 10, 1985: Ed Bradley returns to Cambodia, where he'd done the landmark war reporting that had resulted in his arrival at *60 Minutes* in 1981.

September 1989: The two baby-boomer correspondents, Steve Kroft and Meredith Vieira, were added to the *60 Minutes* staff by a network management starting to worry about the future.

2003: Trevor Nelson, a 34-year-old *wunderkind* producer who collaborated—and clashed—frequently with correspondent Steve Kroft. His unexpected death after a meningitis attack in July 2003 made him the first person ever to die while working at *60 Minutes.* *(Courtesy of Maggie Nelson)*

January 26, 1992: Hewitt giving Bill and Hillary Clinton some last-minute advice on how to handle an interview with Steve Kroft. Clinton had just been accused of adultery by singer Gennifer Flowers, in a supermarket tabloid exposé.

Chapter 14

See You on Television!

For 15 years *60 Minutes* had managed to maneuver its way into great stories and high drama with little second-guessing of its techniques. Sure, there'd been the occasional article or analysis, but for the most part the show had remained immune, both critically and legally, to those who would challenge its basic methods or threaten its approach.

But that was all about to change, thanks to a slander suit against the show and its now-departed correspondent Dan Rather. It was a minor case involving a December 9, 1979, piece called "It's No Accident," about insurance scams in which spurious medical claims are filed in reference to faked auto accidents. In the story, Rather had reported that Dr. Carl Galloway, a California doctor, had signed a fraudulent medical report; Galloway claimed that though his name was on the report, it was not his signature—and that *60 Minutes* and Rather hadn't made adequate effort to prove that it was.

When the case came to trial in the spring of 1983, it offered the public a rare glimpse behind the curtain of the TV newsmagazine. For the first time in its history, the news-gathering techniques of *60 Minutes* would themselves go on trial, in what became something of a media circus—with Rather taking the stand for three days in his own defense in a Los Angeles courtroom. But what really mattered to *60 Minutes*—over and above the embarrassment of having its former star on trial—was one crucial part of Galloway's defense, which (thanks to a favorable court ruling) enabled him to introduce interview outtakes that cast Rather or *60 Minutes* in a less than flattering light.

During the Galloway trial, audiences learned how *60 Minutes* obtained what was known as the "reverse" shot, in which the correspondent was filmed asking a question—sometimes repeatedly—after he'd already heard the answer. Because the reporter was essentially the star, he could redo his questions as often as he liked, until he got it right—a freedom not afforded those answering the questions. (The 1987 movie *Broadcast News,* written and directed by a former CBS News writer named James L. Brooks, did much to malign this particular technique. In one sequence, correspondent Tom Grunick, played by William Hurt, used the "reverse" shot to insert a shot of himself crying during an interview with a victim of date rape; it was later revealed that Grunick had filmed the crying after the interview had been completed.) Overall, the exposure of raw, unedited footage did little to enhance the reputation of the anchorman or of *60 Minutes.* In one instance, someone trying to get away from an unwelcome CBS camera was yelled at by a raucous Rather: "Adios! See you on television!"

A jury ultimately ruled in favor of Rather and CBS; the case went away. But the fallout from the public's peek backstage into the process tempered the victory. *60 Minutes* later instituted a requirement that all interviews be shot with two cameras, in an effort to lessen the public perception that its correspondents were not so much reporters as well-rehearsed actors reading from a script. (However, two decades later CBS News standards still do not explicitly require two cameras to be used for interviews. "There may be times when the reporter or producer feels that reaction shots and reverse questions made out of real-time sequence are necessary," the rules state. "In such cases, the subject must be made aware of what we are doing and why, and, if questions are to be repeated, the subject or his or her representative is to be given the opportunity to be present during the recording of those questions.")

As usual, Fred Friendly—who'd become an éminence grise to the industry, often quoted as an unassailable critic of network news practices—weighed in on the latest *60 Minutes* imbroglio. "We put our cameras on an awful lot of people," he remarked to the *New York Times* after the verdict came in. "I think the fact that we are accountable that way can't help but be good for all of us." That said, Friendly conceded that the presence of Rather on the witness stand had only helped bolster the anchorman's position. "Viewers have seen Dan Rather in a new light and a good light, not just the talking end of a TelePrompTer," Friendly said, "but as someone who is able to cope with a very difficult problem, willing to face his accusers." In the end, the case proved the principle of *60 Minutes* yet again—that the show depended heavily on the performance skills of Hewitt's tigers to keep audiences coming. It would always be the correspondents who turned good reporting into great storytelling.

By the fall of 1983 the other networks had tired of ceding the Sunday night at 7:00 time slot to CBS and were at last gearing up to challenge *60 Minutes*. ABC was bringing in James G. Bellows, a onetime print journalist and now managing editor of *Entertainment Tonight,* to come up with a competing strategy—maybe even starting a new show at 6:30 to give it a head start. Meanwhile, at NBC, the plan was to move *Monitor,* its own newsmagazine, to the Sunday-night-at-7 time slot. *Monitor* had launched the previous March with Lloyd Dobyns as the host, on Saturday nights at 10:00, and quickly plummeted to the bottom of the ratings. NBC News president Reuven Frank promised an overhaul of the show—new music, new sets, new correspondents, even an investigative unit—to draw viewers away from *60 Minutes,* which still owned first place in the ratings.

Hewitt, as always, had nothing but public sarcasm for his would-be competition. "I have seen Lloyd Dobyns maybe once in my life, maybe twice," he told a *New York Times* reporter. "We have lived in this neighborhood for 15 years. It is a nice neighborhood. Mr. Disney used to live across the street. Father Ripley lives down the block. [Hewitt was referring to Ripley's *Believe It or Not!*, the latest family fare thrown up against his show.] I don't imagine a nice man like Mr. Reuven Frank would do anything to ruin our neighborhood."

Behind the bluster, Hewitt was always looking for ways to retain his edge and stay ahead. Not that he feared getting beaten, but just in case, it couldn't hurt to heap a little more star power onto his enterprise. Fortunately for him, CBS News had the perfect piece of talent to give his show the adrenaline boost it might one day need.

Back in 1969 when she was a 23-year-old weathergirl at WLKY in Louisville, Diane Sawyer, having nothing to show for herself but a well-honed sense of gumption and poise, dialed up CBS and asked the switchboard operator to connect her with Don Hewitt of *60 Minutes*. Minutes later, Sawyer was talking with Hewitt—who has always made a habit of answering his own phone. They made an appointment for Sawyer to see him on her next trip to New York. When that day came, Sawyer was granted a 45-minute audience with the executive producer, after which she was politely informed that she would not be immediately joining the cast of the number one show on television— although the meeting presumably did go on far longer than most of Hewitt's interviews with weathergirls from local stations.

"We'll get back to you," Hewitt said at the end of their chat.

It wasn't all that surprising that Hewitt found himself in a room with Diane Sawyer so early in her career. Sawyer, born December 22, 1945, had been brought up to be the best, the brightest, the first. Growing up in Louisville as the daughter of a Republican county judge and a schoolteacher, Diane had singing lessons, walking lessons, and dance lessons. She and her sister, Linda, had looks, height, talent, and charm, and their mother was determined to exploit that in full—without much credit to them. "She's not pretty," Mrs. Sawyer once said of Diane. "My daughter's not the least bit pretty!" That harsh standard still pertains; Sawyer's mother, Jean, routinely calls from her Kentucky home to criticize her daughter's appearance on *Good Morning America*. "To this day," Sawyer said in a 2002 interview, "I get messages about clothes that didn't look good or how I didn't sit in a ladylike position. She thinks that if she just says the right thing, one day I'll get it right."

As the girls grew older and their training program progressed, they entered numerous beauty pageants—Linda winning the Miss Kentucky pageant and Diane later earning the Junior Miss crown in 1963. Her winning essay compared the music of the North and South in the Civil War. Sawyer has said she aspired to a career on the stage, devoting what little spare time she had as a child to practicing show tunes.

In 1963, Sawyer followed her sister to Wellesley College in Massachusetts, where she kept up with her passion for singing and the stage, performing in college productions, including *The Threepenny Opera*. She graduated in 1967 with a degree in English; with no clue how to turn herself into a Broadway star, she headed home to Louisville and found herself a job doing the weather on WLKY, the local ABC affiliate. In 1969, her father was killed in a car crash; a year later, Sawyer decided to leave Louisville and test herself in Washington, D.C.

She met with Bill Small, an old family friend from Louisville who had become the Washington bureau chief of CBS News. He was upbeat about her chances in broadcasting; but she needed a job, not a cheerleader. Through other family connections, she landed a spot in the Nixon White House, working for press secretary Ron Ziegler. She remained there throughout the Watergate scandal, handling press inquiries and reportedly earning her nickname "the smart girl" from Nixon. During that time, she began dating presidential speechwriter Frank Gannon; it was with him that she traveled to San Clemente after Nixon's resignation, to work on the presidential papers. Sawyer was the tall blonde visible to viewers as Nixon boarded the chopper departing the White House lawn for the last time in August 1974.

After Sawyer finished helping Nixon with his memoir, *RN*, she went back to Washington. A job had opened up at CBS News, and Bill Small had risen to CBS News management. With his help, Sawyer was hired in 1978 as a reporter in the CBS News Washington bureau. (Dan

Rather, who'd gotten to know Sawyer while covering the Nixon White House, told the *New York Times* in 1981 that he'd advised against hiring her. "She proved me wrong," he said.) Her experience working for Nixon did little to endear her to her new colleagues, and her lack of on-air experience made her an easy target for sniping. But Sawyer's solid performance covering the Three Mile Island nuclear disaster in 1979 (not to mention her telegenic appearance) earned her a promotion to covering the State Department. She stayed until September 1981, when the latest management team at CBS News—headed by division president Van Gordon Sauter—acknowledged her glamour and skill and handed her the job of co-anchor of the perpetual last-place finisher *CBS Morning News,* along with veteran newsman Charles Kuralt.

It was 1981; Sawyer was 35 years old. That year, a *TV Guide* reporter asked Sawyer if she planned to get married. "Oh yes," she replied. "I'm going to have the world's most rapturous, fun-filled, wise and generous marriage. And I'm going to have the most fascinating and autonomous children. I'm going to have it all." At that time she was dating Richard Holbrooke, a former assistant secretary of state and prominent New York investment banker. But Sawyer's focus seemed to be primarily on her burgeoning career. The morning news— redubbed *Morning*—raised her stature in the industry: the minuscule rise in the show's ratings was attributed to her, and in 1982 CBS replaced Kuralt as her partner with Chicago anchorman Bill Kurtis. The switch brought no further improvement to CBS's long-standing weakness in the morning TV wars.

By 1983, CBS News was in chaos. Under the leadership of Ed Joyce—who stepped in as head of the news division when Sauter was promoted to a corporate post—the network's morning show was one of the most visible symptoms of the news division's lack of direction. A succession of executive producers was recruited to help save the show, but they only cemented Sawyer's growing desire to leave. The last straw was the appointment of Jon Katz, a former print journalist. "The low point of my *Morning News* existence," Sawyer recalled to author Peter Boyer, "was when I interviewed the yo-yo queen of America for about five minutes. I did that. That was a Jon Katz special, which I never let him forget." Meanwhile, Hewitt, infatuated by her obvious star quality as well as her social connections, was angling to get her over to *60 Minutes*. She, too, had cultivated a friendship with CBS chairman William Paley and blended easily into the upper-crust social circuit to which the less-polished Hewitt aspired. Their paths didn't exactly cross, but Hewitt made no secret of his desire to have Sawyer in his company of players.

On August 9, 1982, a young black man in Greenville, Texas, robbed a Kentucky Fried Chicken of $615. The case remained unsolved for weeks, until a white woman reported a suspicious-looking parked car with South Carolina license plates at the park across from her home, which was 31/2 miles away from the restaurant. The Greenville detective in charge of the case, Lieutenant James Fortenberry, traced the license plate to a young black man named Lenell Geter. Fortenberry passed Geter's picture to other nearby police departments, who suspected Geter of similar unsolved robberies in Plano and Garland. Less than two weeks later, a Kentucky Fried Chicken franchise in nearby Balch Springs was robbed. Eyewitnesses picked Geter's photograph from lineups, and before long Geter had been charged with three armed robberies. But Geter insisted he wasn't responsible for any of the crimes. He earned $24,000 as an engineer for E-Systems, a defense contractor, and was engaged to be married. On the day of the Balch Springs robbery—at 3:20 in the afternoon—Geter had gone into downtown Greenville to register to vote and to apply for a loan at a local bank. He'd returned to his office, where coworkers recalled seeing him. Geter adamantly refused to plead guilty, but local authorities were certain they'd found the perpetrator, and the rush to judgment began.

The story first surfaced in the Texas press; as Don Hewitt tells it, a loyal viewer then contacted *60 Minutes* on Geter's behalf. Morley Safer recalls hearing about the story from an article in *People* magazine, though he admits to being uncertain of his memory.

In fact, it should be noted that the exhaustive December 9, 1983, account of the case, "Lenell Geter's in Jail"—which went on to become perhaps the most celebrated single segment in *60 Minutes* history— was a perfect example of how *60 Minutes* often followed the reporting of others, only to receive the lion's share of the credit when the TV version got results. With its bumbling detective, poorly assembled evidence, and victim claiming innocence, the Geter story made for a great narrative. It fit Hewitt's "tell me a story" dictum, plus it advanced the case; after months of on-the-scene reporting, Safer and his producer, Suzanne St. Pierre, left little doubt in their segment of the weakness of the prosecution's case. Interviews with white witnesses who spoke on Geter's behalf, as well as Safer's conversation with the prisoner himself—who was composed and articulate throughout—made for a deeply disturbing and powerful piece.

Four days after the story aired on *60 Minutes,* both the prosecution and the defense moved for a new trial, and Geter was released from prison. For a prosecutor to abandon his own case was as precedent-shattering an event as anyone could remember in the Texas legal system.

For all the print stories that preceded it, none could hope to create the dramatic immediacy of interviews like this one in Safer's piece, which conclusively demonstrated Geter's innocence—or, at the very least, established a reasonable doubt of his guilt.

SAFER: Two people who were not called to testify and did not realize until after the trial that their testimony could have been crucial were Dan Walker and Debra Cotton.

DEBRA COTTON: I talked to [Geter] shortly, right around one o'clock, and then again at a—at three, right at three.

SAFER: At three o'clock?

COTTON *(affirmative):* Mm-hmm.

SAFER: And the robbery took place at three-twenty.

COTTON: Three-twenty.

SAFER: Absolutely impossible to get from E-Systems to Balch Springs?

COTTON: It was impossible for Lenell Geter to be there.

DAN WALKER: No question about it. He came by to use my phone at, right around three-forty-five, somewhere between three-forty-five and four o'clock, that afternoon.

SAFER: No way you could get back from Balch Springs in fifteen minutes?

WALKER: No. No way. No.

Safer's piece—a point-by-point deconstruction that reinterviewed witnesses and closely examined the flaws in the case—showed the unique power of television to shape the national debate. By the following spring, Geter's case had been overturned, and *60 Minutes* had popularized the exoneration of the innocent by crusading journalists. Such stories have become a routine part of media coverage— as well as the frequent subject of movies and plays—but in 1983 the Geter case marked an early instance of a journalistic investigation by a TV show that resulted in a reversal of a conviction.

In July 1984, Diane Sawyer and Don Hewitt found themselves at the same dinner party. They'd both gone to San Francisco to cover the Democratic National Convention, and while there they went to a dinner hosted by Gordon and Ann Getty in honor of Charles Manatt, chairman of the Democratic National Committee. Over the course of the evening, Hewitt learned that Walter Mondale—soon to be the Democratic nominee—was planning to remove Manatt from his party position.

Sawyer, seated at another table, hadn't picked up the news and was happily engaged in small talk with other guests when she felt something tugging at the hem of her skirt. She looked under the table expecting to find the Gettys' dog, and instead saw Hewitt on his hands and knees. (As implausible as this sounds, both Hewitt and Sawyer tell the same version of this story.) "Hey," Hewitt whispered, "I have a scoop!" Sawyer didn't quite know what to make of the sight of the executive producer of *60 Minutes* pulling at her, but it seemed easier to follow him out of the room. Together they slipped into the Gettys' library, Hewitt explaining his news along the way. "We have to call this in to CBS radio!" Hewitt said. "Get it on the air, right away!"

Quickly, the two scribbled out a script for Sawyer to phone in to the radio desk; within minutes, Hewitt's scoop was on the air. Perhaps as a result of their reporting, an embarrassed Mondale later abandoned his plan to displace Manatt. Even in her earliest days as a CBS News reporter, trudging out to Three Mile Island while more fearful (and senior) reporters stayed at home, Sawyer hadn't quite experienced the rush of a Hildy Johnson moment before; she was engaged enough by Hewitt's passion to be certain that *60 Minutes* was where she belonged.

Sawyer accepted Hewitt's offer of a job and showed up at *60 Minutes* in the late summer of 1984. In typical fashion she was greeted warmly by no one at all. No one told her where the bathrooms were, or where to have lunch. She didn't even have an office of her own; for a time, she roamed from office to office while her own was readied. Once she finally got her own digs, various correspondents stopped by to tell Sawyer they were going to help her out by letting her have the best producers from their staff. It all seemed nice enough, until Sawyer saw through the phony Welcome Wagon facade: she was getting the producers the other correspondents didn't want. It wasn't politics, she realized; it was something both impersonal and ferocious, something Darwinian and a little scary. She knew she was on her own.

It didn't help that she was the designated golden girl in an office of middle-aged men. Within weeks, newspapers heralded her arrival with articles detailing her glamorous social life (the *New York Times* told readers of her dinners with Warren Beatty and CBS chairman William Paley) and hinted at her ambition (which she denied) to one day replace Rather as anchorman of the *CBS Evening News*. "I want to do explorations of character as well as investigative pieces that make a difference to consumers," Sawyer told the *Times* in October 1984. Later in the interview, she pointed out the disparity between her glowing media image and her wrinkled clothes and unkempt hair with her characteristically excessive humility to reporter Sally Bedell Smith: "Aren't I the picture of perfection?" she said.

Sawyer's first story aired on October 21, 1984, a compelling profile of a 51-year-old North Carolina grandmother named Velma Barfield, who'd been convicted of murdering members of her family and was scheduled to be executed a few weeks later. The following Sunday, Sawyer interviewed the stepchildren of Claus von Bulow, the Danish aristocrat found guilty in 1982 of the attempted murder of his wife, Sunny, now in an irreversible coma. The piece—called "Did He or Didn't He?"—followed a recent reversal of the verdict against Von Bulow, and might have been expected to deliver some fireworks. Unfortunately, while Sawyer may have had the look of a *60 Minutes* correspondent, her questions lacked the confrontational edge of her colleagues. Talking to Alexander von Auersperg and Ala von Auersperg Kneissl, Sunny von Bulow's children from a previous marriage, Sawyer tried out her Mike Wallace impression with disappointing results.

> SAWYER: If he had the intent to harm your mother, and particularly to harm her with insulin, why would he leave a black bag where people could find it?
> VON AUERSPERG: I don't know why it was there. All I can say is it was there.
> SAWYER: Doesn't it strike you as odd or maybe a little stupid for someone with criminal intent?
> KNEISSL: I don't know. I don't know why Mr. von Bulow did certain things, and I don't know. And does it strike me stupid? Maybe it strikes me stupid, but I don't understand why he did it that way.

That piece was overshadowed on that October 28, 1984, broadcast by Morley Safer's now-legendary interview with Jackie Gleason. Safer again approached his subject with his witty voice and erudite perspective and delivered an interview still remembered as The Great

One's best. The most memorable part of it concerned the train that Gleason had gotten from CBS as part of his contract when his show moved
to Florida—a party train befitting a man of Gleason's stature.

> SAFER: What was on that train?
>
> GLEASON: Everything! *(Dixieland music)* We had two Dixieland
> bands coming from California. They would spell each other. I'd
> say to 'em, "Take five miles." And parties went on twenty-four
> hours. I found out that I couldn't attend the parties.
>
> SAFER: Were the—were there girls on that train?
>
> GLEASON: Were there girls? *(Laughing)* There certainly were, and
> they were very, very nice girls. Nothing untoward happened.
> Might have been because the berths were too small. *(Safer
> laughing)* But regardless of that, nothing happened on that train.
>
> SAFER: And was there a bar on that train?
>
> GLEASON: A bar on—? The train *was* a bar.
>
> SAFER *(laughing)*: I guess that's a classic example of what clout is.
>
> GLEASON: Yes.
>
> SAFER: To say, "A train, please!"
>
> GLEASON: That's right. When you've got good ratings and you're
> one, two, or three in the ratings, there is nothing your little
> heart desires that they don't provide.
>
> SAFER: Doesn't work that way anymore, Mr. Gleason.
>
> GLEASON: Did you have a comedy show?

No, Safer didn't, but there was no overestimating the clout of *60
Minutes* in the fall of 1984, when the salaries of its stars—including
Don Hewitt—had surpassed $2 million a year. Even Sawyer, the new
kid, was making $800,000 a year. If Hewitt had asked CBS for a party
train, management might well have considered it.

Chapter 15

A Whim of Iron

"Mike Wallace said he was feeling better yesterday," reported Peter Kaplan in the *New York Times* on December 21, 1984. "The CBS correspondent had spent most of the last week sick in bed and admittedly depressed. . . ."

The reason for Wallace's apparent recovery was simple: He had learned that he would not be called as a witness in the libel trial currently under way in the federal courthouse in Foley Square. It had been almost three years since CBS News had aired the documentary about Vietnam that had so incensed Gen. William Westmoreland. And nothing terrified Wallace more than the thought of getting on the stand and testifying. He didn't quite know what was wrong; lately he had been feeling distracted, unable to sleep, unable to eat. He'd also had trouble focusing on stories, motivating himself, or doing much of anything at all. He had informally separated from his wife, Lorraine, and moved into a new apartment. The libel suit was dragging on and on, and there seemed to be no end in sight. The highly visible trial had limited his ability to do pieces for *60 Minutes,* and Wallace had described himself to others as feeling "trapped" by the trial. On December 30, Wallace was admitted to the hospital for what a CBS spokesman described as "exhaustion."

It wasn't until mid-February of 1985 that Westmoreland finally dropped his suit against CBS, just before it was to go to the jury. Neither side declared victory; the settlement included an agreement that "the court of public opinion" would ultimately decide the divisive case. For Wallace, it was also an emotional victory of sorts, but it didn't alleviate the odd symptoms he'd been experiencing. On the day the case came to a formal end, Dan Rather, Don Hewitt, and others took Wallace out to lunch at the 21 Club to celebrate. Once again, the *New York Times* account of the occasion took passing note of Wallace's less than jovial mood: "After the lunch, in a taxicab, Mr. Rather, grinning, turned and made a mock-gallant toast to Mr. Wallace. 'To Mike,' he said. 'Congratulations. Your hide has never been thicker and your spine never straighter.' Mr. Hewitt laughed, and Mr. Wallace smiled without mirth."

What his colleagues didn't know was that in December, Wallace had admitted himself to Lenox Hill Hospital to be treated for the disease he now felt certain he had been suffering from for months, if not years: depression. To get through the pressures of the regular courtroom appearances, he had been prescribed Ludiomil, an antidepressant that had begun to help him. But in the aftermath of the trial and against the recommendation of his doctors, he had stopped taking the drug entirely.

It was typical behavior for the stoic, otherwise healthy 67-year-old, who had yet to truly confront the reality that depression was an illness that did not go away. After the trial, Wallace seemed to return to normal levels of intensity and combativeness, but he continued to suffer. He has battled depression ever since, though for years he chose not to acknowledge it to others. He first went public with his illness at 1:30 A.M. on the morning of December 10, 1988, while appearing as a guest on the NBC talk show *Later With Bob Costas,* when he says he realized that the late-night TV audience no doubt shared the insomnia that helped doctors diagnose his depression. He has since become a frequent spokesman on depression, along with his close friend, novelist William Styron—and admits that he will be taking antidepression medication for the rest of his life.

One floor below *60 Minutes* in the office building across from CBS News, Andrew Lack—producer of the now-legendary "Gunga Dan" piece—was gathering a small, relatively young staff of newsmagazine producers and correspondents to create *West 57th,* CBS's first newsmagazine show since *60 Minutes.* So far, nothing about the show made Don Hewitt happy. When the *West 57th* staff moved into the building, Hewitt put a sign in the elevator that read: "Eighth Floor, Video Fluent People Get Off Here" and "Ninth Floor, Yesterday's People Get Off Here." It wasn't clear whether he was mocking the new show or his own, but concern within the network about the image and future of *60 Minutes* began to seep out into the press.

Lack was working with the full support of CBS News and particularly of Howard Stringer, an affable Scot who'd risen quickly through the ranks to become executive vice president of the news division. Stringer was anxious to offer viewers an alternative to *60 Minutes* using the same quick-cutting editing that had recently lured young audiences to MTV. It was clear Lack had been given free rein to create a newsmagazine for the MTV audience that was fresh—and different from *60 Minutes.*

"If we are not going to keep repeating the past," Stringer explained shortly before the show debuted in August, "we have to ask, how do we experiment to pace things differently? With the use of sound and editing and video, television has created something that works terribly well, and *West 57th* is advancing it. . . . We can't just walk away from every new idea just because it isn't the mirror of yesterday's programming." Lack described the show as "audacious and dense." "It's geared to reflect my interest," he told the *Times,* "and the interest of my colleagues whose ages start in their twenties and go through their midfifties."

Lack hired a young, good-looking crew of four correspondents, each of them half the age of Don Hewitt or Mike Wallace. They represented a cross-section of the hottest talent available. John Ferrugia had been a CBS News White House correspondent; Bob Sirott had been a popular Chicago radio personality and entertainment reporter; the women, Jane Wallace and Meredith Vieira, were both attractive and ambitious young CBS News reporters widely considered solid parts of the network's future. They were an appealing bunch of young journalists, part of a rock-'n'-roll *60 Minutes* with a dash of MTV flash.

Right away, TV critics mauled the show for precisely that combination of elements. "Think of a supermarket tabloid set to music," John Corry wrote in the *New York Times*. The opening episode included pieces on an Oregon cult headed by Bhagwan Shree Rajneesh; a profile of the actor Chuck Norris; an organ transplant involving the actor Jon-Erik Hexum, who had been killed in a shooting accident; and famine in Ethiopia. "If CBS is serious about reshaping our definition of news, and it does seem to be serious, it will have to do better," Corry wrote. "A little more sex, a little more violence just to grab our attention; then it can get on to new cures for psoriasis and the latest in diets. We are maybe at a turning point in television journalism." The *Times*, seemingly in high dudgeon over this stab at a new newsmagazine approach, assembled the Great Old Names of television to critique the show, one by one. "It was disappointing journalism, but not as glitzy as I was afraid of," was the kindest comment former CBS News president Richard Salant could summon. Former president Bill Leonard had harsher words. "I thought it was well photographed and attractive to watch, but I didn't think it was journalism by any stretch of the imagination," Leonard said, adding snarkily: "But I don't think that counts anymore."

Hewitt, always ready with a quick barb, chose his words carefully, calling the show "quite good and every bit as entertaining as other light summer fare."

West 57th ended up being too superficial to shape the future of anything except the careers of two future *60 Minutes* correspondents, Vieira and Steve Kroft, a CBS News foreign correspondent who joined the

West 57th team shortly after the show's launch. (Lack's career didn't suffer, either; after several years as president of NBC News, he's now the chairman and chief executive officer of Sony Music, working for his old boss, Howard Stringer, the chairman and chief executive officer of Sony Corporation of America.) Of the four original correspondents, only Vieira has maintained a national television presence, as a cohost of *The View* and host of *Who Wants to Be a Millionaire.*

Hewitt could feel the change in the air. It was being murmured, around the time Sawyer joined the show in 1984, that *60 Minutes* was slipping in quality. Howard Stringer, who'd vigorously supported the idea of *West 57th* as an alternative to *60 Minutes,* stuck with it despite poor ratings when he took over as CBS News president the next year. (*West 57th* wasn't canceled until 1987.) And while the network continued to back Hewitt and his still-successful show, his effort to fight *West 57th* and the powers that be at CBS News signaled his acknowledgment that the threats to his supremacy were real.

When Hewitt got in to work early on the morning of October 11, he spotted fellow early riser Diane Sawyer and burst into her office. "Let's buy CBS News," he said, and explained his plan.

He'd had the idea the night before, watching an *Evening News* broadcast with Dan Rather appearing by remote via satellite. As he looked at the satellite dish from his window atop the news headquarters across the street, he had a thought: What if *I* had a dish? And, more to the point, what if my millionaire friends—and famous TV star colleagues—got together to form our own TV news network to use said dish? Sure, it sounded crazy; but with CBS bleeding assets, maybe it wasn't completely far-fetched to imagine company president Thomas Wyman (a former food industry executive) sensing the business possibilities of such a deal.

"Sure, Don. Yeah," Sawyer said. "Count me in." It may not have crossed Sawyer's mind that Hewitt actually planned to take his idea to the chairman of CBS, Laurence Tisch. With Sawyer's endorsement he returned to his office to make calls. Bill Moyers. Check. Dan Rather.

Check. Morley Safer. Check. Mike Wallace. Check. With five CBS stars on board, Hewitt raced across town to present his proposal to Gene Jankowski, president of the CBS Broadcast Group, at Black Rock. But Jankowski wasn't in yet, so he called James Rosenfield, senior executive vice president of the CBS Broadcast Group, at home; Peter Boyer's history of that period, *Who Killed CBS?*, details that day's developments.

"Jimmy, where are you?" Hewitt asked.

"Don, it's quarter to eight in the morning," Rosenfield replied. "I'm in the bathroom, shaving." Hewitt agreed to wait until Rosenfield could get to the office to pitch his concept. Hewitt laid out the basics— claiming he'd gathered enough big-money backers to foot the bill— and convinced Rosenfield to take him seriously. A series of meetings and phone calls followed, and then Jankowski finally informed Hewitt that the news division simply wasn't for sale. But the message to management was clear, particularly when news of Hewitt's audacious bid became public soon afterward: the leading lights of the news division were unhappy with current management and wanted to see significant change. Leading the revolt was Don Hewitt, a man Morley Safer once described as having a "whim of iron."

Diane Sawyer's contract was running out, less than two years after her arrival at *60 Minutes*. Up until now, the show had been known as a place that people were loath to leave. It had been 5 years since Dan Rather's contract talks with ABC led to his selection as Cronkite's replacement, and 15 years since Harry Reasoner left the show for ABC. There had never been much talk of a raid on *60 Minutes* for the talents of Safer and Wallace. The fact is, no one could have offered them anything nearly as good as what they had at *60 Minutes,* still a top 10 show. The most desirable promotion available to a *60 Minutes* correspondent was the opportunity to anchor the evening news, and those jobs were already taken—Rather, ABC's Peter Jennings, and NBC's Tom Brokaw were all relatively young and new to their jobs.

Even so, speculation began that *60 Minutes* was merely a way station for Sawyer en route to an anchor chair and a million-dollar paycheck. Rather had yet to make the kind of definitive impact on the network's bottom line that would make him irreplaceable. With the glamorous Sawyer increasingly thought of as the next big star of TV news, it was inevitable that she would use her growing clout (and Richard Leibner, the powerful talent agent she shared with, among others, Wallace and Rather) to find her way to something better.

In 1986, with her contract set to expire and all three networks exploring their long-term anchor options, Sawyer was in a perfect position to negotiate a more favorable deal. She discussed with all the major players the possibility of being their chief substitute for the regular anchor, which would put her first in the line of succession. But none of the networks was willing to replace their current anchors—Jennings, Brokaw, or Rather—with Sawyer at any point in the immediate future. In 1980, Rather had negotiated himself veto power over any possible co-anchor; according to a *New York Times* account at the time, Rather used that power to nix Sawyer. "He has said someday, maybe, but not now," a source near the negotiations told a reporter.

Nevertheless, Leibner won Sawyer a new contract with CBS that gave her a nice bump in salary, from $840,000 a year to $1.2 million. The new deal raised the possibility that she might end up hosting one of a number of new possible prime-time CBS News programs—including an update of Edward R. Murrow's *Person to Person*—and meanwhile gave her status as "principal substitute" for Rather, even though his veto would prevent her from taking his permanent place. Still, it seemed likely that the network considered her a logical successor to Rather, if his position ever changed. Though her new contract was said to be for a five-year term, few expected her to last that long at *60 Minutes*—including, most especially, her colleagues on the ninth floor.

Sawyer's negotiations had done nothing to ingratiate her with the *60 Minutes* men. She had no friends among the correspondents at the show—Bradley was the closest thing she'd found to an ally—and seemed unlikely to make any in the near future.

If anything, things were getting worse. Wallace, in particular, seemed to delight in making Sawyer miserable. He had little respect for her work on the show; when interviewers inquired about her qualities as a *60 Minutes* correspondent, Wallace would often refer to her looks. She brought out his competitive streak, and it manifested itself, as always, in pitched battle for producers.

Wallace showed up in Sawyer's office doorway one day with a typical taunt. "All your producers have quit," he said. He was testing her; it was a favorite pastime of his, to see whether Sawyer could take his needling.

"Mike," Sawyer said, looking up from her desk, "how many producers of yours have quit over the last fifteen years?" Her response was pointed enough to leave him without a ready comeback, and he turned and left.

Wallace still speaks harshly of Sawyer. "She never made that much impact on the show, she never did," Wallace said in November 2003. "The reputation of *60 Minutes* was made long before she came along. . . . She was fine, she did a good job here, et cetera et cetera. She's smart as hell, and she's pretty. . . . She doesn't need the money. Or the fame. She does this crap on *Good Morning America*. That kind of a life? What for? What she really wanted at that time was to be co-anchor with Dan, or if necessary take over the whole thing herself." Asked for her opinion of her colleagues at *60 Minutes*, Sawyer responds simply: "There's a masculine definition of what is consequential there."

At the very least Sawyer had distracted Wallace from his previous favorite target, Morley Safer. That was just as well for the low-key correspondent, who hated the *60 Minutes* brand of conflict even as he engaged in it.

Safer remained the antithesis to Wallace in both style and substance. He still banged out his scripts on a manual typewriter in an office piled high with books and art. When he traveled, he spent solitary nights in his hotel room, painting, his subjects the rooms themselves. He led a comparatively quiet life in Connecticut, away from the office and the social whirl that kept his colleagues so engaged. While Safer could do battle with the best of them, he preferred a quiet conversation over a good bottle of wine. Alone among the *60 Minutes* correspondents, Safer seemed to enjoy having dinner on the road with his producers; he was known as a witty storyteller offscreen as well as in his pieces, and producers relished assignments on his team.

Closing in on his twentieth anniversary with the broadcast, Safer had long since set himself apart from the rest of the *60 Minutes* correspondents by the types of stories he chose to do. He loved unexpected stories about odd people and offbeat places, from his June 5, 1977, piece on the *Orient Express* called "Last Train to Istanbul," to "Genius," his October 23, 1983, story about savants—including a man named George Finn, who became the basis for Dustin Hoffman's character in the 1988 movie *Rain Man*. Safer traveled to obscure capitals and talked with Muppets and writers and artists and kings. He disdained the kind of in-your-face reporting that had made Wallace famous, instead perfecting his own unique approach to *60 Minutes* stories.

On January 4, 1987, Safer delivered a classic example of the genre: "Curtain Call," a profile of Casa Verdi, a retirement home for opera singers in Milan built by Guiseppi Verdi, produced by his longtime collaborator John Tiffin. Residents roamed the hallways, singing in phone booths or down corridors.

> SAFER: Casa Verdi is a happy place. If not so rich in talent, it is rich
> beyond measure in the zest for all things musical. One sour or
> possible amusing note: when you put a hundred soloists under
> the same roof, it is not impossible to find a certain amount of
> vanity. Each person I spoke to here said they loved this place,
> but each one wondered what all those untalented others were
> doing here. But, of course, if there was no ego, they would not
> be artists.

To Safer, it must have seemed all too familiar a place.

Nearly a decade into his weekly gig as a *60 Minutes* commentator, Andy Rooney had achieved a level of prominence far beyond anyone's expectations. In addition to being a successful author, he had become what many within CBS News believed to be a key ingredient of the continued influence of *60 Minutes.*

Inevitably, a man with so many opinions began to annoy people. Rooney had been the target of attack by numerous groups who disagreed with his curmudgeonly views, and of parody—again on *Saturday Night Live,* where Joe Piscopo had lampooned him in a series of sketches. Rooney now contends, with some exasperation, that he never uttered the phrase, "Did you ever wonder about . . . ?" that Piscopo popularized in his routine. "We've checked the transcripts and can't find it anywhere," he insists.

In the spring of 1987 he took on his biggest opponent yet: CBS News. The Writers Guild of America had gone on strike against CBS over job cutbacks and other issues, and Rooney—in support of the strike—refused to appear on *60 Minutes.* He also wrote a letter to CBS boss Laurence Tisch attacking the network for cutting more than 215 jobs at CBS News, which he said "has been turned into primarily a business enterprise and the moral enterprise has been lost." He had fought, unsuccessfully, to sit in on a negotiating session as a reporter, and soon afterward went public with a threat to quit CBS News entirely. But despite his sympathies, Rooney—who had always kept his office across the street from the *60 Minutes* offices, in the main CBS News headquarters—had avoided crossing a picket line by setting himself up temporarily at *60 Minutes,* even though he wasn't appearing on the show.

All this wasn't sitting well with Hewitt and others at *60 Minutes,* who saw Rooney's position as hypocritical; he was, after all, continuing to collect his $7,700-a-week salary and camping in a CBS office, despite his refusal to appear on the broadcast. For his part, Rooney insisted he'd met the terms of his contract to warrant getting paid—he wasn't a member of the WGA—and told the press he had no animosity toward *60 Minutes,* though it had been reported that he and Hewitt had engaged in shouting matches. "I like the people there, I even like

Don," Rooney told the *New York Times*. "I don't know whether it'll come to my leaving or not."

A few days later, CBS News announced that it would suspend Rooney's salary. Rooney moved out of the *60 Minutes* offices over the weekend, but Hewitt wasn't mollified, issuing a statement attacking Rooney: "You don't move across the street to another CBS building that for a technical reason is not struck, and sit in an office and draw almost $8,000 a week for doing nothing while his fellow writers are out in picket lines in the cold and wind and rain and snow. I would respect Andy a lot more had he gone out there and walked out on the picket line, and if he'd turned those checks back." Asked by the *Times* if he would be able come up with a segment to substitute for Rooney's, Hewitt said, "I'm sure I will." Fortunately for all concerned, a week later the WGA came to terms with CBS News, and yet another Hewitt battle came to an end. When it came time for Hewitt to take sides in a battle between his tigers and his bosses, it was an easy decision; he wasn't about to take on those who controlled his broadcast. In the end, Don Hewitt always wanted the rich and powerful on his side.

Chapter 16

Getting On

"I think it's quite probably peaked," Harry Reasoner said of *60 Minutes* in a *New York Times* interview on September 13, 1987, as the show began its twentieth season on CBS. "I don't see it as coming suddenly to an abyss, but if anything, as an erosion. But we are, many of us, getting on, and it sometimes produces bad decisions. We tend to do profiles of Lillian Gish, instead of maybe Madonna. I assume that half our viewers are younger than our youngest correspondent. It's the beginning of the twentieth year, and as you get that long, you should be making evolutionary changes. And I assume Don is making them. Something's going to happen. Somebody's going to get tired or quit, or get a better opportunity, or somebody is going to be in a life-threatening situation—it's apt to happen to anyone."

That "somebody" seemed most likely to be Reasoner himself. The lifelong smoker had been diagnosed recently with lung cancer, and in June emerged from his first operation. The Associated Press was told only that Reasoner had undergone lung surgery for a "respiratory ailment." For the first time, there were whispers that Hewitt might want to replace Reasoner; his contributions to the show had lessened, and it pained Hewitt to allow the public to see one of his tigers as less than invulnerable. Compounding the problem was Reasoner's insistence on continuing to smoke in the face of his illness. He was hardly the only smoker among the 60 Minutes staff; Hewitt had smoked cigars and pipes, Wallace had smoked cigarettes, and Safer continued to chain-smoke Rothman Specials. But there was something unsettling about this 64-year-old man, crippled by cancer and still indulging the cause of his illness—and it was beginning to cost him the respect and support of his colleagues, who loved Reasoner and also wanted to preserve the reputation of their show.

On the other hand, it wasn't as though things were falling apart. The *Times* reported that 30-second commercials on 60 Minutes were now selling at between $225,000 and $250,000, delivering approximately $3 million per episode in advertising revenue. With an estimated weekly budget of under $800,000, each new episode of 60 Minutes brought more than $2 million in profit to the network, hardly reason to worry about the show's future. Not long ago, Hewitt had signed a 10-year, $22 million contract for his services—the ultimate endorsement of 60 Minutes by the businessmen who ran CBS.

But the longevity of the show—and of its correspondents Wallace and Safer, who hadn't slowed much despite their age—had still stirred critics and insiders to wonder how much longer the party could go on. Even Hewitt found himself speculating occasionally on the show's limits, telling the *Times* that "there's going to come a year when this format will not be as appealing."

By 1988, it was increasingly clear that the courtship of Diane Sawyer by Roone Arledge—the president of ABC News who'd turned the TV news industry upside down with his willingness to pay big money for stars—would likely result in some changes at 60 Minutes.

Hewitt had no desire for Sawyer to stray from his show. She had quickly become his biggest star, after Wallace. But Sawyer's ambitions were plain to even the most casual observer. She'd appeared in 1987 in a series of Annie Liebowitz photos for *Vanity Fair* (much maligned at 6o Minutes for playing excessively on her sex appeal) and cooperated with articles that reported on her relationships (she married movie director Mike Nichols in April 1988), her beauty queen background, and her days in the Nixon White House. More than any of her 6o Minutes colleagues, Sawyer had become a bona fide member of the celebrity culture. And it was her media star status that prompted Arledge to woo her yet again in 1988—this time, with the promise of a prime-time weekly newsmagazine show of her own and a salary reported to be $1.7 million a year. It was a difficult offer to turn down.

But in the final days of her negotiations in January 1989, Sawyer went back to the network one last time with a request: she wanted clearance from Hewitt to do one news special a year, in addition to her duties at 6o Minutes. Still at least publicly clinging to his belief in the repertory spirit of the show and refusing to accept (or encourage) Sawyer's star status, Hewitt refused.

On February 1, 1989, ABC News announced that it had hired away Sawyer from CBS.

"I would have stayed, you know," Sawyer says in a December 2003 conversation in her ABC News office, still sounding slightly bitter about the final round of negotiations that resulted in her departure from CBS. "I asked for one thing. One little teeny thing. Which is I wanted to be able to do one special a year. . . . I found that the highly successful, extremely intelligent, and pioneering formula of 6o Minutes pieces—the kind of 11- to 13-minute piece, the kind of beginning, middle and end of it all—I thought was great. But I also found that every now and then I wanted to step outside and see if I couldn't tackle something for an hour, and do it a little differently. Just for me. I would have done it under 6o Minutes, that wouldn't have been a problem. I just wanted one thing that felt like me. . . . I wanted to do pieces for an hour and see if I could deliver a different kind of punch. . . . Don said no. He thought that it would undermine the singularity of 6o Minutes. Maybe he was right. I don't know. You had to get a special dispensation, papal level, to appear on the Evening News."

Hewitt still stands by his original position. "You get up in the morning, and you take a shower, and what are you thinking about when you take a shower? I didn't want Diane thinking about anything else but this show. And she wanted to spread her wings and fly higher and wider. And I don't think there is any higher or wider."

In the wake of Sawyer's departure for ABC, CBS News knew it needed a woman on *60 Minutes'*s team—whether Hewitt agreed or not. And no one seemed better suited to the needs of the aging newsmagazine than *West 57th* alumna Meredith Vieira—a CBS News reporter seen by management as star material, even though she wasn't exactly a perfect match for the men's club mentality of *60 Minutes*. By the time the wildly disparate lives of Hewitt and Meredith Vieira intersected in February 1989, Vieira had established herself as a formidable journalist with impressive credentials to go alongside her pleasing television persona. After graduating from Tufts University in 1976, she went to work for WJAR-TV in Providence, Rhode Island. That job eventually led her to WCBS-TV in New York City, where her series on child molestation won her a Front Page Award from the Newswoman's Club of New York. She went to work at CBS News as a reporter in its Chicago bureau in January 1982; within two years, she'd become a political correspondent for the network, covering Senator Alan Cranston's presidential bid and the 1984 Democratic National Convention in San Francisco. In the summer of 1985 she was named a correspondent for *West 57th* and earned notice as a natural; she had an ease in front of the camera that gave her an edge over her less-experienced colleagues. In 1989, she earned four Emmy Awards for stories she reported on *West 57th* during its 1987–1988 season.

These were still stressful times for CBS. For the first time in its history, the network finished that season in third place. In July 1988, Tisch moved Howard Stringer to management as president of the CBS Broadcast Group and replaced him with David Burke, then an executive vice president at ABC News. Burke took an immediate hands-on approach to management of *60 Minutes* and pressed Hewitt to accept his choices of Vieira and Steve Kroft, Vieira's colleague at *West 57th*, as correspondents to set the stage for the show's future. Even if he'd wanted to—and he's never admitted to his true feelings on the matter—Hewitt demonstrated yet again a lack of interest in challenging the authority of his boss.

On February 3, 1989, Burke went to Vieira with his plan to put her on 60 Minutes after Sawyer's sudden departure. Her response came as a bit of a shock. The woman who was arguably the network's hottest young star was being offered a job at television's top news show—and was hesitant to accept.

"It's the one broadcast I really want to do," Vieira said. "But can I go have my baby and then talk about it?" (That quote and many other details of Vieira's period at 60 Minutes come from Divided Lives, by Elsa Walsh, a 1995 account of the struggles of three successful women to balance their personal and professional lives.)

Vieira's first son, Benjamin, was born six days after her conversation with Burke. That pregnancy had followed several miscarriages, and at that point Vieira was uncertain whether she'd be able to have another child. In the weeks that followed, 60 Minutes courted Vieira aggressively; she even got a phone call from Mike Wallace, whose imprimatur had become a necessary, almost ritualistic part of the show's hiring process. Equally crucial was Roone Arledge's pursuit of Vieira, which provided the leverage she needed to negotiate a deal with 60 Minutes. The final step in the recruitment process came in April 1989, when Hewitt and Phil Scheffler took Vieira to Tavern on the Green, the sparkling Central Park restaurant that was a favorite of Hewitt. Vieira brought her infant son to the lunch; he sat in a stroller while the grownups talked and throughout the conversation, Vieira held his hand for comfort.

On May 11, 1989, CBS announced that Vieira and her West 57th colleague, Steve Kroft, would both be joining the correspondent team of 60 Minutes that fall. While Kroft would immediately begin work on pieces for next season, Vieira would not start until the following September, when she completed her six-month maternity leave.

*   *   *

Steve Kroft had entered the TV news business at exactly the wrong time—in June 1972, just as affirmative action pushed white males to the bottom of everyone's hiring list. After graduation from Syracuse University and a stint in Vietnam, and unable to find a decent job, Kroft went to the Columbia University Graduate School of Journalism, hoping to reposition himself for a better shot. He managed to get himself hired as an investigative reporter at WJXT-TV in Jacksonville, Florida, which, as it turned out, was a hotbed of municipal corruption with no tough reporters to cover it. The ambitious Kroft jumped into the job full force. Within a year, his reporting resulted in the indictment of the mayor of Jacksonville along with a slew of other corrupt city officials. This got Kroft noticed by the CBS News bureau in Miami. William Small, then the Washington bureau chief of CBS News, heard talk that Kroft was the best young TV reporter in the Southeast.

By January 1980, Kroft was hired by CBS News. After a stint as a junior reporter in the New York bureau, where he continued to make his mark with hard-hitting stories, Kroft wangled better assignments. Eventually the network moved him to Dallas and Miami before handing him a coveted spot in the London bureau. The overseas job (back in the golden days of the early 1980s, before budget cuts reduced the network's emphasis on foreign coverage) gave Kroft the visibility he'd been yearning for.

Being a young star correspondent at CBS News in the 1980s led to great foreign assignments and prominent placement on the evening news broadcast—the TV news business had become increasingly eager to hire young correspondents in hopes of attracting younger viewers. Under the aegis of Howard Stringer, the news division was developing *West 57th*. Kroft wasn't among the reporters hired for the pilot episode that aired in 1985, but soon afterward he was brought back from London to add heft to a show that seemed to need it. He joined the show's young, attractive cast and stayed with it until it got canceled in 1989—which is when David Burke called.

Kroft was thrilled with his new assignment, and had heard enough stories about the perils of a new *60 Minutes* correspondent to deal with at least one issue in advance: the hiring of his own star producer. He knew exactly who he wanted—33-year-old Jeffrey Fager, a former *Evening News* producer who most recently worked as a deputy to Andrew Heyward, another rising CBS News star producer, during the formation of its latest newsmagazine startup, called *48 Hours*. Like Kroft, Fager was an ambitious and determined young journalist who wouldn't stop until he'd made it to the pinnacle of the news business— which, after all these years, was still *60 Minutes*.

Fager grew up in Wellesley, Massachusetts, the son of a prominent brain surgeon at Massachusetts General Hospital. By the time he grad- uated from Colgate University in 1977 with a degree in English and po- litical science, he'd decided to pursue a career in broadcasting and was hired as a "broadcast assistant"—a gopher—at WBZ, the CBS-owned affiliate in Boston. He moved up quickly to become an associate director and assignment editor, as well as writing news for WBZ radio. That led him to a quick succession of jobs at Boston TV and radio stations before he landed in 1979 as a broadcast producer at KPIX, now the CBS- owned station in San Francisco. In 1982 he moved up to the network level as a low-level producer at CBS News in New York, working for shows like *Nightwatch* (CBS's failed attempt at a late-night news show, with Charlie Rose in the anchor chair), before getting hired as a pro- ducer on the *CBS Evening News* in 1984. Fager worked in New York and London for the Rather newscast, covering the Mideast conflict, the Reagan-Gorbachev summits, and the fall of communism in East- ern Europe, then returned to New York to take the job with Heyward on *48 Hours*. But he wasn't there long, either; when the offer came from Kroft, he grabbed it.

Fager produced Kroft's first piece on *60 Minutes,* a profile of a San Francisco orthopedic surgeon, Dr. Lorraine Day, as a window onto health care workers contracting AIDS through exposure in the workplace. After the first screening of the story—called "Dr. Day Is Quitting"— Scheffler and Hewitt gave the piece a standing ovation.

Fager was gentle and soft-spoken. Although he was supremely confident, could report tough stories, and do battle with the best of his peers, he kept his anger in check and typically brushed off tensions with a smile. He had an easygoing, likable manner that won him friends and respect.

Kroft, on the other hand, was difficult. Known for his propensity to yell and go on the attack, he would routinely berate his producers for writing a lousy script, or not making enough phone calls, or failing somehow to live up to the high standards Kroft had for his work. While his criticisms weren't personal, those who worked for him found it a stressful experience. Nonetheless, many were willing to let his behavior slide; they recognized in him a perfectionist who was himself always willing to go the extra distance to make his pieces better. And few ever argued that a script of theirs hadn't been improved by Kroft's heavy hand; he had a reputation as a skilled TV writer and seemed to have a natural voice for *60 Minutes* scripts. Fager and Kroft had started off on a positive note, but it was anybody's guess whether their relationship would continue without incident.

Andy Rooney was in trouble again.

This time it was over racist remarks that had run in an interview he did with *The Advocate,* a Los Angeles–based gay newspaper, in February 1990. That interview had itself been prompted by other inflammatory comments—this time, ones deemed insensitive to homosexuals—in a 1989 year-end special on CBS, "The Year With Andy Rooney." During that program, the 71-year-old Rooney had remarked: "There was some recognition in 1989 of the fact that many of the ills which kill us are self-induced. Too much alcohol. Too much food, drugs, homosexual unions, cigarettes. They're all known to lead quite often to premature death." When the Gay and Lesbian Alliance Against Defamation (GLAAD) had met with CBS to protest, Rooney apologized for the comment, and his decision to talk to *The Advocate* was most likely a step toward repairing his image.

But in the interview, Rooney was quoted as saying: "I've believed all along that most people are born with equal intelligence, but blacks have watered down their genes because the less intelligent ones are the ones that have the most children. They drop out of school early, do drugs and get pregnant."

Rooney adamantly denied having made those remarks. "I did not say, nor would I ever have thought, that blacks have watered down their genes," Rooney told the *New York Times*. "It is a know-nothing statement, which I abhor." Rooney's friend Walter Cronkite also stepped forward with a statement on his behalf. "I've known Rooney for almost half a century, and I know he is not a racist," Cronkite said. "He is an independent thinker and a courageous social critic." However, Rooney's troubles weren't limited to his comments in the interview. In a letter to the editor of *The Advocate* published in the same issue as the interview, Rooney had written: "AIDS is a largely preventable disease" and referred to "growing public resentment" over the health care tax burden created by what he called "self-inflicted diseases."

CBS News had little choice but to rebuke him publicly. David Burke, the CBS News president, announced that Rooney would be suspended for three months without pay and said, "I have made it clear that CBS News cannot tolerate such remarks or anything that approximates such comments, since they in no way reflect the views of this organization."

Within two weeks, pressure mounted on Burke to cut short the suspension, for the simple reason that the ratings of *60 Minutes* had shown a precipitous drop in Rooney's absence. By the last Sunday in February, *60 Minutes* had dropped from the top 10 to eighteenth place in the ratings, and ranked second in its time slot for the first time since 1978— Rooney's first year as a full-time *60 Minutes* commentator. (First in the time slot that week was a hot new ABC series, *America's Funniest Home Videos*.) Don Hewitt posted news of the ratings drop in a memo, hinting that Rooney might be returning early to the broadcast. "Andy is universally liked," Hewitt told a *New York Times* reporter.

Three weeks after announcing the three-month suspension, Burke restored Rooney to the flagging newsmagazine, in the hopes that the controversy might deliver some ratings luster to the show—which, of course, it did. It couldn't have worked out better had Don Hewitt planned the entire episode himself. But as at least one *60 Minutes* insider muttered to a reporter soon afterward: "Why doesn't he ever get in trouble for what he says on the air? Because what he says on the air is basically innocuous and in keeping with their desire to please people, to be popular."

That criticism reflected the enduring struggle at *60 Minutes* between those who saw it as an investigative tool, and those who appreciated its value as great television. Hewitt and his team achieved ratings success by keeping their focus as tight as ever on compelling personalities and dramatic stories, instead of coverage of institutions or issues. Hewitt's Hildy still preferred entertaining his audience to educating or unsettling them. And for all the carping of reporters and critics who fantasized that *60 Minutes* could bring down corporations and presidents, it remained a potent journalistic force precisely because of its reach—a direct result of Hewitt's formula of finding stories with universal appeal. The guy in the Barcalounger might be flipping channels a little more than he used to, but he was still coming back to *60 Minutes* in the end.

Chapter 17

Never a Noble Moment

Meredith Vieira and Steve Kroft had arrived during a period when, at last, the baby boomer generation found itself fully represented in the population of *60 Minutes* producers. Hewitt still ran the shop, with Scheffler at his side, but the producers were at least a full generation younger. And while the ratings may have declined slightly from the highs of the previous decade, CBS News still valued *60 Minutes* as much as ever, and teams of young producers still roamed the world with seemingly unlimited budgets in search of stories.

While they did so, Hewitt was busily maintaining his status as part of the New York power structure. The man who once aspired to be Hildy Johnson had since become Walter Burns and now wanted the perks that came with being the boss.

Hewitt hadn't yet achieved quite the social cachet he yearned for—the kind that came so easily to Diane Sawyer or Mike Wallace as genuine celebrities—but still counted among his friends Pete Peterson, Nixon's secretary of commerce; Felix Rohatyn, partner at Lazard Frères; and, of course, his good pal Bill Paley. He continued to spend time at his house out in Bridgehampton, but now, instead of driving, he hitched rides for the weekend on private choppers. He'd charmed the billionaire set with the one thing they couldn't buy: control of the media. Hewitt owned an hour of prime network real estate, and some suspected his lifestyle was having an influence on *60 Minutes* itself.

"I once told him I'd written his epitaph," Harry Reasoner said in a *Rolling Stone* interview. "'Don Hewitt: Married on a real-estate magnate's yacht, helicoptered out to the Hamptons on weekends with Bill Paley, invited to all the A-list parties.' And then, in smaller type below, 'executive producer of the first half-hour network evening newscast and creator of a television-magazine show.'" Hewitt's response: "Success hasn't spoiled me."

With Hewitt's attention diverted by his private ambitions, his crew of producers and correspondents saw the opportunity to shape the show by their own passions, at least to some extent. A workaholic of the first order, Kroft had made a quick mark in February 1990 with "Chernobyl," a look at the long-term effects of the April 1986 nuclear disaster. Kroft relished the complex and dangerous assignments that others shunned; he had a passion for big stories. While not a stylist like Safer or a dynamic interviewer like Wallace, Kroft nonetheless had a gift for expressing himself as though speaking directly to the viewer, as he demonstrated with this story.

> KROFT: You can't see the contamination, and you can't feel it. All you can do is hear it on a Geiger counter. In some hot spots we found radiation levels one hundred times normal. . . . To give you some sort of an idea of the effects of the Chernobyl accident on Belorussia, imagine the state of Iowa, a third of it contaminated, a fifth of its land unusable forever.

Vieira delivered one of her most memorable segments on October 21, 1990: "Ward 5A," produced by Paul and Holly Fine, about the nurses in an AIDS ward at San Francisco General Hospital. With the pressures of a young child at home, it hadn't been easy for Vieira to report; she'd brought Ben with her on the West Coast trip. It proved compelling in large measure because of Vieira's sensitive reporting and relaxed on-camera style. Hewitt had attacked her for wearing jeans in some parts of the piece, but it added a touch of humanity to the final product, which showed patients coping with the final days before their deaths, and nurses dealing with severe psychological strain—such as this emotional closing exchange with a nurse named David Denmark.

VIEIRA *(voice-over)*: Now he is talking about leaving because he's lost so many friends to this virus. He's lost so much of himself.

DENMARK: A friend of mine died on the unit. I took care of him, wrapped his body and sent it to the morgue—and since that time—

VIEIRA: What did that do to you?

DENMARK: Since I did this for Ken, I have not been able to cry.

VIEIRA *(voice-over)*: On our last day here, David showed me ward 5A's memorial: a dog-eared book that lists every patient who has died. There are more than 1,200 names. The nurses here have a saying: "Don't regret growing old. It's a privilege denied to many." A privilege Tom, Dorothy, Angel, and Rudy will never know. Their names are now written in that book.

DENMARK: When you look at this, you're kind of overwhelmed because the faces come back.

VIEIRA: You want to close the book?

DENMARK: Yeah.

In December, Kroft offered a piece in the classic *60 Minutes* tradition: produced by Robert Anderson, it revealed how used-car salesmen altered the mileage on odometers to convince buyers of the car's good condition. Thanks in large measure to *60 Minutes,* stories like this had become staples of local news shows; to elevate this one above farm-team standards would require flawless execution and a powerful villain. Kroft knew he had one in obese, sweaty Houston car salesman Bill Whitlow. After filming Whitlow with a hidden camera and getting him to admit to breaking the law, this amusing interchange followed, with Kroft clearly relishing his power to intimidate a bad guy as much as Mike Wallace ever did.

KROFT: I want to show you one thing.

WHITLOW: All right.

KROFT: You know what's back there? . . . It's a TV camera back there. . . . We've been taping this whole thing. . . . The good news is, we're not cops.

WHITLOW: Well, I didn't think so.

KROFT: The bad news is, we're with *60 Minutes.*

Kroft and Vieira were both quickly demonstrating their skills at delivering polished *60 Minutes* pieces. But Kroft lacked an incalculable asset that Vieira (and the rest of her *60 Minutes* colleagues) had in abundance: star power. With his extra-large head and stocky frame, he looked like nothing so much as a sportscaster at a local station—and in fact was sometimes mistaken for one when he traveled for *60 Minutes.* If he wanted the level of stardom that had seemed to have come so easily to his colleagues, it was going to take a while.

True to form, the *60 Minutes* boys' club didn't make Meredith Vieira's adjustment very easy. She had difficult screenings of early pieces and run-ins with her colleagues, including one with Wallace in which he called a recently aired piece of hers "embarrassing" to the show. By January 1990, the other new kid, Kroft, had gotten four pieces onto the air; Vieira had yet to crack the lineup. Vieira told one interview subject how difficult it was "competing with people like Mike Wallace." According to author Elsa Walsh, a publicist present at the interview muttered, "You have nothing to worry about there."

The perception of some of the old hands was that Vieira wasn't committed to her four-year contract. Despite a reported annual paycheck of $500,000 she showed up in jeans, worked only the hours necessary to deliver her pieces, and brought Ben along with her to the office and on reporting trips. About four months into her tenure on the show, another female *60 Minutes* staffer approached Vieira to ask her why she hadn't hired a live-in nanny to take care of Ben so she could commit herself more fully to her work. "I will never ever get a live-in nanny," Vieira replied, "because I'm afraid if I ever did that I would delegate more and more to the nanny." But she feared her point of view was lost on women who felt that she had a singular opportunity to make a mark on television's best news show. Vieira observed that almost no one else at *60 Minutes* had young children at home, and that the mindset of the place was decidedly unsympathetic to the whole notion of parenting.

Still, Vieira continued to pursue the kinds of stories that appealed to her at *West 57th*: human dramas that highlighted social issues of personal importance to her. Some at *60 Minutes* suggested that Hewitt's conflict with Vieira might have more to do with her political agenda—she was seen as a staunch liberal, in stark contrast to Wallace, for example—than her maternal one. Hewitt had always asserted that one of the show's greatest strengths was its lack of a political point of view, but he never gave voice to any accusation. It was clear that Vieira had a strong humanist bent and would not devote her time at *60 Minutes* to pieces that didn't inspire her. That first season, her stories included profiles of the president of Gallaudet University, a school for the deaf in Washington, D.C.; "Thy Brother's Keeper," a touching piece about Rabbi Harold Schulweis of Los Angeles, who promoted the history of non-Jews who fought to save Jews from the Nazis in World War II; and, of course, "Ward 5-A."

Vieira kept to herself the fact that she was trying desperately to have another child, until she miscarried again in the summer of 1990 and told Hewitt. According to Walsh's account of the episode, Hewitt responded to Vieira's confession by asking her, in tone-deaf fashion, "Does this mean you want to have more children?"

By the fall Vieira had become pregnant again, but this time, she knew better than to rush into Hewitt's office with her good news.

Hewitt had been pleased with "Ward 5A." It had earned Vieira the kind of critical praise that led people to think she might just make it at *60 Minutes*.

In the winter of 1991, *60 Minutes* had its first real brush with a breaking-news story of enough importance that it demanded wall-to-wall coverage: the Gulf War. In a series of broadcasts through the first two months of the year, the show pounced on the story, demonstrating its ability to compete in a universe that now included the first 24-hour news channel, CNN. The January 20 broadcast included "Saddam's Bodyguard," a Morley Safer interview with a former bodyguard to the Iraqi dictator; "The Man Who Armed Iraq," Steve Kroft's piece about a weapons dealer; "Inferno," a Mike Wallace story about allegations that Hussein had seeded land mines around Kuwaiti oil wells; and "Iraqi Terror," an Ed Bradley look at the possibility of Iraqi terrorist attacks on the United States. In the weeks that followed, the show continued to produce topical, breaking stories, including "Saddam's Billions," a memorable Kroft piece in March, produced by Lowell Bergman, that reported on the possibility that Hussein had stashed money all over the world to fund his war efforts. While the media obsessed over the impact on the TV news business of round-the-clock coverage, *60 Minutes* was demonstrating the continued value of its approach: narrative, magazine-length features that explored the complexities of an increasingly fractious political environment.

While the show may have been outwardly perceived as a well-oiled machine, Meredith Vieira's future remained unsettled. In January 1991, Hewitt called Vieira one Saturday night to ask her to get on the Concorde to Paris to cover a story. Not wanting to travel so early in her pregnancy—the baby was due in August—she finally had to tell Hewitt the truth. "I have to get off the phone to call Morley," Hewitt said before hanging up.

Thus began an intense round-robin of recriminations and negotiations that continued for weeks, as Vieira struggled to work out a part-time arrangement for the next season. Finally, in March, Hewitt made it clear that there was only one option for Vieira if she wanted to remain at *60 Minutes,* one he was certain she would never accept: a full-time load of 20 pieces a year. Vieira knew there was no way to complete that amount of work with two small children at home. She resigned.

In the immediate aftermath, other women in the news business expressed mixed feelings. "She didn't get fired," Linda Ellerbee, the former ABC News correspondent and outspoken feminist, told the *New York Times.* "That's progress." Others didn't see quite so rosy a picture. "It's a little scary," said Maria Shriver, then of NBC News.

Almost immediately, Vieira and Hewitt began a war of words in the press. Vieira criticized CBS for not accommodating her needs or allowing her to continue to contribute to *60 Minutes* on a part-time basis. "I understand his point of view," she said of Hewitt in *Entertainment Weekly,* "but I think it could have been a trailblazing thing for *60 Minutes.* As women come up in this business, people are not putting families on hold. I would have loved them to say, 'We're in a position to try something creative.' I didn't go into this job misleading anybody."

Hewitt never acknowledged Vieira's pull to parenthood as anything other than competition for her loyalty to *60 Minutes.* He'd given ample evidence over the years of his insistence that his troops commit themselves to *60 Minutes* and nothing else. "If you have six people, they only appear twice a month, and the audience loses familiarity with them," Hewitt said. "The game is played with five people. And to show up once in a while doesn't cut the mustard."

Feeling betrayed, Hewitt chose to cast the decision as a reflection on Vieira's talents as a journalist, with public statements designed to embarrass her. "They just disappeared," he said to *Entertainment Weekly* of her *60 Minutes* contributions. "Do you remember any Meredith Vieira stories? Nobody does. Look, in a nutshell, if Meredith Vieira had created half as much attention working with us as she's created complaining about us, I would have turned handsprings to keep her here." Hewitt kept up the diatribe for days. "For reasons I don't un-derstand, she never made anybody sit up and take notice," he told the *New York Times*. "Your fingertips told you that nobody was talking about Meredith Vieira."

Hewitt's attacks eventually turned personal. "She brought her baby! I set up a nursery so she could nurse her baby in the office," Hewitt said. "You know who was horrified at that? The women around here who had had their babies and gone back to work. They couldn't believe it."

In a September 2003 interview, Vieira disputed Hewitt's assertions: "There was never a nursery. There was nothing. Nothing. Zero. I had brought in some toys, like little squeezy toys that I would throw on the floor. There was nothing, no. Nor would I have expected it. I never asked for a nursery. I wouldn't want a nursery. I would never expect it." Vieira also said that once she returned to work after her first maternity leave, she hired full-time help and rarely brought Ben to the office.

In March 2004, Hewitt took a different stance on Vieira's depar-ture. "If I knew then what I know now about how sick her husband was, how absolutely horrific her life was, I'd have handled it a lot dif-ferently," Hewitt says, referring to Vieira's husband, Richard Cohen, a former CBS News producer who had left the company after being stricken by multiple sclerosis. "I didn't know. I did everything. I went out and bought a fucking—we had teddy bears in there for her kids, and a crib, and a playpen." He went on: "Meredith left because I went to my boss and said, 'My guys cannot take up the slack for the sto-ries she's not doing.' Had she come to me and said, 'Listen, I'm only working here half-time, I'll take half a salary, get somebody else to take half the salary,' that would be great. . . . It wasn't that what she did wasn't good enough."

In the final days before Vieira departed *60 Minutes,* Morley Safer made a rare visit to her office and stood in the doorway, smoking a cig-arette.

"You know, kid," Vieira recalled Safer saying, "my wife and my daughter, to this day, resent the fact that I've spent so much time on the road and wish that I could have been around more. I did a lot of things that were great for me but not so great for my family."

To Vieira, it was Safer's way of saying that if she was questioning her decision, there were a few people around *60 Minutes* who thought it was the right one.

Shortly after Vieira left *60 Minutes,* Harry Reasoner retired. He'd had a second lung cancer operation, and his health had deteriorated to the point where he could no longer contribute to the show.

In May 1991, Hewitt and the show threw a retirement party for Reasoner at the Russian Tea Room. It was not a happy event for those who loved Reasoner, and who objected to the way he had been treated in recent months by Hewitt and his correspondents, men who'd long called themselves his friends. It was felt that his colleagues blamed him for his own illness, resented him for letting down the team, and believed he was no longer deserving of their admiration and kindness.

"They treated him like shit," Jeffrey Fager recalls of that day. "Nobody really got up and gave a good toast except George Crile [by then a Reasoner producer on *60 Minutes*]. It was really odd for those of us who were young producers then to watch it happen. Mike got up and said something snide. Don got up and said something snide. Morley got up and said, 'Never a noble moment.' We all came back and thought, My God. Harry could barely walk. He died a month later. And then, everybody was like, 'Harry was so great, Harry was the best.'. . . He had abused himself. He'd been smoking too much, he'd been drinking too much. And because of that they had no respect for him. You're supposed to be a giant. You're supposed to be immortal. So it was pretty striking. I remember it, because Harry was such a sweet guy."

Reasoner died on August 6, 1991, at the age of 68. A CBS spokesman reported the cause of death as "cardiopulmonary arrest."

Chapter 18

Jesus, Mary, and Joseph!

It's all well and good to take bows and curtsies for being No. 1, but unless you get off your backsides and start working harder, we're going to be lucky to end up No. 51. Nowhere in all of journalism are their [*sic*] news people as well paid and loudly applauded as you are. Come on, for Christ's sake, start turning out stories.

—*Memo to the troops from Don Hewitt in September 1990*

When Lesley Stahl arrived at *60 Minutes,* there was some confusion as to whether she was replacing Vieira or Reasoner. She'd been chosen to take Reasoner's spot, but because of her gender—and Vieira's almost simultaneous departure—many assumed she was taking the woman's slot, even though one news account at the time harshly referred to her as "an honorary man." The notion that Stahl was a token of anything represented a bum rap against a woman who had earned her reputation as a terrific reporter regardless of her sex. In almost two decades at CBS News, Stahl had distinguished herself repeatedly as exactly the kind of journalist Hewitt loved—aggressive, smart, and appealing.

"I was born on my 30th birthday," she wrote as the opening sentence of her 1999 memoir, *Reporting Live,* referring to the beginning of her television career. And 400 pages later she had done nothing to contradict that odd assessment of herself. She'd graduated from

Wheaton College in 1963, junked graduate school in zoology, married a doctor, written speeches for New York mayor John Lindsay, worked as a researcher at NBC, gotten divorced, moved to Boston, and landed a correspondent's job at WHDH-TV in Boston, then catapulted to another one at CBS News. Despite her long career in the spotlight, she has revealed little else about herself to viewers or readers—except, in various spots in her memoir where she allows scattered details about her demanding mother. Like her *60 Minutes* predecessor (and eventual friend) Diane Sawyer, Stahl depicts a mother focused obsessively on her daughter's appearance, despite her considerable achievements and a longstanding reputation as one of the most beautiful women in television news.

"She was always harping on me about my hair," Stahl wrote, describing her early years at CBS News in the early 1970s, having been hired in 1972 in the Washington bureau as a beneficiary of affirmative action policies—her own assessment of how it happened. "'You need to go to New York and get Kenneth to style it. That's where Jackie Kennedy goes.' About my makeup: 'Can't you find something to hide those circles under your eyes?' My clothes: 'Where on earth did you pick up that little number? Get rid of it.' It wasn't that I disagreed with my mother. It was just that her formula for success, being beautiful, had the effect of making people think I was brainless."

But few people mistook Stahl for brainless. She'd landed in Washington just as the Watergate scandal was heating up, and as a junior reporter was assigned to cover the story. Not only did she land numerous TV scoops—and regular appearances on the evening news—she also dated Bob Woodward of the *Washington Post,* then one of the capital's most eligible bachelors. Covering the Senate Watergate Committee hearings in 1973, she met Aaron Latham, then a writer for *New York Magazine,* whom she would eventually marry. After distinguishing herself during Watergate, she was assigned to cover politics, and later the Carter White House—and after that, even more memorably, the Reagan administration. With CBS News still the gold standard, Stahl had become a household name and a fixture at White House press conferences. She earned a reputation as a fearless reporter who would ask anything of anyone; legendary stories of her dogged reporting followed her throughout her career—like the time she was dragged away after cornering then-Nixon chief of staff Alexander Haig on Capitol Hill and asking him about the president's plans to turn over the secret White House tapes.

When Van Gordon Sauter took over as president of CBS News in 1981, Stahl was promoted, replacing George Herman as host of the Sunday-morning talk show *Face The Nation*. By then she'd given birth to a daughter, Taylor, yet seemed unwilling to cut back on her reporting duties. When given the difficult choice between work and family, she preferred to simply do both. She continued as host of *Face The Nation* and as White House correspondent.

Don Hewitt had been courting Stahl with phone calls about her work for years; in 1977, he'd even assigned veteran *60 Minutes* producer Paul Loewenwarter to travel with her to Puerto Rico to do a piece to test her potential. By 1991, he decided he needed her. Reasoner and Vieira were leaving; as a woman and an already-established CBS News personality, Stahl neatly filled both vacancies, and Hewitt finally called her with an offer to come work at *60 Minutes*.

Stahl passed along a hot tip to her producer Rome Hartman: her friend Ray Stark, the Hollywood producer, thought there might be a good segment in the story of Dr. Thoralf Sundt, a brain surgeon at the Mayo Clinic who had operated on President Reagan in 1989 following a horseback riding accident. What made Sundt an appealing subject—aside from his preeminence in the field—was the state of his own health. He had been diagnosed in 1985 with bone marrow cancer but continued to operate on patients—particularly those who'd been deemed inoperable by other physicians. Hartman knew it had the makings of a good story, but he also knew there was a higher bar for a *60 Minutes* piece. Until Stahl brought him with her to work as her first producer at *60 Minutes,* he'd been a CBS News producer on a comfortable path to management. Though he'd never produced a piece longer than a typical evening news segment, he knew the mandate he had to meet: tell me a story. The doctor he found on a reporting trip to Minneapolis was a perfect *60 Minutes* character, the center of one of Stahl's first stories on September 22, 1991.

> SUNDT: Fortunately, the illness hasn't affected my mind. I don't know how great it is, but it's as good as it ever was. And my hands—it's not hurt my hands.
>
> STAHL: Dr. Sundt's bones are so brittle from his disease that he has broken ribs just coughing or rolling over in bed. He must wear a special brace to protect him during operations. But he won't give in to the pain.
>
> MRS. SUNDT: He looks better when he comes home at night than when he left in the morning, because he's doing what he needs to do.
>
> STAHL: Saving lives.
>
> MRS. SUNDT: And they're saving his.

Although the Sundt story appeared, on the surface, to be just another classic human interest story, it also tapped into a private but shared obsession of the men who ran *60 Minutes*—a singular passion for work and its redemptive powers.

It was coming up on a quarter century since *60 Minutes* had gone on the air; Don Hewitt was now almost 70, and Mike Wallace was 75. This season had started off well, with the numbers up over the year before—and neither man showed any sign of wanting to quit working full-time at the jobs they loved. The year before, Hewitt and Wallace had boarded a flight together from Los Angeles to New York; Hewitt had just been inducted into the Television Academy of Arts & Sciences Hall of Fame, and they were returning from the ceremony. Just before the plane took off, Wallace got out of his seat and collapsed in the aisle of the plane. "Oh shit," Hewitt thought to himself, "he's dead. Now we're never going to catch *Cheers* in the ratings." Wallace was fine, though it turned out he needed a pacemaker. If anything, the equipment only seemed to energize him more. Maybe Hewitt and Wallace weren't saving lives, but they surely identified with Sundt and his passion for work as a means of staying alive.

Steve Kroft, still the unlikeliest candidate for stardom in the *60 Minutes* pantheon, was on the phone in January 1992 with George Stephanopoulos, a young press aide to Democratic presidential candidate Bill Clinton.

Over the last few days, the energetic Stephanopoulos had been occupied doing damage control on the latest rumors that swirled around his candidate. In the most recent issue of the *Star,* a weekly tabloid, a cabaret singer named Gennifer Flowers had alleged a 12-year affair with Clinton that ended in 1989. The tabloid—which admitted to having paid Flowers—also claimed to have tape recordings that corroborated her story. Clinton had denied the story, but Kroft had heard that Clinton might be interested in having the platform of a national television interview to defend his integrity. Unfortunately, *60 Minutes* was being preempted that Sunday because of the Super Bowl, which, he explained to the press aide, would mean he couldn't get the interview on unless CBS agreed to make time after the game.

"What time would this run?" Stephanopoulos asked.

Probably not until after 10, Kroft explained.

"That's awfully late," Stephanopoulos replied. "I'm not sure anybody would be watching."

"Well, we can't do it any earlier because of the game."

"What game?" Stephanopoulos asked.

"The Super Bowl," Kroft said, barely able to contain his reaction to Stephanopoulos's ignorance.

"The Super Bowl is on this Sunday?"

"Yes."

"On CBS?"

"Yes."

"We're interested," Stephanopoulos said, the excitement suddenly rising in his voice.

Kroft quickly reached Hewitt at the San Francisco airport. Hewitt made a bunch of calls and arranged for a short, special segment of *60 Minutes* to air immediately after the game; he then spoke to both Stephanopoulos and Clinton aide James Carville, before flying to Boston to meet Kroft at the Ritz Carlton Hotel, where the interview was to take place that Sunday, only hours before airtime.

Just before the interview began, Hewitt approached the candidate and told him that honesty and direct answers would win him votes. "I think at some point you're going to have to be as candid as you know how," Hewitt counseled Clinton, "and then from there on you say, 'I said it on *60 Minutes.*'" Hewitt wanted Clinton to make sure he understood: this was going to be history in the making. Hewitt and Kroft both understood the implications of catching Clinton at this perfect moment, and giving him a platform to speak to the American people for the first time.

The session itself lasted an hour. Its most eventful moment came 40 minutes in, when a 50-pound klieg light toppled over and nearly hit Mrs. Clinton before crashing onto the floor. "Jesus, Mary, and Joseph!" the candidate's wife exclaimed. Clinton took her in his arms and clutched her while the cameras still whirred. Those terrifying seconds did not make it into the original broadcast, and have been shown only a few times since on *60 Minutes* anniversary shows. When Clinton signed on to do his "Point-Counterpoint" debate with Bob Dole, he referred to Don Hewitt as "the man who tried to kill me."

As soon as the interview ended, Hewitt, Kroft, and producer Frank Devine rushed to edit it into a nine-minute segment to air in just a few hours. They all knew the obvious pieces to use, yet just moments before the piece was finalized for broadcast, Devine reminded everyone of their plan to include a neglected clip of something Mrs. Clinton had said:

MRS. CLINTON: You know, I'm not sitting here as some little woman standing by my man, like Tammy Wynette. I'm sitting here because I love him and I respect him and I honor what he's been through and what we've been through together. And, you know, if that's not enough for people then, heck, don't vote for him.

The rest of the interview somehow managed to make news, too, though not quite at the level of Mrs. Clinton's comments. It also demonstrated, for the first time, the full extent of Kroft's skills as a questioner; a combination of Wallace's pointed digging and Stahl's repertoire of quizzical expressions, with no respect given to a politician's right to privacy. If there seemed to be little or no compassion or hesitation in Kroft's performance, it was no doubt due to his awareness that Clinton was fighting for his political life. Kroft seized the historic opportunity with apparent relish.

KROFT: Who is Gennifer Flowers? You know her?

CLINTON: Oh yeah.

KROFT: How do you know her? How would you describe your relationship?

CLINTON: Very limited, but until this—you know, friendly but limited. . . .

KROFT: She's alleging—and has described in some detail in the supermarket tabloid—what she calls a 12-year affair with you.

CLINTON: It—that allegation is false. . . .

KROFT: You've been saying all week that you've got to put this issue behind you. Are you prepared, tonight, to say that you've never had an extramarital affair?

CLINTON: I'm not prepared, tonight, to say that any married couple should ever discuss that with anyone but themselves. I'm not prepared to say that about anybody. . . .

KROFT: You're trying to put this issue behind you, and the problem with the answer is, it's not a denial. And people are sitting out there—voters—and they're saying, "Look, it's really pretty simple. If he's never had an extramarital affair, why doesn't he just say it?"

CLINTON: That may be what they're saying. You know what I think they're saying? I think they're saying, "Here's a guy who's leveling with us." You may think that we should say more, and you can keep asking the question, but I'm telling you I think that we've told—I'll come back to what I said. I have told the American people more than any other candidate for president. The result of that has been everybody going to my state, and spending more time trying to play Gotcha!

MRS. CLINTON: There isn't a person watching this who would feel comfortable sitting on this couch detailing everything that ever went on in their life or their marriage. And I think it's real dangerous in this country if we don't have some zone of privacy for everybody. I mean, I think that's absolutely critical.

KROFT: I couldn't agree with you more, and I think—and I agree with you that everyone wants to put this behind you. And the reason it hasn't gone away is that your answer is not a denial, is it?

CLINTON: It's interesting—let's assume—let's—

KROFT: But it's not a denial.

The Kroft interview is often cited as a foreshadowing of Clinton's conduct as president. It's worth noting that the issue that ultimately led to Clinton's impeachment was not infidelity, but rather the question of a sitting president lying under oath. In the Kroft interview, the subject on the table was whether a presidential candidate had a responsibility to affirm or deny an extramarital affair to a representative of the press. If (as Kroft and others have since observed) that interview contributed to Clinton's eventual victory that November, then voters must have rewarded Clinton's position that his private life was none of Kroft's business.

Whatever the interview did for the Clintons, it accomplished the short-term goal of another ratings triumph for *60 Minutes* and clearly established Steve Kroft as a formidable player on a still-relevant team.

*   *   *

One week later, *60 Minutes* offered up "Anita Hill," the first television interview with the woman who'd accused Clarence Thomas of sexual harassment during his confirmation hearings to become a U.S. Supreme Court justice. It defined a *60 Minutes* scoop—a conversation with a formidable newsmaker who chose the broadcast to make an exclusive statement that the world was waiting to hear. In this case the scoop belonged to Ed Bradley.

In his dozen years at *60 Minutes* Bradley had perfected a deceptively easygoing but, in fact, intense conversational style that could intimidate or relax in equal measure. He had an innate sense of phrasing and intonation, and he used his hands as instruments. Perhaps it was his off-camera passion for music that enabled him to find the perfect point of emphasis in every sentence, every question. It probably didn't hurt that he had jazz music playing at all times in his *60 Minutes* office and everywhere else he could. The music relaxed him—he called it his "bliss." And he loved skiing at his home in Woody Creek, Colorado, which he was careful to distinguish from Aspen. He didn't mind reminding a visitor once or twice that Hunter Thompson remains a friend. He went to the New Orleans Jazz Festival every year and picked all his destinations carefully. (One day recently, Steve Kroft was planning a trip to Orlando and went to Bradley's assistant, Paulettte Robinson, to ask if Bradley had a hotel preference there. "Ed doesn't go to Orlando," Robinson explained to Kroft.)

Bradley exhilarated and exasperated his producers. They loved using his prodigious gifts as an interviewer and relished the moments when he would peer down over his glasses at a subject like a bemused district attorney, eyebrows raised in disbelief—or when his hands would chop through the air like a knife or punctuate his points like a conductor's baton. Not interested in maintaining the usual anchorman's poker face, Bradley used an array of expressions; his eyes would widen and narrow to underscore his thinking, and no one doubted the sincerity of his smile. To top it off, he'd been blessed with a melodious voice that added weight and nuance to everything he said, with an orator's sense of just how to emphasize. He might have made an impressive politician or actor—skills that were central to a *60 Minutes* correspondent's craft.

If it was Bradley's love of music and leisure that made him such a deft interviewer, it was that same passion that made him difficult to work with. In his early years Bradley traveled constantly, but by the mid-1990s, his pace had slowed somewhat. Producers always had to work around his considerable and increasing need for personal time. He had a daily gym workout, and interviews had to be scheduled around his appointments with his personal trainer. Bradley also considered his Colorado ski trips an inviolable part of his schedule—this made it tough on producers trying to squeeze reporting trips onto his calendar. He didn't like to become involved in a story until it was fairly far along in the process, didn't relish long talks with his producers about interviews, and preferred to read research materials on his own time. Nor did he write drafts of his stories; he rarely set pen to paper except to rewrite the work of others. It wasn't that he was lazy—anyone looking at his list of produced pieces would have to admit that Bradley worked hard. But he refused to give over his entire life to work the way Wallace did. As much as possible his nights and weekends were his own—and sometimes, so were parts of his weekdays. And the lack of social interaction with his colleagues suited him just fine.

When it came to interviews with people like Anita Hill, Bradley brought all his talents to the table. The end result was a serious conversation that lent new understanding to the underlying issues of sexual harassment for women in the workplace.

BRADLEY: People say, "Well, I sat there and I watched her, and I wanted to believe her, but I don't understand how she could say nothing for ten years. I don't understand how she could stay with him. I don't understand how she could follow him to another job." How do you make those people understand?

HILL: I cannot make those people understand. But I can share with those people what others have experienced. One of the things that women do when this happens is to examine themselves—

even to the extent of blaming themselves, their own behavior, their own actions, their own words. And so that is a factor in women not coming forward. Another thing that happens very often is that women are told, either by their harassers or by others, that they won't be believed if they come forward. And they know of enough experiences of other women where, not only were they not believed, but they were actually made to be the culprit.

Once again—and this time with great irony—a *60 Minutes* piece resonated not only with the audience, but with those who knew the inside story of the show itself.

On the Saturday morning after the Los Angeles riots began in May 1992, Rome Hartman went into the *60 Minutes* office and was summoned to Don Hewitt's office. That was almost unheard-of; he'd always been told *60 Minutes* doesn't even have meetings. Hartman raced down and discovered people gathered around Hewitt's desk, discussing how the show should cover the riots that had followed the acquittal of four Los Angeles policemen in the videotaped beating of a black motorist named Rodney King.

In a matter of minutes, it was decided that Hewitt, Stahl, and Hartman would immediately go to Los Angeles to interview Daryl Gates, the outgoing police chief. This was the kind of crash journalism that Stahl and Hartman had been doing for years, and with Hewitt now leading the charge, it was guaranteed to deliver a reporting high. The true thrills came the next day, as Gates interrupted a roving interview to get out of his car, holding a nightstick, and brandished it at a group of youths in full view of the *60 Minutes* cameras.

Stahl's interviews were just as revealing as the camera work. Her style as a questioner reflected her own aggressive and somewhat intimidating nature; she had little patience or tolerance for mistakes, either by those she was interviewing or those who worked for her. In a matter of months, Stahl had become known around the *60 Minutes* offices as a tough, demanding boss. She ran her life according to a precise and rigorous schedule—determined, as she was, to make her mark on *60 Minutes* just as she had in Washington. Inevitably, producers who didn't enjoy the experience of working with her or according to her rules dubbed her a "bitch." Other producers praised Stahl's style, citing her determined work ethic and personal compassion for their family issues. Many ultimately found her to be a generous and thoughtful boss in ways that mitigated the impact of her demanding temperament. Still, some felt Stahl had an overdeveloped ego and was excessively concerned with her appearance on camera; others resented her detail-heavy demands, including a requirement that all papers be assembled for her with paper clips, not staples.

Even her detractors had to admit that Stahl had a natural rapport with the camera and an instinct for making news. Soon after the Gates piece aired, she followed up with scoops for *60 Minutes* that included a June 1992 interview with Russia's president, Boris Yeltsin, and one in October of that year with Ross Perot—interviews that revealed not only Stahl's stern side as a rugged questioner but also her talent for nailing down truths from evasive public figures. She had quickly shown Hewitt that she fit in perfectly with a dysfunctional group of correspondents who'd become as famous as the stories they covered and used their celebrity to further the cause of their show. It was only those behind the camera who occasionally felt they were handling a newly minted and temperamental movie star, rather than a network news correspondent.

Chapter 19

Reporting, Not Crusading

It had been another great season for *60 Minutes,* ending in June 1993 as the number one show on television for the fourth year in its history. That tied it with *I Love Lucy* and *Gunsmoke* and left only *The Cosby Show* and *All in the Family* ahead of it on the all-time list. On an average Sunday, more than 31 million people watched *60 Minutes,* which by then had broadcast 2,299 original segments.

The show had just survived a momentary scare: Ed Bradley threatened to quit and join a new ABC prime-time newsmagazine. At the last possible moment, during a boat cruise around Manhattan to celebrate a successful season, he told his producers he'd changed his mind. That flirtation with another network eventually netted Bradley a salary increase that put him at the level of Mike Wallace and Don Hewitt—both thought to be making in the vicinity of $4 million a year.

In the 1992–1993 season, the show had reached a 21.9 rating and was number one; by 1994, though it remained in the top ten, its ratings were starting to slip. The blame was put on football. In a clever counterprogramming move, Fox, which now owned the broadcast rights to the NFL, was scheduling Sunday games to end at 7:30, cutting into *60 Minutes,* still CBS's top-rated show. But there was also a glut of newsmagazines, more than ever before: NBC had finally launched a successful one, *Dateline NBC*. ABC had added *Turning Point* (the show Ed Bradley was to have hosted) to *Prime Time Live* and *20/20*. CBS now offered both *Eye to Eye With Connie Chung* and *48 Hours*. All this competition led to an increase in tabloid topics; this, at least, gave *60 Minutes* an exclusive hold over viewers who liked their newsmagazines to contain some actual news.

CBS itself was facing new challenges; the median age of its audience was rising just as advertisers were putting an increasing premium on the 18–49 market. Even with the ongoing success of *60 Minutes,* there was no ignoring the fact that its audience (and, of course, its cast) was aging rapidly enough to create some long-term concerns. In the fall of 1995, as speculation grew that Laurence Tisch was considering the sale of CBS, NBC decided to challenge the supremacy of *60 Minutes* directly by programming an hour of its profitable new newsmagazine, *Dateline NBC,* on Sunday nights at 7:00 P.M. Other shows that had tried to go head-to-head with Hewitt had left the lineup battered, but given his show's recent ratings decline, it seemed like a propitious time to take him on again.

One day in the spring of 1993, Wallace producer Lowell Bergman opened the door of his house in Berkeley, California, and discovered that someone had dropped a bundle of tobacco industry documents on his doorstep. Bergman, a big bear of a man, was considered one of the best investigative producers ever to work on *60 Minutes*—good enough for the show to allow him to live 3,000 miles away from his bosses.

Needing help to decipher the documents, which were a tangle of legalese and scientific jargon, Bergman went to Jeffrey Wigand, a biochemist who had been hired in 1989 by Brown & Williamson, a tobacco company that makes Kool, Lucky Strike, and other brands, to develop a "safer" cigarette. Over the next few years he became acutely knowledgeable about the addictive properties of nicotine; his outspoken opinions led to his dismissal in March 1993. Bergman had long been interested in the dangers of smoking, and saw in Wigand great potential for a *60 Minutes* story. Wigand agreed to consult for CBS on a 1994 piece on fire safety and cigarettes, but Bergman—a gruff, obsessive, and unstoppable reporting machine—realized that if he could convince Wigand to go public with his knowledge of the inner workings of Big Tobacco, it could make a far bigger story.

The story Bergman wanted to tell—an exploration of Brown & Williamson's chemical manipulation of nicotine—was important and timely, but complex and highly technical as well. Wigand's presence in the piece—as scientist and discarded employee—would offer the perfect humanizing touch. But when he approached Wigand to talk, he discovered a man in fear. Wigand had signed a confidentiality agreement with his former employer. He claimed he had received death threats and insisted that he couldn't and wouldn't talk until at least March 1995, when his severance package with Brown & Williamson expired. Bergman was relentless, however; he wasn't going to let the story slip away.

Finally, in August 1995, he convinced Wigand to come to New York for an interview with Mike Wallace. After he had written a rough draft of the piece, Bergman was summoned to a meeting at Black Rock on September 5 and told to suspend work on the Wigand story for a week until he and his *60 Minutes* bosses could meet with a CBS lawyer to discuss the legal implications of the story.

On September 12, Bergman, Hewitt, Wallace, and Phil Scheffler crossed the street from the *60 Minutes* offices to the CBS Broadcast Center and went into a meeting in the conference room of Eric Ober, then president of CBS News. There the *60 Minutes* crew first encountered Ellen Kaden, the woman who set into motion the events that made the Wigand story a crossroads in the show's history: Kaden, who was general counsel of CBS Inc., told the crew that the Wigand piece was too risky to air because of a relatively obscure legal concept known as "tortious interference." She wanted a three-week delay (though Bergman could continue to work on the piece) while CBS sought an opinion from outside counsel.

As Kaden explained, Wigand had a contract with his former employer, as part of his severance, that prohibited him from revealing inside information about the company. Any attempt by CBS to induce Wigand to break that contract was considered tortious interference. More important, it was the stuff of a potential multibillion-dollar lawsuit against CBS News. Airing the interview with Wigand would put the entire corporation into jeopardy. If the *60 Minutes* crew needed convincing, they only had to consider the mess ABC had gotten into as a result of a tobacco investigation.

A month before, ABC News had announced settlement of two multibillion-dollar lawsuits against its own weekly newsmagazine *Day One* brought by Philip Morris and R. J. Reynolds. In that case, ABC agreed to withdraw its previously reported assertion that Philip Morris and R. J. Reynolds added significant amounts of nicotine to their tobacco. "That was a mistake that was not deliberate on the part of ABC," were the carefully chosen words of substitute anchor Diane Sawyer on ABC's *World News Tonight*, which aired on Monday, August 21, 1995, "but for which we accept responsibility and which requires correction. We apologize to our audience, Philip Morris, and Reynolds."

ABC's apology was seen by outsiders as a cave-in to the legal threat of the huge tobacco companies seeking damages that could have had a dire effect on the network's financial picture. It was also strongly rumored that CBS would soon complete a merger with Westinghouse; current owner Laurence Tisch didn't want any multibillion-dollar lawsuits gumming up the deal.

After the meeting, Bergman recalls, he, Hewitt, Wallace, and Scheffler stood together for a few tense moments in the long, narrow hallway outside Ober's office. "She has great tits," Hewitt said finally, of Ellen Kaden. "I'd like to fuck her."

A little more than two weeks later, on September 29, Ober, Wallace, Hewitt, Scheffler, and Bergman watched a rough assembly of the Wigand story. Ober felt the piece wasn't finished; he wanted corroboration of Wigand's story from another source. But Hewitt loved it. The following week, on October 3, Kaden's office informed *60 Minutes* that outside counsel agreed that the story was too risky to pursue—at which point Bergman was expected to stop work on the piece.

"We've got a gun pointed at our head," Hewitt told the National Press Club in Washington, D.C., on October 17. "We've got a story we think is solid. We don't think anybody could ever sue us for libel. There are some twists and turns. And if you get in front of a jury, in some state where all the people on that jury are related to people who work at tobacco companies, look out. That's a $15 billion gun pointed at your head. We may opt to get out of the line of fire."

The next day, the *Wall Street Journal* published a front-page story that delved into essentially the same charges that Wigand would have made on *60 Minutes* about the chemical manipulation of nicotine. Bergman explained to Hewitt and Wallace, who felt they'd been scooped, that in the wake of the Kaden decision he had released Wigand from any obligation to *60 Minutes*. Hewitt then told Bergman he wanted him to pursue "a story about the story"—so the producer went back into his material, hoping to find some way to salvage a *60 Minutes* piece without naming Wigand. In early November, Wigand reported to Bergman that several newspapers were trying to talk to him about what he knew—and also about possible censorship of the story by CBS.

On Tuesday, November 7, Bergman and Wallace screened their revised segment, set to air the following Sunday. The piece examined the way tobacco companies covered up information about cigarettes and health, but it did not include the sensitive inside information provided by Wigand.

That Thursday, the front page of the *New York Times* carried this stunning headline: "*60 Minutes* Ordered to Pull Interview in Tobacco Report." The story, written by Bill Carter, reported that CBS lawyers "ordered the news program *60 Minutes* not to broadcast a planned on-the-record interview with a former tobacco company executive who was harshly critical of the industry." Carter attributed the move to "an atmosphere of heightened tension between cigarette manufacturers and the press," alluding to the recent ABC settlement and apology.

Carter reported that both Hewitt and Wallace "agreed with" the CBS lawyers' order to suppress the Wigand interview. "I'm very comfortable with the decision," Hewitt told Carter, as definitive a statement as the reporter could have wanted; Hewitt was aligning himself with the corporation's censorship of his own broadcast. "We just knew that ABC had looked into the barrel of a gun," Hewitt said. "The ABC lawsuit did not chill us as journalists from doing the story," Wallace told the *Times*. "It did chill the lawyers, who with due diligence had to say, 'We don't want to, in effect, risk putting the company out of business.'"

The story had an immediate and explosive effect. Suddenly *60 Minutes* appeared to have sacrificed a legitimate and hard-hitting piece of journalism to management bean counters. Hewitt and Wallace looked a bit like cowards—or at least could be now portrayed that way by journalists secretly gleeful not to be in their position. It was widely assumed within CBS that Carter's source for the *Times* story was Lowell Bergman. ("I have never met Bill Carter, nor have I ever spoken with Bill Carter," is all Bergman will now say on the matter, declining any other comment about possible contact between them.) It didn't matter who leaked it; for the next 24 hours, few in the *60 Minutes* office talked about anything else. In the wake of the *Times* story everyone had an opinion, and many of them opposed Hewitt and Wallace's stance.

Steve Kroft went to talk to Hewitt, deeply concerned about morale around the office. "You've got to do something," he said. The correspondent—who, like most others at *60 Minutes,* had only just learned the details of the Wigand story—had observed widespread confusion among producers and support staff and believed Hewitt needed to address them directly, and soon. Hewitt agreed. The next day, a Friday, he convened a rare *60 Minutes* staff meeting in Screening Room 164, which, as usual, degenerated into screaming and walkouts.

In the piece that finally aired that Sunday, Bergman focused less on the substance of Wigand's accusations than on how the tobacco industry had historically misled the public—Wigand, referred to only as "the insider," was hidden, his voice disguised. Wallace had experienced a change of heart over management's position and expressed it with this new ending to the piece:

WALLACE: We at *60 Minutes*—and that's about one hundred of us who turn out this broadcast each week—are proud of working here and at CBS News, and so we were dismayed that the management of CBS had seen fit to give in to perceived threats of legal action against us by a tobacco industry giant. We've broadcast many such investigative pieces down the years, and we want to be able to continue. We lost out, only to some degree on this one, but we haven't the slightest doubt that we'll be able to continue the *60 Minutes* tradition of reporting such pieces in the future without fear or favor.

The next night, Wallace was invited to appear on *Charlie Rose* to talk about the story. At the last minute he asked Morley Safer to tag along—a favor Safer came to regret. "The question of whether Mike and the producer induced this guy is out of the question," Safer told Rose. "He wasn't paid, he wasn't threatened, he wasn't promised anything." Safer later learned that Wigand had, in fact, previously been paid a consulting fee and fired off an angry memo to the entire staff retracting his comments.

The *Charlie Rose* appearance served to further divide an already fractured staff; it precipitated yet more conflict between Safer and Wallace—and Bergman—that might have otherwise been avoided. Safer came to believe that Bergman and Wallace had made a deal with Wigand that they shouldn't have, and his statement said as much. The *New York Times* editorialized against the show's handling of the story. None of the show's insiders seemed certain of anything about their positions except that they wished the entire mess would go away—Hewitt most of all. A few weeks later, Ed Bradley invited the correspondents to his Central Park West apartment for a private breakfast—without Hewitt—to try to bring an end to the divisions created by the story.

Bradley told his colleagues that they had to stop going off in different directions. They were a splintered group, afraid the divisions created by the Wigand story would become permanent. Their efforts helped to restore order to the show, but some believed the wounds would never completely heal.

It was December 4, 1995, only 10 days before Hewitt's seventy-third birthday, but there appeared to be no immediate prospect of Mike Wallace wheeling in cake and champagne.

Hewitt was tense; his show had been shaken to its foundation by the media's incessant coverage of the Wigand story. He hated the ongoing portrayal of *60 Minutes* as having caved to corporate power. Ever since it landed on the front page of the *New York Times*, the Wigand story had been a nightmare for Hewitt. He had to defend the story publicly, again and again, even before it aired. Hewitt had fought relentlessly over the years to protect the reputation of his creation, but some stories he could not control, and this was one of them. At the same time, he had to maneuver delicately around the power structure at CBS, which issued his rather substantial paycheck.

When Hewitt got tense, he liked to write someone a memo. He might not ever send it, but the process helped him to crystallize his thoughts into a coherent form. Often he would show it around and get the opinion of others before sending it. So, early on this Monday morning, before anyone else arrived for work, Hewitt sat down at his desk and typed a memo to a man whose office was less than 50 yards away, and whom he had worked alongside every day of his professional life since 1968.

In the letter—copies of which were sent to Eric Ober, the president of CBS News, and Peter Lund, the president of the CBS Broadcast Group—Hewitt described what he called the "obsessive nature" of the show's reporting on Wigand, which he said "caused us damage far in excess of any good that could have come to us" from airing the piece. Hewitt said that while *60 Minutes* "committed no glaring crimes against journalism," he professed disappointment that the story led to "disclosure of information that was nobody's business but our own."

He then cited Shakespeare's famous "admonition" (as he described it) from *King Lear* that "discretion is the better part of valor" and concluded that "until the right moment presents itself I would like to put the Jeffrey Wigand story on the back burner and get on with our business—which is reporting, not crusading." It was signed: "Sincerely, Don."

Hewitt had at last articulated a feeling that had consumed him since the beginning of this controversy. He measured the value of this story itself against the damage it had caused his creation, *60 Minutes,* and the answer was simple.

Kill the story.

In suggesting this, Hewitt's position ran counter to his star correspondent, Mike Wallace, as well as Wallace's longtime producer, Lowell Bergman—not to mention Hewitt's own public stance. This was Hildy Johnson quitting, after all—turning in his badge to Walter Burns. He knew journalists expected them to fight the corporate bosses to death over the Wigand story, not put it aside. But Hewitt cared deeply about his show and the epic divisions the battle had already created. He worried the wounds would show in his beloved broadcast. By stopping the fight now—by putting the Wigand story on the back burner and getting on with our business, as Hewitt put it—he believed there might be some chance *60 Minutes* could save itself.

In January, the *New York Daily News* identified Wigand by name as the *60 Minutes* source, and the *Wall Street Journal* then published a Wigand deposition that freed *60 Minutes* and CBS from any culpability in airing its interview. In late January, Wigand returned to New York for another *60 Minutes* interview; and on February 4, 1996, the show broadcast a two-part segment, "Jeffrey Wigand, Ph.D.," that at last told the entire story as Bergman and Wallace originally intended to tell it.

At the end of 1999, *The Insider* was at last set for release. This was the movie the *60 Minutes* crew had all dreaded, a semifictional account of the Wigand crisis based on Marie Brenner's exhaustive account in *Vanity Fair* and directed by Michael Mann. No one knew quite what to expect, particularly since the central character—the hero—was not Jeffrey Wigand but Lowell Bergman. He would soon come to represent the notion of the dashing *60 Minutes* producer, thanks to Al Pacino's performance and much to the chagrin of Hewitt and Wallace.

The movie came out in December 1999, with Christopher Plummer as a reptilian Wallace and Philip Baker Hall as an ineffectual Don Hewitt. ("That's not an actor," Hewitt became fond of saying. "That was a dormitory.")

There was no way for *The Insider* to reopen old wounds, because they'd never healed to begin with. The battles between Wallace and Hewitt had escalated, becoming more volatile and personal than ever before. The movie left what many at *60 Minutes* consider a permanent stain on the show's reputation, only made worse by the movie's mediocre performance at the box office.

Without question, *The Insider* took liberties with the truth in representing Bergman as the one who quit CBS in moral high dudgeon at the end of the movie—perhaps Hewitt's most loudly voiced criticism of the film. Bergman had, in fact, remained at CBS long after the Wigand controversy and was hoping to become Jeffrey Fager's number two producer during the start-up of *60 Minutes II*, a scenario approved by Fager but ultimately blocked by Hewitt and Wallace.

Bergman now acknowledges that the movie misrepresents the truth in some respects. "I didn't like the way the movie ended, the way that they did it," Bergman says. "I told them it was going to cause me trouble. That didn't change Michael Mann—it's his movie. He said, 'You left *60 Minutes*.' I said, 'Yeah, but it makes it look like I left CBS.' And so that's a criticism of the accuracy of the film, I'll grant it to them. But it's no more of a fiction than what's actually produced on *60 Minutes*. And presented by Don every week. His correspondents never make a mistake, never lose an argument; they never look like they need any help from anybody."

Wallace describes Bergman's attitude as that of a producer frustrated with a lack of proper credit. "He always felt he didn't get enough attention," Wallace says. "Which I can understand. I mean, come on. You do all the reporting and it says, 'Produced by Lowell Bergman.'"

By the time *The Insider* came out, Hewitt had just turned 77, and Wallace was 81. For all their endless battling, they still relished the control they had over the institution they'd created together, and neither showed any sign of wanting to give it up or sharing a piece of it with the likes of Lowell Bergman or anyone else.

Chapter 20

The Tin Eye

Andrew Heyward may owe his longevity as president of CBS News in part to an act of loyalty performed for his then-boss Dan Rather on the night of September 11, 1987, one that forever cemented the bond between anchorman and producer. On that memorable night, it had been announced that a U.S. Open tennis semifinal match might run over into the 6:30 P.M. time slot and delay the start of the evening news broadcast. Furious, the bullheaded Rather stormed off to call Howard Stringer, then president of CBS News, in protest. The game ended at 6:32 P.M.; since Rather was not in the anchor chair, the entire CBS network went black.

While the *Evening News*'s executive producer Tom Bettag (now executive producer of ABC's *Nightline*) tried to reason with Rather, senior producer Heyward—sitting in the control room in New York—was being strongly urged to press the button to broadcast a taped version of the opening of the evening news. That opening had been taped within the last hour, as a standard precaution against technical failure. "If Heyward had pushed the button, he would have done the right thing by CBS News but would have been Rather's lifelong enemy," recalls a producer present that night. "Obviously, he made the right decision."

Heyward had been an *Evening News* junkie his entire life. It surprised no one when he landed at CBS News. He'd grown up in New York as the son of an executive at UNICEF. After graduating from Harvard, he went directly into television journalism and produced the local newscast at Channel 5 in New York before moving to CBS News in 1984, where he rose quickly through the ranks to become a producer for the evening news. In 1988 he became the original executive producer of the weekly newsmagazine *48 Hours*, with Rather as its anchor. The show's original format—an hour devoted to a single story—caught on and hastened Heyward's ascent. Even the failure of *Eye to Eye with Connie Chung*, launched in 1993 with Heyward in charge, didn't slow his progress.

In 1994 he took over as executive producer of the evening news, during the period of the experimental Rather-Chung evening newscast, and although the ratings never quite took off, it strengthened his alliance with Rather—then, as now, the 800-pound gorilla of CBS News. When Eric Ober lost his job as head of CBS News at the end of 1995—having presided over the ill-fated pairing of Rather and Chung, not to mention the Wigand episode—Heyward got the nod to replace him as president and has remained ever since.

Heyward was not someone you would expect to find running the news division of a network. He had the well-spoken manner of a college professor, or perhaps a psychologist. (In fact, he married the daughter of Dr. Willard Gaylin, a well-known psychiatry professor and medical ethicist at Columbia University.) But Westinghouse had just completed its acquisition of the network from Laurence Tisch, and perhaps that was what the new management of CBS was looking for.

Heyward's ascension came amid turmoil in the news division, and at *60 Minutes* in particular. The show was suffering from the deep divisions inflicted by the 1995 tobacco story. NBC News—under the leadership of president Andrew Lack, the former *60 Minutes* producer who had clashed with Hewitt as executive producer of *West 57th*—was about to challenge *60 Minutes* by putting on another edition of its *Dateline NBC* broadcast up against it on Sunday nights at 7. Asked by a reporter in January 1996, right after taking the job, whether that counterprogramming might result in changes to the *60 Minutes* format to keep its audience, Heyward replied: "Anybody who would tinker with the most successful program in television history and say, 'Uh-oh, *Dateline* is coming,' would be nuts." Within four months, *60 Minutes* had nevertheless announced several changes, including new, hip commentators (Texas journalist Molly Ivins, humor writer P. J. O'Rourke, and acerbic black columnist Stanley Crouch) to complement Andy Rooney and a revised weekly format with an emphasis on breaking news. As with most attempts over the years to fiddle with the *60 Minutes* format, these lasted less than a season.

Heyward also reached out for young, good-looking new correspondents and respected, well-known commentators to shake up the status quo. From MTV he hired a correspondent named Alison Stewart to contribute youth-oriented stories. As commentators (to be used throughout the news division) he hired the former New Jersey senator Bill Bradley from the left and author and analyst Laura Ingraham from the right. He also brought in Christiane Amanpour, the CNN star, for part-time *60 Minutes* duty. "This is not your father's Oldsmobile," an anonymous CBS News executive told the *New York Times* of Heyward's changes in May 1997.

As it turned out, Heyward had one flaw in his otherwise stellar list of achievements, what colleagues jokingly referred to as his "tin eye"— his seeming inability to recruit to CBS anyone who might develop the stature or staying power of an existing network news star.

Heyward's first demonstration of the tin-eye problem came in the spring of 1997 when he lured Susan Molinari, then a Republican congresswoman from Staten Island, out of politics to cohost a new Saturday morning news and talk show—"a sort of *60 Minutes* meets *Rosie O'Donnell*," as Molinari described it. The move came up for instant ridicule. Maureen Dowd parodied the move in a May 31, 1997 *Times* column written in Molinari's voice: "The only person at CBS who was really upset—she came at me one day in the cafeteria with an ice pick—was Laura Ingraham, who thought if Andy wanted a GOP blonde with no experience to star in this show, it should be her." The reviews weren't particularly warm, either. "A television star was not born," *New York Times* television critic Caryn James wrote in her morning-after review.

In June 1998, less than a year later, it was announced that Molinari would be leaving. "I think she missed the political arena—not being in politics per se, but political commentary and analysis," Heyward explained when Molinari left. "There's very little of that on a Saturday morning show."

In March 1997, Heyward announced his biggest move yet: he'd hired NBC *Today Show* star Bryant Gumbel with a five-year deal said to be worth at least $5 million a year. Heyward desperately hoped the move would inject life into a news division in major decline. There was just one problem: no one knew what do to do with Gumbel once they had him. First Heyward handed him a newsmagazine called *Public Eye*. It launched in October 1997 and to most observers lacked a distinctive personality—a hybrid of *Nightline* and *Dateline*, with the ratings pull of neither. Production shut down in August 1998.

Heyward was now stuck with a multimillion-dollar player with no important tasks to perform. The next idea he floated was to make Gumbel an integral part of something he'd been discussing with his bosses: a second edition of *60 Minutes*. It was a notion the network brass loved—to use the brand name of *60 Minutes* to launch another newsmagazine. It made perfect economic sense, but there was just one problem: selling the concept of *60 Minutes II* to Don Hewitt and the ornery, stubborn correspondents of *60 Minutes*.

Leslie Moonves wanted it to happen, and that meant it probably would. To the CBS entertainment chief it was only logical—to spin the hugely successful franchise into a second show. It had already worked for NBC; by 1997, *Dateline* had expanded to four nights and become highly profitable. But to Hewitt and the correspondents, it was nothing more than a misguided attempt by the network to diminish the value of the franchise by going "down market" with a *Dateline* clone. The immediate suspicion of the 60 Minutes crew was that Moonves and his corporate cronies would do anything to squeeze another buck out of the news division, even at the risk of destroying the credibility built up over three decades by Hewitt and 60 Minutes.

Moonves went to a birthday lunch for Mike Wallace in the spring of 1997 and was a bit surprised when some of the correspondents used the occasion to corner him, furious about the plan. They continued to spill their venom at a series of meetings meant to mollify the angry stars. "All you guys want to do is use the brand." Morley Safer fumed at Moonves. "And what you're going to do in the process is destroy it." More nasty meetings followed; at one point the correspondents told Moonves that none of them would appear on his proposed new show. Then Hewitt and Wallace took their case upstairs to Moonves's boss, Mel Karmazin, making their adamant opposition painfully clear.

But Karmazin—a shrewd businessman who at that point held the title of chairman and chief executive of CBS—wasn't going to be told by anyone, even Mike Wallace and Don Hewitt, what he could or could not do. He was not, he said, going to override Heyward and Moonves. "We're putting on 60 Minutes II whether you like it or not," Karmazin reportedly said. "If I have to slap the title 60 Minutes II across The Nanny, I'll do it, but you're going to have 60 Minutes II."

By late spring—after endless meetings, endless calls among the correspondents, and endless leaks to the press—the correspondents had a final meeting with Moonves and Heyward at Black Rock. As Safer recalls it, attempts at consensus went nowhere until, as it was breaking up, he said to the assembled executives: "Look, if you guys want to do another 60 Minutes, you take the best producers you have at CBS News and the best correspondents you have at CBS News, you call that 60 Minutes II, and I don't see a way we can argue with you. But at the top you need that kind of uncompromising guy to run the broadcast." At which point, according to Safer, Hewitt stood behind Heyward, pointing at himself. (Hewitt denies ever having wanted to be in charge of the new show, and Heyward has no recollection that Hewitt ever wanted to run it.)

In any case, Heyward's choice was Jeffrey Fager, the former *60 Minutes* producer now running the CBS *Evening News*. Within weeks (and after a meeting that June in the *60 Minutes* screening room with Karmazin and the correspondents to help smooth things over) Fager was installed in the job as executive producer of *60 Minutes II*—and that battle, at least, was finally over.

CBS News was hoping to use the new show to anoint Mike Wallace's son, Chris, as his possible *60 Minutes* successor; he'd been a correspondent for ABC News for several years and bore a strong superficial resemblance to his father. But at the last minute, negotiations between the younger Wallace and CBS broke down when ABC News refused to let him out of his contract—a move, according to Mike Wallace and several other sources, that was engineered directly by Sawyer to spite her old *60 Minutes* antagonist.

Finally, Hewitt and his rattled tigers acquiesced (at least nominally) to a fate that was probably sealed before they ever protested it. When the official announcement of *60 Minutes II* was made at last in July 1997, Hewitt declined to comment except to issue this statement: "I think that under Jeff Fager, *60 Minutes II* is a natural to be the second-best broadcast of its kind on television. Inasmuch as I can help, without shortchanging the first-best broadcast of its kind on television, I'm hoping to do that."

Kathleen Willey had a story to tell, and she fit all the Hewitt standards of a perfect *60 Minutes* character. What could be more interesting than an attractive, well-spoken woman claiming to have been sexually harassed by the president of the United States?

In the context of Hewitt's own troubled history with the subject, of course, the notion of interviewing Kathleen Willey—and lending credence to her invasive, privacy-shattering charges against Bill Clinton—presented certain glaring ironies. Just as the Clinton scandal unfolded publicly, CBS was privately negotiating the settlement of a harassment charge against Hewitt by a former *60 Minutes* editor. But if anyone at CBS felt uncomfortable with the possible hypocrisy involved in the coverage of the growing Clinton scandal in the winter of 1998, they did not speak up. And so when Michael Radutzky, Ed Bradley's producer, informed his bosses that he had nailed down an exclusive interview with the president's latest accuser, there was never any doubt that *60 Minutes* would run with the story.

By the time Willey sat down for an interview with Ed Bradley for the March 15, 1998, broadcast of *60 Minutes,* there were differences—some subtle, some significant—between what she was now charging and how others described her response to the incident at the time. Willey had alleged (in her deposition in the Paula Jones case against the president) that Clinton had made sexual advances toward her in the Oval Office; however, one of her corroborating witnesses—a former friend named Julie Steele—had since claimed in an affidavit that Willey asked her to lie to a *Newsweek* reporter about having been upset over the presidential encounter, which had taken place in the Oval Office in late 1993. Likewise, Linda Tripp had told *Newsweek* that Willey was "joyful" after her private encounter with Clinton. The president had denied any inappropriate behavior during his meeting with Willey.

All that paled by comparison to the fact that Willey would be the first woman to go public in an interview format with allegations against Clinton. Radutzky had met with Willey's attorney several times in advance of the session, and once with Willey herself, before Bradley arrived in Virginia to do the interview in a hotel suite on the Thursday before broadcast.

In 17 years at *60 Minutes,* Bradley had become a master of this kind of interview. He knew how to use his body language and empathetic demeanor to coax answers from nervous or reluctant subjects. He had a way of putting people at ease if he needed to, or on edge if that was required. In this case, he wanted to relax Willey so that she would tell her story in the most dramatic possible way. This was not, he felt, an occasion for confrontation or tough questions.

BRADLEY: And what happened next?
WILLEY: Well, he—he said that he would do everything that he

could to—to—to—help, and w—I turned around, and out of the—out of the office, and he followed me to—I thought he was going to open the door to the—to the Oval Office. And right as we got to the door, he stopped me and gave me a big hug and said that he was very sorry that this was happening to me. And I—I had no problem with that because when I saw—every time I saw him, he would hug me. He used—just does that—is like that.

And I remember I had—still had this coffee cup in my hand, and it was kind of in between us and I didn't want it to spill on him or me, and it just was this—it was just very strange. And he— he took the coffee cup out of my hand and he put it on a bookshelf and—and he—this hug t—lasted a little longer than I thought necessary, but at the same time—I mean, I was not concerned about it.

BRADLEY: Mm-hmm.

WILLEY: And then he—then he—and then he kissed me on—on my mouth, and—and he pulled me closer to him. And I remember thinking—I just remember thinking, "What in the world is he doing?" I—it—I just thought, "What is he doing?" And I—I pushed back away from him, and he—he—he—he— he's a big man. And he—he had his arms—they were tight around me, and he—he—he—he touched me.

BRADLEY: Touched you how?

WILLEY: Well, he—he—he touched my breast with his hand, and I—I—I—I was—I—I was just startled. I was—I—I—w— j— was just . . .

BRADLEY: Thi—this wasn't an accidental, grazing touch?

WILLEY: No, no. And then he—he whispered—he—he w—he said in—in my ear, he said, "I've—I've wanted to do this ever since I laid eyes on you."

After going over several more intimate details of their encounter— including Bradley nonchalantly asking Willey of the president of the

United States, "Was he aroused?"—Bradley probed briefly into the nature of her response.

> BRADLEY: Did you feel intimidated?
> WILLEY: I didn't feel intimidated. I just felt overpowered.
> BRADLEY: Did you ever say, "Stop. No. Get away from me"?
> WILLEY: I just—I—I pushed him away. I pushed him away and—and I said, "I think I—I'd better go."

After that, Bradley established with Willey that the story she'd just told was the same as the testimony she'd given to the grand jury, under oath.

Bradley then briefly referred to the reversal of position by her former friend Julie Steele, who now denied Willey's account of her having told Steele of Clinton's unwanted advances at the time—and claimed that Willey had been pressuring her to lie to a *Newsweek* reporter. Willey's explanation of the Tripp description of her as "joyful": "I think when I am in—if I get into a very tense—tense situation I try to—fall back on my sense of humor. I think when I said, 'You are not going to believe this one,' maybe she took that as joyful."

Toward the end, Bradley gently inquired as to Willey's motives for going public with her accusations.

> BRADLEY: You—you were a reluctant witness. You didn't want your story to go public.
> WILLEY: No.
> BRADLEY: Why not?
> WILLEY: I just knew that it was a bad story. It was just horrible—ha—horrible behavior on the part of the president, and I did not think it was my place to make it public knowledge.
> BRADLEY: You didn't walk away. You didn't lodge a complaint anywhere.
> WILLEY: No. That's right. That was the choice I made. . . .

BRADLEY *(voice-over)*: Then why did she decide now to go public?

WILLEY: I just think that it's time to tell this story. I think that there—too many lies are being told, too many lives are being ruined, and I—I think it's time for the truth to come out.

That apparently satisfied Bradley's curiosity on Willey's motives. The president's lawyer, Bennett, had declined to be interviewed for the story. But on Saturday he changed his mind: the White House contacted *60 Minutes* and asked for unedited time on the show to refute Willey's comments, or the chance to review her comments in advance. Instead Bennett was invited to a CBS studio in Washington, where he was interviewed by Bradley via satellite.

Bennett was apparently unfamiliar with the setup and didn't know where to look; producers told him to look away from the camera, as though Bradley were in the room with him. (Bradley never disclosed on the air that it was a satellite interview.) As a result, he appeared on camera to be uncomfortable—and to some observers dishonest. CBS News president Heyward later acknowledged to a reporter that the piece should have clearly disclosed Bennett's location. Bennett told Bradley, in the limited time he was allotted, that the president "hugged" Willey and that "he may have given her a kiss on the forehead."

BRADLEY *(voice-over)*: Mr. Bennett concedes that Kathleen Willey is not part of what he calls the "get-Clinton" crowd. And like all lawyers, he's confident his client will be vindicated.

BENNETT: My client is the president. He says it didn't happen. I believe the president, okay? I believe him. The day is going to come, Ed, either because Judge Wright throws the Paula Jones case out, as I hope and believe she may, or a jury of—of twelve people—not Ed Bradley, not Bob Bennett—are going to sit there and listen to all of the evidence and decide who is or is not telling the truth.

*   *   *

The next day, the White House released to reporters a series of friendly letters written by Willey to Clinton after the alleged harassment incident, some of them seeking a job and one that referred to herself as his "number one fan." It was also revealed that Willey's lawyer had been pursuing a $100,000 book deal, raising the possibility that her motivations may not have been so pure as she represented them to Bradley and *60 Minutes*. Critics attacked the interview for being too soft; Hewitt's pleasure at scoring a coup was diminished by the media's response, not all of it positive. *60 Minutes* denied knowledge of the letters or the book deal, and Phil Scheffler, the show's executive editor, later publicly attacked Bennett for holding back information about the letters during his *60 Minutes* interview. According to a *60 Minutes* insider, Radutzky called Willey directly and asked her bluntly why she had failed to disclose the letters to him in advance of the interview. (The source said she claimed to Radutzky that she didn't think they were of any significance.)

But one subsequent press account suggested that *60 Minutes,* in its zeal to get Willey onto the air, might have intentionally overlooked information. At the very least, the team's feelings about the piece went from pride over the scoop to slight embarrassment at having perhaps rushed the interview onto the show without enough reporting.

Howard Kurtz, the media writer for the *Washington Post,* reported in a *Brill's Content* article in August 1998 that according to an unnamed Willey associate, "Willey told a *60 Minutes* producer about letters she had written to the White House seeking a job." Kurtz's source insisted that the producer never followed up on that knowledge—"directly contradicting statements by *60 Minutes* executives that the program knew nothing of the letters." A *60 Minutes* source told Kurtz that producers didn't want to dig too deeply into Willey's credibility, for fear of alienating her and losing the interview. "When you're trying to convince somebody to spill their guts on the air," a *60 Minutes* staffer told Kurtz, "you don't want them hearing from the neighbors."

In a letter to the editor of *Brill's Content* published in September

1998, Hewitt ridiculed Kurtz for his use of unnamed sources. He condescended and blustered—"As a newcomer to investigative journalism," he wrote, "perhaps you wouldn't mind a tip or two from an old-timer about the business you have just embarked upon"—but did not take issue with the substance of Kurtz's reporting, that *60 Minutes* had advance knowledge of the Willey letters or that the show went easy on Willey so as not to lose the interview.

Even Andy Rooney—who had declared on *60 Minutes* on the night of the interview that Bradley "did a good job"—later backed off that assertion in an on-air commentary after reading hundreds of letters from viewers. "If you think it fell short of *60 Minutes* standards," Rooney told the show's audience, "you may be right."

By the time Hewitt approached Candice Bergen to join the *60 Minutes* staff in 1998, she had firmly established herself as a prominent contributor to a highly rated network newsmagazine called *FYI*. Unfortunately, the show—and her journalism experience—was fictional. Bergen's journalism experience was limited to what she got playing a character by the name of Murphy Brown—a hugely famous and highly endearing character, but nevertheless the creation of sitcom writers in Hollywood. At the beginning of her career as an actress, she had briefly flirted with photojournalism, but after a 1970s audition for Hewitt, she never produced a *60 Minutes* segment—or any news segment at all, for that matter.

Murphy Brown had gone off CBS that spring after 10 seasons, but not before creating controversies that had blurred the line between fiction and reality. Vice President Dan Quayle had inserted her into the political debate in 1996 by attacking the character for being a single mother. Other social issues, like breast cancer, were raised on the show and thus in the national conversation. But was this enough to justify the elevation of Bergen to the status of real-life *60 Minutes* correspondent? Hewitt thought enough of the idea to call Grace Diekhaus, a former longtime producer for *60 Minutes* now living in Los Angeles, and ask her to meet with Bergen to discuss the possibility.

Diekhaus went to lunch with Bergen to talk about ideas. It was the belief of both women that to pull it off, Bergen would have to demonstrate to her future colleagues the ability to get big interviews—the kind that could be gotten only by a celebrity of Bergen's caliber. So she set to work: her first tries were John F. Kennedy Jr. and TV producer David E. Kelley, both famously reluctant. Unfortunately for Bergen, they remained so. When word leaked out to the other *60 Minutes* correspondents that Bergen was a potential candidate to join the staff, they rose up as one to protest what they perceived as yet another boneheaded Hewitt idea.

The Bergen plan was quickly scuttled, but not before Hewitt's correspondents were reminded, yet again, of their boss's fundamental weakness: He desperately needed someone to remind him that despite his proven record of great ideas, he seemed to have an even greater propensity for bad ones. As recently as 2003, Morley Safer said that he couldn't recall the last good idea he got from Hewitt. "You just take them and put them gently under another piece of paper on your desk," Safer said. "You know another whim will strike and he will have forgotten all about it." Then, as always, Phil Scheffler played perhaps the most crucial role in Hewitt's professional life—censoring the worst ideas before they reached beyond his office. God forbid Hewitt should ever be alone at the top, the correspondents thought often and aloud, without Scheffler there to keep him from jumping off the ledge into the abyss.

Chapter 21

This Is Wrong!

On the morning of October 7, 2001—the day the United States began a rigorous bombing campaign in Afghanistan—Don Hewitt woke up in the hospital. He was here for an angioplasty. Nothing serious—just a tune-up to keep the old man moving. It was less than a month after the attacks on the World Trade Center and the Pentagon. These were troubled times, and he needed to get back to work as fast as he could.

Plans for an entire fall season of new pieces on *60 Minutes* had been scuttled on the morning of September 11, 2001; instead, the show's correspondents produced three weeks' worth of stories related to terrorism and the attacks. On September 16, 2001—the first episode to air since the attacks—Ed Bradley reported from a New Jersey community that lost several of its citizens at the World Trade Center. Steve Kroft examined weaknesses in U.S. airport security. Lesley Stahl led a roundtable discussion with General Electric chairman Jack Welch, former treasury secretary Robert Rubin, and investor Warren Buffett on the impact of terrorism on the nation's markets. Mike Wallace explored the flaws and errors in U.S. intelligence that allowed the attacks to take place. Producers worked nonstop and the office took on a dead-line atmosphere not felt at *60 Minutes* since the Gulf War in 1991.

Hewitt worked as hard as he ever had to make his show indis-pensable in a world of wall-to-wall news coverage. On September 23, Stahl returned with a Laura Bush interview; Kroft examined problems with immigration policies; Bob Simon explored the mind of a suicide bomber; and Ed Bradley reported on the Arab world's reaction to the events of September 11. On the following Sunday, Wallace focused on U.S. preparations for a chemical or biological attack; Bradley did a story on differences between American Muslims and those involved in the attacks; and Morley Safer went to West Point to look into the future of the American Armed Forces.

Looking back on the last four weeks from his hospital bed, Hewitt had to admit to himself that the skills of the *60 Minutes* crew didn't do crash reporting as well as they used to. Any way you looked at it, Wallace was too old to cover a story as aggressively as a decade ago. Same with Safer. He could still count on Kroft for a great hard-hitting story. Stahl knew Washington better than any of them. Bob Simon al-ways delivered a first-rate foreign piece, but was he one of the *60 Min-utes* correspondents or not? Not really. Not yet. Hewitt would have hired him full-time, but that would have meant wrestling him away from Jeff Fager, where Simon was a 20-pieces-a-season correspondent for *60 Minutes II*. Then there was Christiane Amanpour, who'd been recruited for part-time *60 Minutes* duty in 1997 but in wartime was contractually owed to CNN for breaking news.

Hewitt needed to figure out how to distinguish himself and his show—not only for the show's benefit but also for his own. He knew that sooner or later, Heyward wanted to replace him at *60 Minutes*. No one had yet raised the issue with him directly, but he'd heard the rum-blings. Was Moonves gunning for him? It probably wasn't Mel Kar-mazin, the number two at parent company Viacom. Karmazin was a pal. Still, Hewitt realized he had to put together some classic *60 Minutes* broadcasts fast, and prove to everyone that it wasn't yet time for him to leave. The newsmagazines (aside from *60 Minutes* and *60 Minutes*

II) had been neglecting hard news to focus on stories like the murder of JonBenet Ramsey. In theory, then, *60 Minutes* ought to have been positioned better than anyone else to cover these tragic events. Whether it had remained a matter of debate.

That night's show would probably go smoothly enough. If any last-minute emergencies arose, Phil Scheffler would be around, as always. For 50 years, that had been a big part of Scheffler's job: to be around. Hewitt and Scheffler had a working relationship resembling that of a blind man and a seeing-eye dog. Scheffler's only purpose was to serve his master. It remained Hewitt's impulses that guided *60 Minutes,* and Scheffler primarily functioned to help his boss achieve that vision.

Scheffler owed Hewitt his career, starting from their first encounter in 1951 when Scheffler was a student at the Columbia University Graduate School of Journalism. One day, Hewitt had taken a couple of hours off from running *Douglas Edwards With the News* to spread the gospel of television to eager students. Scheffler boldly asked Hewitt if he could come down to watch them do a broadcast; once he got to the newsroom, Hewitt offered him a job as a news assistant. Within two years, Scheffler was a street reporter for CBS News—perhaps the first such reporter in the history of television news. The two men stayed tethered, and when Palmer Williams retired as senior producer of *60 Minutes* in 1981, Hewitt promoted Scheffler, by then a seasoned and respected producer for several correspondents at *60 Minutes,* including Dan Rather, to the number two spot.

And if for some reason Scheffler couldn't handle that night's show by himself, there was always Josh Howard, who Hewitt promoted last year to the job of senior producer. In this news shop, the 47-year-old Howard was the equivalent of a baby-faced teenager. But fortunately for Hewitt, Howard had way more tenacity and drive than Scheffler—and that would come in handy for Hewitt in the dark days ahead.

The previous afternoon, senior vice president Betsy West had gotten word from reporters covering the Defense Department for CBS News that the war would begin the next day. She and Heyward had spoken immediately about plans for coverage. Heyward's initial plan had been to broadcast that night's *60 Minutes* episode (already geared to the topic of terrorism) with a news opening to report on the latest developments. Knowing that Hewitt was in the hospital, West had phoned Scheffler to explain the situation.

"What do you expect me to do about it?" Scheffler had responded in what colleagues described as a typically downbeat response— "Doctor No" had lately become Scheffler's nickname around the *60 Minutes* office. "Let the special events unit handle it," he said. It was an odd attitude to take, considering the likelihood that Hewitt would disagree, and perhaps explains why Hewitt didn't hear about that night's plans until Sunday morning.

Meanwhile, CBS News management moved ahead on its own, acknowledging that Scheffler was neither ready nor willing to tear up the next day's *60 Minutes* to reflect the breaking-news development of imminent war.

On Sunday morning, management turned the task of producing that night's *60 Minutes*—now extended at Heyward's request to a two-hour special—over to Jim Murphy, the executive producer of *CBS Evening News* with Dan Rather.

"We'll do it," Hewitt said to West when he arrived at CBS from the hospital. "We'll do all the things you want to do, but let us package."

Hewitt's argument came too late. By the time he'd reached the CBS Broadcast Center, the CBS crew had already started putting together that night's episode of *60 Minutes*. It would feature reports from various CBS News correspondents with no connection to the Sunday night show. Hewitt was helpless to stop it and furious that his show had been taken away.

In the late afternoon, Hewitt was standing around the "fishbowl"— the central area of the *CBS Evening News* where newswriters and producers gathered to work on the special that would emanate from the nearby anchor desk. It was in the fishbowl, a generation ago, that Hewitt had once been the first man to executive-produce the evening news.

Now Murphy and his producers were working feverishly, and Don Hewitt was a bystander.

"This is wrong!" he yelled at the busy producers, according to an eyewitness. "You shouldn't be doing this! Everyone ought to walk out right now!" Hewitt genuinely wanted—in fact, expected—everyone to stop what they were doing and get up and leave. Finally, Hewitt had to be asked to leave, to allow the *Evening News* team to proceed with the broadcast as planned.

The show aired that night under the *60 Minutes* logo, complete with the ticking stopwatch; but to Hewitt it was, in his words, not *60 Minutes* but "a fucking abortion."

Chapter 22

Across the Road

One afternoon several months later, Andrew Heyward left the CBS Broadcast Center, crossed West 57th Street, entered the BMW car-dealership building where *60 Minutes* had its headquarters, flashed his CBS News badge to the front desk security, rode the elevator to the ninth floor, and proceeded left past the dull-gray carpeted reception area, with its facsimile of the *60 Minutes* stopwatch on the wall across from a Ben Shahn drawing of TV antennas, toward Room 177, Hewitt's corner office.

Heyward had picked this March day in 2002 to begin the delicate matter of removing from his job the man who had been running *60 Minutes* for the last 34 years. Heyward wanted to tell Hewitt his proposal for the future. It called for next season to be Hewitt's last as executive producer, and for Phil Scheffler to leave a year earlier—by this coming June. For several years there had been a clause in Hewitt's contract allowing CBS News to remove him as executive producer of *60 Minutes* at the corporation's discretion; Heyward now wanted to exercise that contractual right. Heyward's plan was to replace Hewitt and Phil Scheffler with Jeff Fager of *60 Minutes II*. This meeting was to begin that process. Heyward would be joined for this meeting by Betsy West, who oversaw production on *60 Minutes,* and would help explain to Hewitt their plan for the future of the show.

However, this was not the plan Don Hewitt envisioned, at least not now. Not yet. When he'd signed his most recent contract with CBS, he told one correspondent that he would leave when it expired; at that point he would be 79 years old. But now that he had passed his seventy-ninth birthday, he'd shown no inclination toward leaving anytime soon. Anyway, Hewitt had his own successor in mind—Josh Howard, who'd been the senior producer (the show's third in command) since 1996. The good-natured Howard had begun at *60 Minutes* as a producer for Mike Wallace, and had also worked on the *CBS Evening News* with Dan Rather and even served a stint at New York's local WCBS affiliate. He had friends throughout CBS News, in part because he was one of those people who always seemed on the verge of a chuckle.

Heyward believed he had a legitimate case for Hewitt's removal. As a corporate manager, he needed to prepare responsibly for the transition of power that was inevitable, given Hewitt's age. It was clear that Hewitt was slowing down in the afternoons. Knowing this, correspondents and producers vied to schedule screenings of their pieces earlier in the day; by 4:00 P.M., Hewitt was frequently yawning, if not asleep. On top of everything else, he remained as intractable and difficult as always, at least from management's point of view. For example, he had never been willing to discuss in detail with CBS a clear and definitive plan for a handover of authority at *60 Minutes.*

Making matters more complicated for Heyward was the astonishing longevity of everyone at *60 Minutes.* As a group, they defied science with their amazing looks and health. Wallace, at 83, looked and acted like a man 20 years younger. Morley Safer drank and chainsmoked (Rothman Specials) but at 71 years old looked vital. Andy Rooney—born in 1920—in some ways looked better than any of them; his thick shock of white hair and his remarkable analytical mind continued to define his persona, and though his walk had grown a little shaky, he continued to function as a sharp and cynical observer of

American life. Lesley Stahl and Ed Bradley (she of the leather miniskirt, he of the earring) had both just celebrated their sixtieth birthdays and still traveled the world with the energy of far younger reporters. Steve Kroft, at 56, remained the kid of the bunch, a fact that regularly amazed him as he approached retirement age. He too smoked—Merits—and sometimes enjoyed a glass of wine with lunch. But the median age of a *60 Minutes* viewer hovered near 60. To a generation raised on journalists like Tabitha Soren and John Norris on MTV, the *60 Minutes* crew looked like the guests at their parents' fiftieth wedding anniversary party.

Like most of the American news media, television now focused its attention on finding and nurturing young talent; but at *60 Minutes,* there was rarely any attention paid to finding someone under the age of 50 (or 60, for that matter) who could one day lead the show after Hewitt died. In 1996 the promotion of 41-year-old Josh Howard to senior producer had marked the first time a member of the baby boomer generation entered the show's top management circle. Otherwise, in 2002 Hewitt still headed a staff of cronies he'd worked with for decades and planned to keep near him indefinitely. Despite Hewitt's age and the presence of grandchildren in his life (by then he had three, ranging in age from 2 to 31), he had no desire to stay at home and pursue hobbies. Work had always been his hobby. In 35 years he'd never once seriously considered leaving control of *60 Minutes* to anyone else.

"I want to die at my desk" was rapidly becoming his catch phrase.

With Hewitt's new work schedule, though, that was starting to seem unlikely. He had always gone to his house in Bridgehampton for long weekends; but the weekends were getting even longer, and the workdays were getting shorter. It was rare to find Hewitt in his office on a Friday or a Monday, making the notion of dying at his desk at best a figure of speech.

Heyward and West sat down in the overstuffed black leather armchairs that Hewitt kept directly opposite his large, immaculate glass desk. Hayward seemed ready, at last, to act for the sake of the show's future—and his own.

There was no disputing that *60 Minutes* had become less profitable in recent years, primarily because of the huge salaries paid to the show's biggest stars. That included the salary paid to Hewitt himself, close to $6 million by one estimate. Wallace's salary reportedly hovered in that vicinity. Ed Bradley had reached the salary A list after his 1993 flirtation with ABC News, and Safer's salary was estimated at $3 million. Stahl and Kroft were believed to earn between $1 million and $2 million. Then, of course, there was the healthy expense account for each correspondent; this included first-class airfare (often on the Concorde), as well as high-end hotels and transportation. Add to these fixed costs the highly paid producers of *60 Minutes,* who earn anywhere from $100,000 to $300,000 a year, depending on seniority and importance to the show. Stories themselves typically cost a minimum of $70,000 to produce, and could cost as much as double that, depending on location. With 24 producers working behind the scenes, the total salary allotment for *60 Minutes* amounted to an estimated two-thirds of the show's annual budget—double that of other TV newsmagazines.

Heyward needed to recover at least some of that money. Because of the September 11 terrorist attacks in 2001, the news division had spent far more than could have been anticipated to deliver wall-to-wall coverage; now Heyward had to find a way to make up for those unexpected costs. In November 2001, two months after the attacks, CBS News had ordered each correspondent to cut one associate producer. To most people at *60 Minutes* the cuts seemed not so much invasive as pointless.

Now, four months later, Heyward was sitting in Hewitt's office about to propose the most difficult cut of all.

"We need to start planning for the future of *60 Minutes* after you leave," Heyward told Hewitt. "And we need to start that process right now."

The meeting did not go well. After it was over, Hewitt went to Wallace, Bradley, and other correspondents to tell them that Heyward was trying to fire him. (Hayward denies this but concedes, "He'd pass a lie detector test, he truly believes it.")

The correspondents were conflicted about the future. They knew Hewitt was getting tired, and there were days they wanted him gone. But at other times, they reminded themselves that he'd created this show, their jobs, everything. They owed him for their huge salaries, their perks, their fame, their clout. He'd said vicious, hurtful things to all of them, but he always apologized, and there was no one quicker to credit their achievements or to defend their honor. They knew he would protect their secrets and their jobs and their livelihood for as long as humanly possible. Most of all, however, they didn't like the idea of management—"the folks across the road," as Safer referred to them—telling them what to do.

After the meeting with Hewitt, Heyward thought he had at least the understanding, if not support, of Hewitt to push forward with a plan for Scheffler to leave at the end of the 2001–2002 season, an act to be followed at the end of the 2002–2003 season by the retirement of Hewitt himself.

But then—in a move that took management by surprise, after weeks of friendly retirement talks between Scheffler and management Scheffler seemed to change his mind about leaving. At that point, according to Safer, Hewitt (to the annoyance of management, which knew differently) acted as though he knew nothing of CBS's intention to get rid of Scheffler. The correspondents were unnerved by the idea of Scheffler leaving so soon; they knew Hewitt couldn't function without him around. As long as Hewitt remained in charge, *60 Minutes* needed Scheffler to function as a buffer between Hewitt and the outside world—and them.

Word of the correspondents' concern filtered back to Heyward, who called a meeting in his office. The meeting was to deal specifically with a retirement plan for Phil Scheffler, but hovering in the background was the matter of the eventual departure of Hewitt himself.

"Scheffler's hard to deal with," Heyward explained to the group, shortly after they settled in his office. Heyward had always been appreciated by many as a plainspoken, intelligent man, but this observation made no obvious inroad with the correspondents.

"Of course he's hard to deal with," Andy Rooney said "We're all hard to deal with."

Both knew that wasn't what Heyward meant. He was trying to address a deeper issue between him and *60 Minutes* than the obvious personality quirks of its staff. As the head of a news division that had seen its profits erode year after year, Heyward was looking for any way possible to make *60 Minutes* a more highly rated, less expensive show. Getting rid of Scheffler (and then Hewitt) would accomplish two main goals: it would lower the salary budget of *60 Minutes* and open the avenues of communication between CBS News management and the people who shape the show.

"Don doesn't function without Phil. Phil makes it possible for Don to be Don," one correspondent explained. "To get rid of him is a huge mistake." The two men functioned as more than just a team, the correspondents told Heyward. Scheffler operated as a governor on Hewitt's impulses; without him, Hewitt might easily spin out of control.

Heyward and the correspondents agreed on this much: Hewitt couldn't care less about an orderly transition and would probably be just as happy if *60 Minutes* died on the same day he did. That was the common ground of self-interest that led Heyward to assemble this group, without Hewitt, in the hopes that together they could pull off a management shift to keep *60 Minutes* alive—and somehow manage to preserve, for the future, the oldest and still most successful news show on CBS.

Chapter 23

All Due Respect

Ever since the 1970s, the staff of *60 Minutes* had enjoyed a peculiar perk not shared by anyone else at CBS News or anywhere else in the world of television news. It was one treasured by all those who worked there, described in hushed, reverent tones as perhaps the single best thing about the job: the July vacation. Instead of everyone juggling to squeeze rest into the tiny gaps between the constant editing, reporting, and traveling that came with producing 30 fresh episodes of *60 Minutes* every season, they all waited until the season ended in June, then shut down the office completely and took off. After three decades of this, the vacation period had recently begun to slide backward, extending into late June. By mid-June of 2002, many *60 Minutes* employees were already taking long lunches, going shopping in the afternoons, and solidifying travel plans. By July 1, the office was completely shut down except for a skeleton crew in place for emergencies. Otherwise, everyone had disappeared.

But on July 6, 2002, an article appeared in *TV Guide* that disrupted the vacations of several members of the *60 Minutes* team. The article, headlined "The Clock's Ticking," carried a telling subtitle: "CBS Insiders Suggest *60 Minutes* Has Lost the Old Hewitt Edge." The piece, written by J. Max Robins, contended (based on anonymous quotes from a "CBS insider," a "*60 Minutes* insider," and a "Hewitt supporter") that *60 Minutes II* was "journalistically sharper" and speculated that its executive producer, Jeffrey Fager, would have control of both shows by the 2003–2004 season. This marked the first time Heyward's plan for an eventual transition had made it into print. Despite vehement denials from CBS management, it was clear that someone with a lot of inside information—someone who wanted Hewitt out—had talked to Robins.

The most explosive elements of the story were the news that the Fager succession plan was already in place and the suggestion that Hewitt would not accept a forced retirement from his job without a fight. "Everybody would like an orderly transition, but Don may not make that so easy," Robins quoted his ubiquitous "CBS insider" source, characterized as neither a friend nor a foe of Hewitt. "[CBS News president Andrew] Heyward knows this all too well, so he's been tiptoeing around the situation for months." The article even mentioned the specifics of Heyward's plan to put *60 Minutes II* senior producer Patti Hassler in charge of day-to-day operations for that show, while *60 Minutes* senior producer Josh Howard would handle similar duties for the flagship show. It even reported Scheffler's imminent retirement—which had been pushed back, after all the protest, until June 2003.

Months later, after constant steaming to colleagues and friends about the *TV Guide* article and Heyward's plans to remove him as executive producer, Hewitt at last decided to go public with his campaign to keep his job. He invited Jim Rutenberg, a television reporter for the *New York Times*, to his office on November 19, 2002, for an interview in which he handed the reporter a blueprint for his planned defense strategy. He was hoping to garner public outrage of the sort that surfaced a year earlier, after the *Times* reported that ABC was considering the possibility of replacing its beloved *Nightline* and Ted Koppel with late-night comedy host David Letterman.

"CBS Wants *60 Minutes* Chief to Hand Over Stopwatch," read the headline of the Rutenberg piece, which ran across the top of the business section the next Monday, right before Thanksgiving. Not exactly the story Hewitt had counted on, it portrayed Hewitt as a difficult manager who "sometimes has trouble hearing in the screening room" and was not yet willing to consider an orderly transition to a new team. It quoted correspondent Ed Bradley as advocating more flexibility from Hewitt: "Whoever the successor to Don is," Bradley told the *Times*, "maybe Don could walk with him part of the way. . . . I'd like to see Don welcome somebody. Is that going to happen? I don't know, that's up to Don."

While the story went to some length to note Hewitt's considerable achievements, its ambivalent tone ended up leaving both sides unhappy. CBS in particular wasn't pleased with the chart on the front page of the *Times* business section that illustrated the steady decline of the show's ratings in recent years. Josh Howard told colleagues he was annoyed that Heyward hadn't given any quotes at all in support of *60 Minutes,* let alone Hewitt. It's likely that those complaints led to Betsy West's letter to the editor published in the *Times* a few days later, filled with praise of *60 Minutes* and, specifically, its coverage of the World Trade Center attacks.

Hewitt professed to be happy with the piece, but, ever mindful of the importance of spin, realized he needed to provoke a second burst of media interest to keep his campaign afloat. He arranged to go on *Larry King Live* for the full hour on the night of December 2, 2002. Hewitt had been on Larry King's show before, of course; all the *60 Minutes* correspondents gathered, with Hewitt, for a 1998 appearance in connection with the show's thirtieth anniversary. And from time to time, correspondents appeared individually as guests, as did Andy Rooney. But this would mark the first time Hewitt by himself had ever commanded the entire hour.

King launched the interview (on a split screen from Los Angeles) by reading a quote from the *Times* story:

KING: "Mr. Hewitt likes to say that he would die at his desk before relinquishing his position, and that he really means it. But

CBS executives are insisting that he prepare to step aside, seeking to put new zest on the venerable program. They want to replace him most probably with the 47-year-old Jeffrey Fager, a former Hewitt protégé and the producer of *60 Minutes II*."

Mr. Hewitt, the stage is yours. What about this?

HEWITT: Well, I still intend to die at my desk. I never said where that was. I would like it to be at CBS.

Later in the interview he told King that he'd "already had two job offers." One of them, it was suggested later, was an offer from Fox News executive Roger Ailes, for the 7:00 P.M. Sunday night time slot on Fox. The nature of the second offer was never made clear.

HEWITT: I think the problem is that they don't know that I'm not the ordinary, run-of-the-mill, everyday 80-year-old. . . .

KING: Knowing you, you must have picked up a phone when the story ran and called the powers that be and said, "What's the story?"

HEWITT: Well, I know what the story is, but I have a feeling that whatever they've sort of decreed, I think they're having some second thoughts. I mean, that may be wishful thinking and I may find out tomorrow morning that I was kidding myself, but I got a feeling that—I can't believe Mel Karmazin and Leslie Moonves are going to run a network based on not how good you are, but how old you are.

Hewitt then launched into his standard defense of the show, citing ratings, demographics, and his endlessly repeated hunch that the emphasis of advertisers on the 18–49 age group is the result of "a bunch of kids in advertising agencies getting even with their parents" for not letting them watch TV on a school night.

As King pressed him on his reaction to the *New York Times* piece, Hewitt implied that the story was planted by CBS News—and revived the J. Max Robins *TV Guide* piece as evidence that someone in the news division was out to make him look bad. As for the *Times* report that his hearing has suffered, Hewitt declared testily, "That's absolutely untrue."

Even King's callers seemed fascinated by the succession issue, with questions like this one from a viewer in Birmingham, Michigan.

CALLER: Mr. Hewitt, with all due respect to your fabulous career—hello?

HEWITT: Anything that starts with all due respect, look out.

CALLER: O.K. With all due respect to your fabulous career, don't you think it's time for you, Morley Safer, Mike Wallace, and Ed Bradley to step aside and let a younger group come in and take over where you left off in such great grace?

HEWITT: Why do you want a younger group to take over? Are you dissatisfied with what you see on *60 Minutes*?

CALLER: A little bit.

HEWITT: Well, I'm sorry to hear that.

KING: How about the old adage, which is what she's calling about, hey, sometimes it's time to move aside?

HEWITT: Yeah. And what, and let them do to you what the network did to Ted Turner? I mean, it wasn't time for Ted Turner to move aside, but somebody decided that maybe they ought to move him out of here. That guy was as close to being a broadcasting genius as there ever was and he's not around anymore. No, I think the part—why doesn't somebody start a younger *60 Minutes*? Go ahead. Take a *60 Minutes* and find a whole bunch of young guys and program it for younger people.

KING: Is that what *60 Minutes II* is?

HEWITT: No, *60 Minutes II* is a carbon copy of us. Now, if they are unhappy with the demographics that we reach, why do they make a carbon copy? Why didn't they do a different show? I don't understand that.

*　　*　　*

Andrew Heyward, watching the show, didn't agree at all with Hewitt's contention that CBS wanted him out because of his age; he had great respect for Hewitt and the show he'd created. But he just needed to ensure its longevity by lining up a successor. Why couldn't Hewitt understand that? It was clear to Heyward that Hewitt wanted a battle and would continue to play it out in public in the worst possible way.

But for fun, Heyward was contradicting Hewitt's answers in his head—imagining what Hewitt would say if he were being completely honest. He was especially amused when King asked Hewitt about his reaction to the *New York Times* article. King presumed that Hewitt would immediately call his bosses to ask them if the story were true. "But you did not pick up a phone," King asked Hewitt, sounding incredulous, "and call and say, 'What's the story?' You did not do that?"

Of course he did not do that, Larry, shouted the voice in Heyward's head, laughing. Because he planted the story himself!

On the night of December 14, 2002, less than two weeks later, Heyward headed downtown for what promised to be the most awkward social event of the season: Don Hewitt's 80th birthday party.

It had been decided by management that the event should take place in public, not in some private room somewhere; and so several tables had been reserved in a private alcove at Eleven Madison Park, an elegant East Side restaurant with high ceilings, strong drinks, and rich desserts. The guest list included all the correspondents of *60 Minutes,* of course, as well as the senior producing staff of the show—Phil Scheffler, Esther Kartiganer, Merri Lieberthal, and Josh Howard. The CBS contingent included not only Heyward and Betsy West but also CBS chairman Leslie Moonves and his boss, Viacom vice chairman Mel Karmazin. Hewitt was seated with the CBS honchos, while the rest of the correspondents were scattered at smaller adjacent tables.

Much time was devoted to a series of gifts and toasts that deflected attention from the acrimony between Hewitt and the network that was paying for his party tonight. Foremost among the gifts was a large pink elephant brought to the restaurant by Betsy West, meant to symbolize the proverbial unseen 800-pound elephant that was filling the cavernous restaurant. West had neatly captured the spirit of the dinner, a boisterous and friendly affair of drinking and toasting and celebration—albeit with an undertone of odd discomfort. A signed *60 Minutes* cover from Heyward included the inscription "Let's celebrate your 85th together"—a statement that could have been construed as wishful thinking in light of Hewitt's threat on *Larry King Live* to leave CBS if he was removed from his job at *60 Minutes*.

Aside from friendly jokes and knowing winks in the various testimonials to Hewitt that night, the dinner did nothing to resolve the differences between Hewitt and CBS. The next day, Hewitt sent Heyward a thank-you note; in it, Hewitt couldn't resist an allusion to the very issue he believed was behind Heyward's desire to remove him from his job: his age.

"It made me feel twenty years younger," Hewitt wrote, "which means I'm now 60."

A few weeks later, in early January, Andrew Heyward took Don Hewitt to lunch at Gabriel's, a neighborhood favorite for CBS honchos, and told him, in amicable but definite terms, that the time had come for him to leave *60 Minutes*.

The *Larry King Live* appearance had failed to galvanize the pro-Hewitt forces the way he had imagined. Hewitt's rage against CBS management had elicited nothing like the groundswell of support for Koppel in 2002—nothing, in fact, but more resentment. It was clear to everyone, including the correspondents, that the time had come for change. And to most *60 Minutes* insiders, the notion of Jeff Fager coming in as their new executive producer was not nearly so dangerous or destructive as Hewitt had tried to make it seem.

A year had passed since Heyward first suggested that Hewitt step aside. Scheffler had eventually agreed to retire a year later, in June 2003: that meant it was time for Hewitt to formally sign a new contract as well, spelling out the precise terms and timetable for his departure. After years of reluctance to do battle with an acknowledged giant of the TV news business, Heyward knew he must now act and accept the consequences, which would no doubt be acrimonious and ugly.

Heyward had made Hewitt a final offer: He could remain at CBS News as a well-paid consultant but only if he agreed to cede total control of *60 Minutes* to Fager at the end of the 2003–2004 season. From CBS's point of view, it was a generous arrangement; having pushed back the Scheffler retirement, the network was also giving Hewitt an extra year to make his exit. That extension also benefited CBS, in that it allowed Phil Scheffler's successor, Josh Howard, a full year as Hewitt's number two man before his likely appointment to succeed Fager as executive producer of *60 Minutes II*.

Unlike all the previous negotiations, however, this one offered no room for equivocation, no possibility for Hewitt to wangle another year at the helm of the show—no more chances to delay the transition to new leadership that CBS had been trying to pull off for years, and now needed to nail down. The days of delicate maneuvering were over.

Predictably, the negotiations turned briefly difficult—at one point, one high-level *60 Minutes* insider said he believed Heyward threatened Hewitt with dismissal unless he agreed to CBS's terms. But before matters reached the breaking point, according to the *60 Minutes* insider, Hewitt's longtime attorney, Ronald S. Konecky, entered the discussions and helped avert a crisis. In a matter of days, the tough postures were set aside; the deal was done. Hewitt would officially leave *60 Minutes* in June 2004 and remain at CBS with the title of executive producer, CBS News, for 10 years—at which point he'd be 90. His new contract (including an estimated $1 million annual salary) would retain all the perks of his current job, including health insurance, car service, and a liberal expense account.

After Heyward and Hewitt left Gabriel's, they walked back to CBS together. Along the way, Hewitt told Heyward an amusing anecdote about Henry Kissinger and Walter Isaacson, Kissinger's biographer and former president of CNN.

"Isaacson got a phone call from Dr. Kissinger's assistant saying that he'd like him to come to Thanksgiving at his apartment," Hewitt said.

"Isaacson was kind of amazed. He said, 'Let me talk to my wife.' He was very flattered. Meanwhile Kissinger comes back from lunch. The secretary tells him that Isaacson would be getting back to them about Thanksgiving. 'I didn't say Isaacson!' Kissinger said. 'I said Isaac Stern!'" The two chortled over that all the way back to the office, almost as though they hadn't just battled over Hewitt's future in a way that did neither of them proud.

On the morning of January 28, 2003, readers of the *New York Times* got the news of Hewitt's new contract from a story in the bottom right-hand corner of the newspaper's front page—stunningly prominent placement for a story reporting on the transfer of power at a single network television show.

"Man Who Made *60 Minutes* to Make Way for New Blood," read the headline on the story by Jim Rutenberg, the same reporter Hewitt had enlisted in his campaign against CBS two months earlier. Rutenberg's story reiterated Hewitt's earlier hard-line position against leaving *60 Minutes* and attributed the quick turnaround to, among other things, the CBS birthday dinner.

"A lot changed at that party," Hewitt told Rutenberg. "I could feel a warmth in the room."

The story represented Hewitt's decision to relinquish power as a "compromise," and incorporated anonymous praise for Heyward's "deftly handling a potentially explosive situation." Choosing his words with obvious care, Rutenberg avoided stating what was obvious from the events themselves—that Hewitt had, at last, been removed from the helm at *60 Minutes*—but he did note Hewitt's unexpected shift in position. "Still, the deal that Mr. Hewitt has accepted is similar to the one that he would not accept earlier," Rutenberg wrote. "It surprised those on the staff who believed that by going public with his desire to keep his job, Mr. Hewitt had painted CBS into a corner. 'Two weeks ago, I was telling people, he beat those bastards—they can't find it in their hearts to make him go,' Mr. Rooney said."

CBS successfully put a happy face on the events. But within the news division—and particularly inside *60 Minutes*—it was obvious that Hewitt has been forced to leave the very job he'd loudly declared to all concerned, barely one month earlier, that he would never, ever quit.

Buoyed by his own spin—"How many 80-year-olds do *you* know who just signed a ten-year contract?" he was fond of asking people—Hewitt snapped back into action.

Within weeks of the announcement, he was back in the newspaper with the announcement of his latest media stunt; this time, it was the return of the "Point-Counterpoint" format, with former President Bill Clinton and former Senator Bob Dole agreeing to 10 weekly debates on *60 Minutes* for the bargain price of $1 million apiece. The news stunned everyone, including the correspondents and producers at *60 Minutes,* who'd been hearing about cost-cutting for years and were shocked at the price tag for something with such limited potential. Mike Wallace moaned about the money—he'd been cut back like everyone else—and the dubiousness of the idea, which he'd heard about only the night before the announcement.

Nevertheless, the media were immediately enraptured with the notion of Clinton and Dole squaring off. After two years of speculation about a possible Clinton TV career, it seemed incredible that the telegenic former president could have been convinced to become an ensemble player on Hewitt's show rather than the star of his own. Rather than call it "Point-Counterpoint," Hewitt planned to call it "Clinton-Dole" or "Dole-Clinton," depending on who spoke first each week. "When you've got a name like that, you don't waste it," Hewitt told a reporter. Media observers speculated in print that the addition of Clinton and Dole could spark the show's ratings. And it did—for exactly one week, which is how long it took for most viewers to realize that the idea wasn't going to work. Due to the constraints of schedules, Clinton and Dole didn't appear together on camera; they filmed their segments separately and faxed opening statements to each other for reply. There wasn't a nanosecond of spontaneity in either man's performance; in their two-minute debate about President Bush's proposed tax cuts, neither managed to engage the other—or the audience.

The reviews were terrible. Instead of bolstering Hewitt's status, the idea seemed to have backfired in his face. "Bill Clinton wore a dark red tie," wrote Tom Shales in the *Washington Post.* "Bob Dole wore a bright red tie. And that was about as striking as the contrast got last night when the two preening politicos made their debut as a debating team on *60 Minutes.*" Shales called it a "bore" and noted the amusing irony of Andy Rooney's commentary that night—about the shrinking content of everything, including *60 Minutes,* which according to Rooney now included only 42 minutes of programming and 18 minutes of commercials. "Don Hewitt can't even produce good TV with Bill Clinton and Bob Dole," Democratic political consultant James Carville sniped to the *Philadelphia Inquirer.* "That's the real crime against television."

The shows that followed grew even worse; one week, the two politicians actually announced that they agreed with each other. By May, rumblings in the press predicted cancellation—and Hewitt started to ruminate publicly about the segment's faults. "It could have been livelier if they had been in a position to talk about issues that separate right and left," Hewitt admitted, instead of devoting so many weeks to deadly discussions about Iraq and foreign policy that offered nothing new. But in fact it illustrated nothing so much as Hewitt's desperate efforts to catch lightning in a bottle yet again, as he had so often before in his long career.

One afternoon in June 2003, Don Hewitt showed up in Jeff Fager's doorway for a surprise visit. He'd never been prone to strolling all the way across the ninth floor to say hello—but that was before Fager had been given Hewitt's job.

"Hey Jeff, how are you," Hewitt said. "I just thought I'd—"

"Hi, Don!" Fager said. He got up to shake hands with Hewitt. "We're just watching a Steve Hartman piece. Want to see it?"

"Sure," Hewitt responded. Hartman was the CBS News correspondent and humorist hired by Fager to fill the spot at the end of *60 Minutes II* once held by Charles Grodin. Fager had been struggling to find the right voice for the segment; Hartman had lately been alternating with Bill Geist, a reporter for CBS's *Sunday Morning*. Rumor had it Fager had been turned down by both Jerry Seinfeld and Jon Stewart. The piece he was watching showed Hartman going to a high school reunion—not his own—to see whether people would act as though they remembered him.

Hewitt and Fager sat and watched that short segment on Fager's office TV. When it ended, Hewitt turned to Fager and asked, "Who was that?"

"Steve Hartman," Fager said.

"Hartman," Hewitt repeated. "Hartman?"

"Hartman," Fager said. "Steve Hartman."

"I don't know anyone's name," Hewitt said, and then added: "He gives it away." Hewitt meant that Hartman gave away too early in the piece the fact that he didn't really go to the school whose reunion he attended. "I wouldn't give it away," he went on. "I would start with—"

"It's good, though," Fager said, cutting him off. "He's good, isn't he? What do you think of him?"

Hewitt shook his head, unimpressed.

"You're not sure about him," Fager said. "He's a talented guy."

"You don't know with these things," Hewitt said. "With Rooney you didn't know. Rooney was writing for Reasoner. And I said, 'You know what? What if we took a news person and make a little cartoon character, looked like Andy Capp.'" Hewitt was referring to an animated character that Rooney helped create in the early days of *60 Minutes*. It was a typical conversational reference for Hewitt; he was often more likely to mention what happened 30 years ago on *60 Minutes* than on last night's show. "Rooney was thoughtful," Hewitt went on. "You have to be thoughtful."

"He's pretty thoughtful," responded Fager, a little testily—speaking of Hartman, not Rooney. "This is sort of a funny one. But he's a pretty thoughtful character. It's tough to be like Andy. You have to be able to have that kind of body of work behind you to just say things."

Hewitt nodded. "You don't go out looking for an Andy Rooney," Hewitt said. "You have an Andy Rooney. You look for a guy. I think that's the problem. You have to start with the guy and say this is my guy, now what do I do with him?"

"Good point," Fager said, not looking much like he thought so. Hewitt headed toward the door.

"Grodin worked really well," Fager cracked. He knew that Hewitt hadn't thought much of Grodin, either.

"Grodin . . . Grodin was worse," Hewitt said at the door.

"You're right," Fager said as Hewitt left, "I can't fuck up again."

Chapter 24

None of These Men
Can Speak at My Funeral

On the afternoon of Tuesday, June 5, 2003—precisely two hours after Howell Raines and Gerald Boyd delivered their bombshell resignations in the *New York Times* newsroom only 17 blocks away—the entire 125-person staff of *60 Minutes* was getting smashed at Gabriel's, the site of Hewitt's final negotiation last winter with Heyward. They'd only been here 20 minutes and already they were behaving like a bunch of rowdy teenagers on vacation, the wine pouring freely throughout the cavernous dining room. Today, for the first time in anyone's memory (and the guest list included people who remember the Hoover administration), every single member of the *60 Minutes* team was gathering for lunch. Andrew Heyward had invited the staff to lunch on the network's nickel, to celebrate the retirement of Phil Scheffler.

Now that management had achieved its goal of removing Scheffler from his full-time job, *60 Minutes* insiders worried how life with Hewitt would continue without him. The whispering at Gabriel's today revolved almost exclusively around this topic. How many days a week would Scheffler be coming in? What would it be like with Scheffler not there to stop Hewitt from going wild? Why would anyone want

Scheffler to leave before Hewitt's own retirement a year from now? These confusing questions fueled a current of anxiety in the room; it was hard to say who was celebrating and who was drowning their tears. After lunch, a series of toasts from the correspondents added to the odd, disquieting nature of this boozy event.

"You never wanted to go into a screening without Phil Scheffler there," Steve Kroft said to the crowd at Gabriel's. "That sort of became the rule for the last three, four, five years that I've been here. Because he always understood as a producer what you wanted to do. So if Don sometimes thought maybe there wasn't a story there, Phil always understood the amount of work that went into it, and had good ideas, and always meaningful suggestions on how to complete it. He's the only one who could talk Don off the ledge. Even though you sometimes didn't always agree with what he said, you were willing to put up with the occasional disagreement for the wisdom that he brought into the room every day."

Kroft paused and looked around the room. He was ready to deliver his final valedictory, every word chosen with considerable care.

"The fact is that the show has been able to maintain its standards over thirty-five years when there is so much going on in television news that does not," Kroft said. "And the person who I think is singularly responsible is Phil Scheffler. I don't think there's any doubt about it. He always kept his eye on the ball, he's always kept us in line, and it's the biggest loss to the show since Harry Reasoner left. And it's a challenge to everybody to make sure those standards are still here when Phil's not there."

Kroft looked down at Scheffler, seated at a table only a few feet away, and began to cry. And as Kroft wiped the tears off his normally stoic, butcher-block face, others in the room marveled to themselves how bold and direct his comments were—how pointed and unmistakable his reference was to Scheffler's singular contributions.

Wallace's testimonial to Scheffler echoed Kroft. "Phil was the only man who could disagree with Hewitt in a screening," he said, "and make it stick."

Safer also agreed. "At 60 Minutes," he said a few minutes later, "we have 'bad cop, worse cop,'" referring to the Scheffler-Hewitt team. He failed to specify who was who in that formation, but it wasn't a big mental leap for his audience to make the division. Soon after finishing his remarks, Safer headed outside for a smoke.

Then came Stahl, who followed the men. She appeared to have come directly from the airport, wheeling a suitcase behind her as she walked into the restaurant at 12:45, a little late.

"None of these men can speak at my funeral," the 61-year-old correspondent declared, which earned her the biggest laugh of the lunch. She then went on to emphasize Scheffler's unique importance to the show; she implied that Hewitt's style was to personalize the battles that were a routine part of the show's backstage drama, whereas Scheffler kept things steady.

"We have the drama . . . we have the Jewish hysterics . . . but whatever we've gone through, my impression is that Phil maintains his sanity and keeps us on an even keel," Stahl said. "I can't remember a time where it ever got personal. It was always about the story."

The outpouring of love and respect for Scheffler was to be expected; after all, this was his farewell lunch, the final chance for the men and women of 60 Minutes to express their appreciation for Hewitt's longtime deputy. It was less expected to hear these famous news stars, even in the relative privacy of Gabriel's, use Scheffler's departure as a moment to stick it to the boss. It is as though they wanted to remind those listening—including Hewitt—that there were two ways to manage the show, and that the departing Scheffler's was the one they preferred.

At 1:50 P.M., the door to Gabriel's swung open to reveal a terrifying glimpse into the show's mortality, in the person of a pale, limping shadow of a man barely recognizable as perhaps the show's beloved Ed Bradley.

It had been five weeks since the 61-year-old Bradley was rushed to Mount Sinai Medical Center for a quintuple heart bypass surgery on April 29, following several weeks of unexplained chest pains. While it wasn't unusual for the seasoned correspondents at *60 Minutes* to need medical help, the reality of Bradley's condition came as a huge shock to his friends and colleagues. A health nut known to work out for hours every day and to eat little besides fruits and vegetables, no one figured Bradley for an incapacitating hospital stay anytime soon. ("We're all quitting our gym memberships and eating donuts for breakfast," joked then-senior producer Josh Howard a month after Bradley's operation. "I mean, what's the point?") The surgery came suddenly in the final weeks of the 2002–2003 season and left pieces unfinished, interviews undone. And while no one wanted to say it, everyone at *60 Minutes* was afraid that Bradley's condition could mean an early, precipitous departure by a man who had been expected to stay and contribute to the show for at least another decade.

Which is why, when Bradley stepped gingerly into the Gabriel's dining room, the guests jumped to their feet and cheered their colleague with sustained applause and whooping. "I'm sorry I'm late," he said once the ovation died down, and he took a seat at a back table with his team of producers. "I'm getting more like Don, with a short attention span."

More laughter, more applause, before Bradley offered a few remarks that bore an uncanny resemblance to what his colleagues had already said. If ever one needed evidence that the *60 Minutes* correspondents never consult each other much about things, the similarities of these testimonials proved it beyond a reasonable doubt.

"I remember Phil for a lot of things," Bradley said. "Among them that strength . . . that fortitude. He can say, 'Don, you're wrong.' I can't tell you how much I appreciated that frankness. That fortitude in pointing it out so many times when he was wrong." Bradley paused. "I'll miss him," Bradley said finally, placing his hand over his heart. The crowd leapt to its feet once again and cheered. Bradley sat down, and then realized he had a few more words to say.

"My heart is fine," Bradley told the roomful of colleagues anxious for an update on his condition. "My lungs aren't fine. I have lesions."

Bradley didn't dwell on his health, or reminisce much more about Scheffler, save to relate one story of the two men hanging out at a dive under a highway near San Francisco. He was clearly tired, and wrapped his remarks up quickly with an odd, off-key signoff. "Lest I forget . . . for all the trips that Patricia [Blanchet, Bradley's wife] and I have made to Italy, for all the restaurant recommendations you've given us, many thanks." That oddly impersonal farewell may have been just a reflection of the correspondent's weakened state; but it also served as yet another sign of the emotional distance and lack of intimacy among the personalities of *60 Minutes*. The correspondents had formed no real friendship with one another over their decades of working together—all they shared was a commitment to their continued longevity and success.

The final testimonial of the day came from Hewitt himself. He followed the remarks of Scheffler's successor, Josh Howard, and Betsy West, who engagingly referred to herself as "management scum."

"I had known and admired Phil for a long time," West said, "and for a long time I thought that he admired me, too. Then I came to work for CBS as a vice president. Phil has a bit of a thing about management. Some say he derives some perverse pleasure from thumbing his nose at any suit that dares to patrol the hallowed halls of *60 Minutes*. But I have to say that despite your valiant efforts to pose as a disruptive, antimanagement, pain-in-the-ass curmudgeon, Phil, you have failed miserably."

Howard followed up with his own recollections. "Phil Scheffler's management rule number one. When a vice president calls to speak with you, don't take the call. Rule number two. When Mike Wallace calls to speak to you, pretend you're too busy because you're on the phone with a vice president. And finally the most important sentence to remember: 'No, Don, you can't do that.'"

Hewitt then went to the podium.

"The best way I know how to add my two cents to what everyone else has said," Hewitt said, "is to use a word that television all by it-self—with no help from anyone else in the civilized world—managed to change from a verb to a noun: the 'get.' As in '*20/20* got a get' when it got Hillary Clinton. Or '*PrimeTime Live* got a get' when it got Jennifer Lopez.

"I can murder the language just as well as they can," Hewitt continued. "I got a get when I got Phil Scheffler. Many years ago I fished him out of a pond at 116th Street and Broadway called the Columbia School of Journalism. He cleaned up after me while I cleaned up after a guy named Douglas Edwards. Among other things, what he's been doing for the better part of half a century is cleaning up after me. And making sure no one at *60 Minutes* ever used 'get' as a noun. . . . I envy the next guy you sign on to clean up after." As the crowd applauded, Scheffler got up out of his chair and hugged the man he'd served for his entire adult life.

As the final year approached—and with Scheffler mostly gone (his retirement package included the right to serve next year as a three-day-a-week consultant), the fears had increased about Hewitt and how he would function as executive producer. And none felt those fears more acutely than Mike Wallace.

After 35 years, the relationship between Hewitt and Wallace still defied explanation even by most of those who knew them well. One theory had it that Hewitt had always wanted to be Wallace's friend, and was chagrined by Wallace's ongoing, tacit refusal. Another popular notion was that each one believed he was more responsible for the success of *60 Minutes* than the other—and resented the other's claims of credit. Others speculated that Hewitt and Wallace were competing to outlast each other at *60 Minutes,* a battle to the finish line based on health and longevity. Certainly, they loved to point out each other's medical infirmities. Wallace never lost that competitive streak and used it as a weapon against Hewitt whenever he felt like it. They had become, in the common parlance of those who worked at *60 Minutes,* the quintessential "grumpy old men"—two elderly neighbors who seemed to thrive on endless battles and arguments and misunderstandings.

But underneath all that, most of Wallace's close associates believed that he'd never entirely recovered from the scars of the Wigand war. Many of their fights since then included comments about Wigand; Wallace never stopped feeling that Hewitt had resigned himself to the will of the network, and Hewitt believed Wallace had hung onto his righteous indignation for too long. Each blamed the other for the crisis that had left their show so fundamentally scarred.

The fights between them in the post-Wigand era struck most observers as more painful and personal than ever before; one producer described a battle between Wallace and Hewitt (one that began over a small issue in a piece) as having gone to such an extreme that Wallace insisted their relationship was over. "That's it," Wallace told the producer. "Finished." The two men then went days without speaking until finally Hewitt (characteristically the first to apologize) made an overture that Wallace accepted. Still, though, when the fights were finished, they were forgotten—at least until the next one started up.

The fights would typically begin over something small; perhaps Hewitt would find some flaw in the first screening of a Wallace piece.

"This sucks," he would say, or, "You've told it backwards," or, "I don't get it." A lesser ego might be stopped cold by such direct criticism; for Wallace, it only energized him to fight back.

"What do you mean you don't get it?" he would reply. "It's right there. Right there."

"Right where? Not in the fucking piece I just saw."

"Well, maybe if you were looking at the piece instead of . . ."

"Fuck you!"

"Fuck you!"

Before long one or the other would head to the exit of the screening room and walk out—Wallace was often the first to leave. One producer recalled remaining behind after a Wallace walkout and discussing more calmly Hewitt's objections to the story, until about 20 minutes later Wallace stormed back into the screening room, still in a lather.

"What the fuck are you still doing here?" Wallace yelled at his producer. "When I walk out, my producer walks out too!"

*   *   *

At a lunch the day after the Scheffler retirement party, a *60 Minutes* correspondent was asked whether Don Hewitt could still perform the job of executive producer.

"No," the correspondent answered definitively. "He can do it to a certain degree if it doesn't go past noon. He doesn't hear, he doesn't comprehend. This doesn't mean that he's a basket case. What I mean is that his sensibilities are not what they were by any means." The correspondent paused for a moment, then added: "His sensibilities were extraordinary."

Chapter 25

Still Climbing

Trevor Nelson, who at the age of 29 became a producer at *60 Minutes* in 1999, was the kind of guy who easily earned a 4.0 grade point average at the nation's finest prep schools, like Andover and the Putney School, only to be tossed out for partying. Wild and intense and charming and brilliant, he loved to flaunt his contradictions. He carried a briefcase to his classes at the University of California at Berkeley, and wore jackets and ties that hid the wild man underneath. Nelson's intelligence and self-confidence carried him past every obstacle, all the way to the staff of *60 Minutes* at the age of 27—a young, gifted producer in the hothouse of television news, destined for greatness in an industry always ready to worship the eager face of a young man who knows what he wants.

Nelson arrived at *60 Minutes* in 1996, after a five-year tour of duty at the *Christian Science Monitor* radio network in Boston. A friend had tipped him to an opening in Washington, working for Lesley Stahl as an associate producer; only 18 months later, Nelson was transferred to New York and Ed Bradley's team. He made a dramatic impression; his quick sense of humor and storytelling talents made him an immediate force to be reckoned with. Nelson became a full-fledged producer for Steve Kroft in 1999, having completed his climb to the pinnacle of TV news in near-record time.

Nelson quickly made his mark with the kind of sharp-edged investigative pieces that distinguished *60 Minutes*. His stories sparkled; he tore through topics like dotcom millionaires, terrorism, and investment scams without breaking a sweat. A 2003 piece on the Halliburton company drew special notice; it drew damning connections between Defense Department contracts and the Bush administration's roster of former Halliburton executives, most notably Vice President Dick Cheney. It won the special attention of Don Hewitt, who saw in Nelson the bright, energetic future of a show desperately in need of a new adrenaline supply. Hewitt wanted producers who could tell complex stories in simple, elegant ways; he loved flash and respected substance, and Nelson's stories had both.

In September and October of 2001, Nelson shared bylines with other producers on a series of distinguished Kroft pieces that followed the World Trade Center attack. Those included stories on airport security, immigration policy, and the survivors of Sandler O'Neill, an investment banking company headquartered in the World Trade Center that lost one-third of its employees. In the midst of crashing stories on September 11, Nelson produced a Kroft piece for the November 18, 2001, edition on allegations of criminal activity at the U.S. Border Patrol. On March 10, 2002, he delivered another hard-hitting investigation by Kroft on problems at the U.S. Immigration and Naturalization Service. "Con Man," on April 14, 2002, profiled a Frenchman who represented himself as a Rockefeller to steal from a high-profile crowd. Nelson's segment on New York State Attorney General Eliot Spitzer on October 6, 2002, would earn him an Emmy.

Nelson distinguished himself by dedication, not just to the show but to his life outside it. He left his Upper West Side apartment for work each morning promptly at 9:30, and returned home by 6:30 every night to be with his wife, Maggie, and their sons, Conrad, 2, and George, 1. He ran 6 miles every day in Central Park and maintained a large network of friends. After the death of his father in early 2003, Nelson committed himself to spending as much time with his two little boys as he could.

It appeared, to those who knew Nelson only from a distance, that by the summer of 2003 the wild man had achieved a rare measure of happiness and peace. But those close to him knew that for all his success, not everything in his life was as peaceful as it seemed.

One day in the spring of 2003, Trevor Nelson walked back to the office of the graphics designer at *60 Minutes* to take a first look at The Book for a piece he'd assembled on Saddam Hussein and his secret stash of billions. The Book was *60 Minutes* slang for the graphic depiction of the story's content and headline that appeared behind the correspondent, on screen, as the story was being introduced. Producers took a particular interest in The Book because that was the one place their names appeared on *60 Minutes,* where the jolt of ego gratification came after months of hard, anonymous work.

"Saddam's Money" hadn't been Nelson's idea—Kroft had dropped it on his desk some weeks earlier—but he'd reported it nonetheless and found a legitimate story there. As with most of his stories, Nelson had the help of an associate producer at the show, in this case a woman named Dana Miller. Although Miller had helped considerably throughout the reporting and research process, Nelson had been the one to write the script and shape its content.

Which is why Nelson was stunned to see Dana Miller's name above his own on The Book. When two producers worked together on a story—or when an associate producer shared a credit—the order of the name was always the same: the primary producer's name got top billing, and the secondary contributor went below. An associate producer's name almost never went above that of a producer, except in extraordinary circumstances.

"How did that happen?" Nelson asked the designer. He knew that when he'd put the credits on paper for the graphic artist who designs The Book, he'd put his name first.

"Steve switched the names," the designer explained.

Nelson was stunned. For the last three years he'd been a full-time producer for Kroft and had endured every form of verbal abuse imaginable. Kroft rarely read a Nelson script without tossing it back at him, telling him in the bluntest terms it was defective in some form. Nelson learned to live with it, for the simple reason that he loved working for *60 Minutes*—and he respected Kroft's ability to craft a great script, to take a draft and rework it incessantly until it was brilliant. Also, unlike most Kroft producers, Nelson wasn't afraid to yell back. Though Nelson never instigated the fights, he never shied away from them, either, and gave as good as he got.

That said, Nelson hated the harshness of it, but he loved the results. He'd been nominated for two Emmys and was considered by everyone, including Hewitt, as one of the show's rising stars, so he figured he'd keep living with it for a little longer. His three-year contract with CBS News was up in the summer of 2004. Maybe he'd find another job in television, or maybe he'd quit TV news altogether and follow his passion for politics and social issues in an entirely different direction.

But this time, when he saw what Kroft had done with the credits on The Book, he couldn't take it any longer. He decided he had to quit—not in August, but right then. He went immediately to find Josh Howard, then the show's senior producer but about to become the show's number two, and told him what happened. Howard told him he was right—that it wasn't fair, that it shouldn't have happened, and that he had every right to quit. But Howard persuaded him to resist resigning from the show; they'd work it out. Sure enough, by the time the story aired, on March 2, 2003, "Saddam's Money" carried the credit as originally intended.

Still, the rocky relationship between Kroft and Nelson never really repaired itself. As the summer approached, Nelson began weighing his options; he talked to people at other networks and vaguely considered doing what producers do when their contracts expire—entertaining offers from other programs, and using them as leverage for more money or status. Because Nelson had been promoted from within the ranks, he earned far less than most other producers at *60 Minutes*—and he wanted, if nothing else, enough of a raise to justify remaining in a job that had often made him miserable. Besides, he loved *60 Minutes*—he'd been watching the show every Sunday since his days at Berkeley and considered it a privilege to be producing stories for the greatest TV newsmagazine show around.

On the night of July 24, 2003, Trevor Nelson died suddenly of complications from meningitis, at the age of 34. He'd been on vacation with Maggie and the boys in Massachusetts. It was the first death ever of a current member of the *60 Minutes* family.

Because it was July, the entire staff of *60 Minutes* was on vacation; the offices were empty. But everyone quickly assembled to pay their last respects to Nelson. By the next afternoon, both Hewitt and Kroft had issued statements to the press. "He was the most talented young producer I ever worked with," said Kroft. "He was destined for great things." Hewitt went even further in his praise. "Trevor Nelson was a guy who had star written all over him," he said. "I thought one day he might be the executive producer of this broadcast."

In early August, a letter of condolence came in the mail to Maggie Nelson from Lesley Stahl. "Many years ago," she wrote, "an expedition of the hardy reached the top of Mount Everest and were surprised to find a lone cross with an inscription. It said merely: "Died While Climbing." That, Stahl wrote, was also the message of Nelson's life, tragically interrupted on his route to the very top of the tallest mountain in his world.

On August 9, nearly three weeks after Nelson's death, Mike Wallace was heading to the mailbox of his oceanfront home on Martha's Vineyard, where he had been a summer fixture for years. He took the same path he always did, over a rock jetty across the beach. He was hoisting himself up about 5 or 6 feet. It was around noon; after he got the mail, he was supposed to meet a reporter from the *Vineyard Gazette* for an interview.

As Wallace was making his way, he slipped and came crashing down on the rock, where he lay unconscious for several moments. When he came to, he was alarmed to realize that he was covered in blood. He'd slashed his ear and his head, broken an eardrum, and taken a bad enough blow to the head that a local doctor decided immediately that he needed to be taken by helicopter to New York City. He ended up in Lenox Hill Hospital in Manhattan, where he stayed a few days—not as long as his doctors would have liked, but as always Wallace couldn't stay still.

He tried to resume normal function but right away, he observed a few significant changes in himself. His memory (until recently, remarkable for a man of 85) seemed far more faulty than usual. His hearing wasn't as good as before, nor was his sight. It was a strange, difficult experience for a man whose physical well-being had been the subject of marvel and envy for so long. He still maintained his trim, athletic figure, but behind the facade Wallace was suffering. He'd previously been diagnosed with gastric reflux disease—hardly a killer ailment but nonetheless cause for him to have to clear his throat with uncommon frequency at times. Now, coping with the setbacks from his fall, he seemed less secure about himself than he had in years.

At the beginning of September, the *60 Minutes* correspondents and Hewitt were honored by the National Television Academy of Arts and Sciences with an Emmy for lifetime achievement. Even for a group of journalists as celebrated as this one, this particular award marked a special distinction, and as a way of commemorating the event, the correspondents agreed to appear on a panel discussion at Fordham University, to talk about their careers at *60 Minutes*. The panel was run by William Small, the former CBS News executive who'd discovered Diane Sawyer. Ed Bradley didn't come—he was still recuperating from his own illness—but Wallace showed up, along with Safer, Stahl, Rooney, Hewitt, and Bob Simon.

Simon was there despite his ongoing lack of the formal title of *60 Minutes* correspondent. He had been doing pieces for both shows, but his only official status was as a full-fledged member of the *60 Minutes II* family—even though he had the dashing looks and reporting chops to qualify as a correspondent on the more prestigious show. Simon's face—and the words, "I'm Bob Simon"—were only a part of the show's opening credits when Simon had a piece airing that night. That appeared to be the main distinction between Simon and his *60 Minutes* peers.

Simon, who lived in Jerusalem, had been at CBS News most of his adult life; after college and a brief stint at the United Nations, he stumbled into broadcasting and discovered a natural gift for television. Born in the Bronx, he nevertheless managed to cultivate the lilting voice of a man who has lived most of his life in more elegant ports of call; he preferred to keep his foreign base, to remain atop the constantly breaking stories in the Middle East that had been his métier for two decades. Simon shot to stardom in 1991, when he was taken hostage for 40 days by Iraqi forces near the Saudi-Kuwait border, but by then he'd already been a distinguished correspondent in London, Vietnam, China, and India. "Simon is me, 20 years ago," Wallace had said the previous spring.

The crowd (mostly students) at Fordham University was so enraptured by these *60 Minutes* stars that most of them missed the moment when Mike Wallace almost fell apart. What was barely perceptible to a casual observer was terrifying to his colleagues.

Wallace had started on a rambling recollection of his controversial 1999 Jack Kevorkian interview, which had included the broadcast of an assisted suicide. After a few minutes, it became clear he'd lost his train of thought. He was repeating himself, speaking vaguely. After pausing for an unusually long time in the middle of a sentence (with his colleagues looking over at him with compassion, knowing all too well that his behavior was the result of his recent accident), Wallace suddenly shifted gears, and felt the need to explain his behavior.

There would, after all, have been no way for this audience to know anything had happened to Wallace. For some reason the *Vineyard Gazette* hadn't printed the news of the fall, even though its own reporter was on the scene for the previously scheduled interview. CBS

News hadn't disclosed it, either; not knowing the seriousness of the injuries, there hadn't seemed any need to alarm the public with an announcement.

"I'm having a bit of difficulty," Wallace said at last. "I should explain. About two or three weeks ago, I fell. Landed here." He pointed to his head. "As a result of which my hearing, memory, and sight have suffered." He paused again, and then resumed his Kevorkian comments as though nothing had happened, but in the same halting, confused manner as before. At the first possible moment, the moderator Small jumped in to interrupt, and Wallace said little else all morning.

Afterward, there was a special Emmy lunch to honor the show's producers; and by that afternoon, everyone at *60 Minutes* had heard what happened to Wallace. The show's press spokesman, Kevin Tedesco, arranged for the story of Wallace's accident to go out, at last, over the Associated Press wire, where it was picked up in many papers around the country, including, at last, Wallace's hometown paper, the *Vineyard Gazette*.

Chapter 26

It's Not Who You Know

In a glen plaid suit, white shirt, and red-patterned tie, Don Hewitt leaves his 17th-floor apartment in the spectacular San Remo, a sprawling building on Central Park West at 75th Street. On this October morning in 2003, a car service picks him up and takes him to the corner of 116th and Broadway, a 15-minute trek to the Columbia University Graduate School of Journalism. At 9:00 A.M., he is to speak to a group of graduate students in the World Room, an ornate lecture hall on the third floor with wood paneling and stained glass windows.

The students trickle in slowly. By the appointed hour every seat is full. Hewitt, holding in his hands two videocassettes, sits down at a table in front of the students. "I'd like to show you these tapes," he says, "of two pieces I consider among the best we've ever done." He holds up one cassette and then looks over helplessly at the student who escorted him to the lecture hall. "Can you help me? I'm terrible with these things." The first tape, from the 2002–2003 season, is called "All in the Family." It's the investigative piece by Steve Kroft, produced by Trevor Nelson, about close ties between Halliburton and Defense Department contracts. The second piece, "Musically Speaking," is a Lesley Stahl story, produced by Shari Finkelstein, about a young musical savant.

Hewitt watches the stories with the students and then opens the floor to questions.

"How do you make pieces that good?" one student asks.

"It's a lot of work," Hewitt explains. "It's a casting process. Just like a movie or a TV show. You need just the right element, the right personality to tell the story. A writer in a magazine can use his writing talents to make the subject interesting. Not in television. In television, dull is dull is dull."

Hewitt clearly enjoys his time on campus. As he leaves the World Room, an enterprising female student approaches him with a smile and says, "I've waited all my life to meet you, and I want to work at *60 Minutes*, so I'm going to take advantage of this opportunity and give you my resumé." Hewitt smiles, folds the résumé, and puts it in his pocket. "Well, I'll read it!" he says in a way that sounds sincere enough.

Hewitt heads back downtown. He has a meeting at the corner of 60th and Madison at 11:00 A.M. to discuss his latest inspiration: three-dimensional TV. He says he's found a guy who can do realistic 3-D visuals on a television screen.

"The 3-D still requires glasses, so people tell me adults won't go for television that way," Hewitt says. "But kids will. Kids will wear the glasses and play video games. I've already talked to Sony about it. This is going to be big." He reaches into a FedEx envelope next to him on the car seat and pulls out several pictures. The first is a three-dimensional photograph of Penelope Cruz. After that, a 3-D Van Gogh painting. "I'm going to talk to Graydon Carter about this," he says, referring to the editor in chief of *Vanity Fair*.

Hewitt reaches into his pocket for his cell phone, opens it, and says "office" into it; the phone speed-dials the number of his *60 Minutes* office. His secretary isn't around, so he asks to speak to Josh Howard, now executive editor of the show.

"Hey, kid," Hewitt says. "I'm going to a meeting at eleven, and I'll be in by noon. What's going on?"

Howard tells him he'll be going out to lunch today, but he reviews the schedule of afternoon screenings with Hewitt, mentioning the fact that newspapers reported this morning that Barbara Walters will be interviewing Martha Stewart on ABC. That was one of the big "gets" of the past year, and the loss of it pains Hewitt; at the moment his show could use all the gets it can get. Two weeks ago, the show aired a Steve Kroft interview with Sam Waksal, the convicted head of ImClone who prompted Martha Stewart's interest in the company's stock. Under Kroft's fierce cross-examination about his spreading of insider information, Waksal struggled to defend himself, making for passably good TV. But the interview lacked the emotional dimension that Walters was famous for finding in her celebrity conversations. It comes as no surprise to Hewitt or Howard that Stewart will go with Walters instead of anyone on the *60 Minutes* crew. Still, Stewart is the kind of interview that makes Andrew Heyward and Leslie Moonves happy—if that's anyone's concern.

"It's ridiculous that they're pushing me out," Hewitt says after hanging up the phone. "I'm still doing the job. Have you seen the show? It's great. It's just great. We're doing some great work. It's just ridiculous."

Hewitt has talked to several people about reviving "Who's Who," the one-season failure of the mid-1970s. He had in mind his *60 Minutes* star Ed Bradley to host it. But Bradley remained weakened by his quintuple bypass surgery and subsequent lung problems; it isn't likely he could still be considered for the job.

Still, there are other people out there who might work. Perhaps Hewitt is considering Matt Lauer, the genial cohost of the *Today* show, whom he met for breakfast earlier this week.

"Lauer told me the reason they think the *Today* show has been dropping in the ratings recently is because WNBC dropped Jane Hanson as the early-morning local anchor," Hewitt says. Hanson had been WNBC's *Today* show lead-in local anchor since 1988, until the affiliate announced in July 2003 that Hanson was being "promoted" to host news specials and replaced by Darlene Rodriguez, who'd joined the station in 1998. "People want stability. They don't want to see change for the sake of change."

Hewitt's observations tend to echo his own experience. As anyone will tell you who has spent more than five minutes in Hewitt's company, he loves, more than anything, to talk about himself. In spite of a long career that by definition required a curiosity about the outside world, he continues to live an almost completely self-referential life; even his closest friends say he talks too much about himself, tells the same stories too often, seems too enamored of himself. But at the same time, it is impossible to be in Hewitt's presence without finding yourself in awe of his legend. You look at him and want to have seen the world through his eyes, to have experienced the history he watched and made. No other journalist alive today comes close to having the résumé of this man, and it would be a pleasure to discover this about him if it wasn't so likely that he would soon tell you himself.

His car reaches 60th and Madison. He opens the car door and bounds out onto the Manhattan sidewalk. Across the street, cameras are filming a scene from the sixth and last season of *Sex and the City* in front of Barney's department store.

"One last thing," he says, standing in the bright midmorning sun. "Osborn Elliott, a great journalist, used to say this at the end of the graduation ceremonies at Columbia. To the students. It's not who you know . . ."

Hewitt smiles the wicked smile of a man who knows he's still a master storyteller, the best in the business, and pauses for the perfect interval of time.

"It's whom you know," he says, dancing off into the crowd of pedestrians, teeming with life.

Don Hewitt's eighty-first birthday begins at 5:15 A.M. with a call from Betsy West, alerting him to the news that Saddam Hussein has been taken into American military custody. A new episode of *60 Minutes* is scheduled to air in 14 hours. West—who lives only minutes from the office by taxi—launches into action with the assistance of executive editor Josh Howard, whose willingness to help strikes a notable contrast with Phil Scheffler's nay-saying when the Afghanistan war story broke. By the late afternoon, the three of them—one from the old guard, two from the new—have completed a show that ends up completely replacing the one previously scheduled for that night.

Hewitt calls Andy Rooney, who is in town and agrees to put together a new commentary. He then reaches Ed Bradley, who comes in to anchor the broadcast. Lesley Stahl's producer in Washington, Rome Hartman, says he can deliver Secretary of Defense Donald Rumsfeld—but only if it can be a live interview. This is extremely rare but not unprecedented, and everyone agrees it's worth it to get the government's top military strategist for what appears to be an exclusive with Stahl. The decision is made to entrust the lead piece to David Martin, who covers the Pentagon for CBS News and who, it is agreed, can deliver a better overview than anyone else. Hewitt was arguing for a news opening, but he is persuaded that Martin could cover breaking developments in his piece. Mike Wallace was pushing for an interview with the UN's secretary general, Kofi Annan, but it appears doubtful it will make it in.

Late in the day, as the show is being readied for air, Andrew Heyward and a birthday cake arrive in *60 Minutes* Control Room 33 to commemorate the occasion. "I can't think of a happier way to spend my eighty-first birthday," Hewitt says, "than right here in this control room."

The next night is the *60 Minutes* Christmas party at Tavern on the Green. The party has been held at various places over the years, ranging from a lavish spread in Hewitt's apartment to sipping champagne from plastic cups in the office. Most staffers find that *60 Minutes* parties are stiff, cold affairs with awkward, cringe-inducing toasts. This year, it ends up being slightly more festive—no toasts, no farewells, just mingling and drinking and gossiping about next year. Much of the talk still centers on Hewitt's plans. His friends and colleagues believe that it will take something on the order of the Jaws of Life to remove Hewitt from his office next June. Yes, he has told people he is comfortable with the transition plans in place. But he has also continued to say that there's no logical reason for him to go—not now, not while the show is having its best season in years.

There's no arguing with Hewitt on that point; the 2003–2004 season of *60 Minutes* has marked the first time in several years that the ratings have improved, not declined. After losing a million viewers a year for four straight seasons—the steady audience decline that helped push the Hewitt replacement plan into action—the show has recently landed back in the Nielsen top 10 several times. But while the renewed ratings vigor have given Hewitt and CBS bragging rights, it is mostly irrelevant as an indicator of the show's financial value to the network. Since the late 1970s, networks have sold advertising based on demographics; NBC and ABC use the 18–49 age group as the basis for their rates, while CBS prefers the 25–54 market measure, in part because the network has always attracted an older audience. There's no question that *60 Minutes* remains television's most-watched TV newsmagazine, but not in the 18–49 bracket. For a show like ABC's *PrimeTime Live,* advertisers will pay a premium to get those viewers—particularly when the network ad salespeople assure them that host Diane Sawyer will produce a number of "specials," with guests like Jennifer Lopez or Jessica Lynch, that deliver big numbers.

How does CBS sell *60 Minutes?* Networks never reveal their sales strategies, but analysts conjecture that CBS might induce an advertiser to buy a 30-second spot on, let's say, *The Handler*—a low-rated prime-time network series—by also offering them a reduced rate for a commercial on *60 Minutes,* considered a "prestige" buy. The show earns that status in part because of the total households it attracts and in part because of the number of its viewers who earn over $75,000 a year—coveted "premium" viewers for some advertisers. This way the advertising sales force can bypass the issue of the show's aging demographics. Such calculations make it difficult for anyone to figure out the real profitability of *60 Minutes*. It isn't enough to know the show's editorial budget; you also need to know how much revenue it produces for the network. Those numbers are so closely guarded that even Don Hewitt can't get access to them. (During his 2002 campaign to keep his job, Hewitt called Tom Wolzein, a noted media analyst at Sanford C. Bernstein, to see if Wolzein had any profit numbers to bolster his case.)

The season begins well enough, with an opener that includes an Ed Bradley interview with the undercover drug officer from Tulia, Texas, accused of targeting the town's black community. It continues with provocative interviews with disgraced ImClone founder Sam Waksal and former HealthSouth CEO Richard Srushy. A two-part Steve Kroft examination of pornography lands in the November sweeps. But the first blockbuster doesn't come until November 30, when Mike Wallace's interview with former New York Giant star Lawrence Taylor (tied to the release of Taylor's book) lands the show in the number four position for the week in total viewers—thanks in large measure to blanket promotion during the CBS football games that preceded it that day and to Taylor's sensational revelations about sex and drugs in the NFL. The show even manages to end up in the top 10 shows of the week in the coveted 18–49 demographic, with a 6.4 rating for that age group.

Buoyed by its success, *60 Minutes* follows up the next week with another piece aimed at the youth market: "The Look," a Morley Safer segment about discriminatory hiring practices at upscale retailer Abercrombie & Fitch. The story, prominently featuring shots of scantily clad women, draws an unusually large audience to the show. The special broadcast about the capture of Saddam Hussein wins even bigger numbers.

With the show experiencing its biggest success in years, Hewitt is feeling in a better position to accept his fate at last.

It's a lazy Friday afternoon in early December 2003. Outside, a blizzard has just descended on Manhattan. The picture window behind Mike Wallace's desk shows nothing but a wall of white, with snowflakes floating upward as they seem to do when they fall particularly hard. Elsewhere at *60 Minutes,* staffers are packing up purses and briefcases and backpacks to leave early for the weekend, but not Wallace. He doesn't even notice the snow. He's at his desk, working; it is the place he loves the most, and he shows no particular desire to get home before dark.

"Did you read Liz Smith's column from a couple of days ago?" Wallace asks, referring to the famous gossip column that appears in the *New York Post* and is syndicated around the country. Wallace presses the buzzer on his phone that signals to his secretary. It takes her a while to respond, so he keeps buzzing, annoyed. When she finally answers, he says, "Do you have that Liz Smith column?" She enters and finds it on his cluttered desk.

"Here," Wallace says. "Read it, and then I'll tell you a funny story."

The December 4, 2003, Liz Smith lead item is about Michael Jackson. After describing network plans to cover the forthcoming Jackson trial, Smith recalls similar overkill in the O. J. Simpson story.

It hasn't been lost on a single network executive that the people who pursued the O. J. Simpson trial from the get-go, the ones with the most pizzazz, push and perseverance, were the ones who left the others, the more fastidious ones, in the dust. (I do recall when *60 Minutes* producer Don Hewitt sniffed at coverage of O. J. and took his show out of the running. I don't think the great news magazine has completely recovered even yet.)

But this time they are *all* going to mix it up; they are going to war like you can't imagine. As Al Jolson said: "You ain't heard nothing yet!"

"Don went nuts when he saw that item," Wallace whispers, in the conspiratorial tone he often takes on when talking about Hewitt. "Nuts! He called Liz's office three or four times yesterday. Yelled at her assistants. Screamed at them! He was furious. Liz wasn't there. Who knows if she even wrote the item? Anyway, she wrote Don this letter, and she sent me a copy. I've known Liz for years. She worked for me a long time ago as a secretary, in the 1950s."

Wallace hands over a faxed copy of a letter from Smith to Hewitt. Written in her chatty, friendly voice, she chides Hewitt for exploding at her over the item and mentions that she has resisted the temptation to do the same with him in the past, when she'd felt his show had slighted her.

"You want to know the real reason we didn't cover O. J.?" Wallace leans forward to whisper again. "The true story is, the whole O. J. thing happened during the summer. We were on vacation. We didn't want to come back in. It had nothing to do with anything but the fact that we didn't want to come back in. Who wants to come in and cover the goddamned O. J. story? Everybody's going to be all over it, all the time, anyway. So it was concocted . . . along with everybody else. Don sniffed at coverage of O. J. and took the show out of the running."

Wallace leans back in his chair again. The snow has started to fall even heavier now.

He is asked to reflect on how he and Hewitt are getting along these days.

"Better, these last couple of months," he says. "Finally."

For a moment Wallace glances toward the wall of his office, in the direction of where Hewitt would be if he hadn't already left for the weekend. By now the entire office is empty except for Wallace.

"We were like brothers," Wallace says softly. "We were such good friends for such a long time. I said to Don, 'You have it all. You have all the money in the world. You have all the reputation in the world. Don't get angry. If people criticize you, the criticisms are like this'"—Wallace holds his hands close together—"'and the accomplishments are like this'"—his hands spread wide apart. "'For Christ's sake, why get so excited about this?'"

Wallace holds up the Liz Smith column again. "For him to get that excited about that kind of thing," he says, shaking his head. "On the phone to her, apparently three or four times."

Wallace rests the column on his desk and looks as though he's about to cry. "For Christ's sake," Wallace says. "He's a major figure in TV history. Isn't that enough?"

By then darkness has fallen outside the window. It is almost evening, and time at last for Wallace to leave for home.

*   *   *

Early on the morning of December 16, 2003—the morning after the Christmas party—Hewitt sits down at his computer and bangs out a memo to the entire *60 Minutes* staff. At 11:30 A.M., the message appears in the e-mail in-boxes of everyone on the show.

> Dear 60 MINUTES:
>
> On this, our last Christmas together let me get a little "mushy" and say this morning what I wanted to say last night at our Christmas party but frankly didn't seem appropriate to the occasion.
>
> Having been for more than 35 years on the receiving end of an untold number of "Dear Sixty Minutes" letters it doesn't seem unreasonable to pen one of my own—to *you*, the heart and soul of the best broadcast of its kind anywhere on earth.

After praising the talents of his staff—and patting himself on the back for his own 55-year television career—Hewitt finally acknowledges that the show he created will soon continue with new leadership.

> One of the more rewarding things about that long tenure is leaving this extraordinary broadcast and its offspring in the hands of two extraordinarily good guys—Jeff Fager and Josh Howard who will soon become the new managing directors of a company I like to think of—even if no one else does—as "Don Hewitt & Sons."

At which point Hewitt at last addresses the issue of his own departure and eventual destination, to a staff that wasn't sure Hewitt would ever leave voluntarily.

> I'll be downstairs on the eighth floor in a corner office even bigger than the one I'll be vacating with a fancy new title and a mandate to come up with new ideas for broadcasts and old ideas to improve the new ones we already have . . . and if they're real lucky not second-guessing Jeff and Josh . . . and trying, with all my heart, not to be a pain in the ass.
>
> How can anyone be sad about basking in the warmth of the largest and most talented television family anyone ever gave birth to?
>
> Don

It is the first hard evidence that Hewitt will indeed leave his office as promised in June. While it contains lines that may annoy one person or another (one could easily imagine that the image of "Don Hewitt & Sons" might bother his successor), it leaves everyone with at least the possibility that, come June, he would stick to his word and go downstairs at last. "I figured it's almost Christmas," Hewitt explained that afternoon, "and I didn't want everyone spending the holiday worrying about me." It was not at all surprising to know that Hewitt assumed his staff would spend their two-week vacation worrying about his future.

As it turns out, everyone will be thinking about Hewitt and *60 Minutes,* though hardly for the reasons he might have hoped. What was supposed to become a quiet and dignified denouement for Hewitt is about to become one of the most tumultuous and controversial moments of his career.

Chapter 27

Bending the Rules

"Goddamn it! God-fucking-damnit!"

It's 4:49 P.M. on Sunday, December 28, 2003, slightly more than two hours from the scheduled start of *60 Minutes,* and Don Hewitt is furious. For much of the afternoon, he has been wandering Control Room 33 in the CBS Broadcast Center, waiting desperately for the arrival of "Michael Jackson," Ed Bradley's two-part exclusive interview with the beleaguered pop star. The final version has yet to be fed from Los Angeles, where Bradley is still feverishly working with producer Michael Radutzky to finish a story that will surely result in the highest-rated *60 Minutes* episode of the season. Jackson, under increasing media scrutiny due to the latest round of rumors and accusations against him, finally met with Bradley three days ago, on Christmas afternoon in a suite at the Beverly Hills Hotel, surrounded by a phalanx of whispering lawyers and managers. After 23 minutes of on-camera questioning, the pop star abruptly stood up and walked out, claiming he was in too much physical pain to continue.

Under normal circumstances, an interview with a prominent newsmaker that ends in a walkout might result in a delay or cancellation of the piece. But these are not normal circumstances. Hewitt has to run the piece that Sunday night, no matter what, or risk violating an agreement made between Jackson and CBS Entertainment to air the interview prior to a Jackson musical special the following Friday. The interview and the special has been linked by CBS, in an unorthodox arrangement that will earn Jackson millions of dollars' worth of free network promotion for a new album that might have otherwise been lost.

"My show is being held hostage!" Hewitt screams at Radutzky, with Josh Howard and Betsy West in the background. "Where the fuck is the piece? This is fucking ridiculous! God-fucking-damnit!!!"

Hewitt is frustrated, but he isn't about to let the interview slip away. The Jackson segment represents a potential ratings bonanza for *60 Minutes*—and high ratings, after all, remain Hewitt's obsession. High ratings are the main reason Hewitt is still, at 81, sitting in a CBS News control room and not on a golf course somewhere.

It might not seem unusual for other network news divisions to agree to extraordinary demands in return for access to Michael Jackson. But CBS News (and *60 Minutes* in particular) has always prided itself on adhering to a higher standard. This eyebrow-raising agreement between CBS and Jackson reflects the desperation of CBS News to keep *60 Minutes* popular and relevant—and profitable—in the face of declining ratings and demographics.

This moment, and the circumstances that led to it, is totally in keeping with the approach of Hewitt his entire career—to grab the attention of the TV audience, no matter what the price.

Thirty-eight days earlier, Michael Jackson was arrested in Santa Barbara, California, and charged with seven felony counts of child molestation involving an overnight guest at his sprawling Neverland Ranch. These latest charges sparked a level of media and public interest in Jackson that transcended any previous moment of his two decades in show business. While news organizations—including Bradley and *60 Minutes*—had long been pursuing a sit-down interview with Jackson, the arrest made him an even more coveted prize for the newsmagazine. Every major talking head, from Diane Sawyer to Katie Couric to Larry King, desperately wanted the chance to ask him about the charges. An exclusive on-camera sit-down would pull in huge ratings for whoever managed to land him first.

Hewitt wanted Jackson as much as anyone. But in recent years it had become more problematic than in Hewitt's early days for network news divisions to make deals with subjects without arousing suspicion. Only six months before, Betsy West had written a controversial letter to the family of Private Jessica Lynch, the putative war hero, raising the possibility of tie-ins with other units of Viacom (CBS's parent company, which also owns MTV) as part of her pitch for an exclusive CBS News interview. Despite his own controversial track record, Hewitt liked to insist that *60 Minutes* would never make deals with anyone to get an interview.

"We don't play that game," Hewitt had barked to Leslie Moonves, the chairman of CBS, at a meeting in Moonves's New York office in November 2002. Moonves had called the meeting to scold Hewitt and his counterparts at the other CBS prime-time newsmagazines—Jeffrey Fager of *60 Minutes II* and Susan Zirinsky of *48 Hours Investigates*— for not having gotten an interview with Jennifer Lopez. The actress-singer had just appeared on *Primetime Live* in an hour-long conversation with Diane Sawyer that had garnered huge ratings for the network, particularly in the coveted 18–49 demographic. Those numbers made Moonves angry.

"I want those stories," Moonves told his assembled staff, which included West and her boss, Andrew Heyward. "I don't want to see her on ABC. I want to see her on CBS." But Hewitt (who described the meeting as the first time in 55 years that he'd been "summoned" to CBS corporate headquarters) explained that to get Lopez on CBS would have required making deals that went beyond the network's rules. The *60 Minutes* bosses left Moonves's office bruised and battered. They'd basically been admonished for not sacrificing standards and not bending the rules the network news division had supposedly always held sacrosanct—all for the purpose of ratings.

It seemed an ironic pose for Hewitt, who'd been bending the rules of television news for the last half-century—to replace the dull presentation of news headlines and the tired rhythms of documentaries with something not only informative but also entertaining. In doing so, Hewitt had transformed TV news into a profitable enterprise that would forever depend on ratings for its continued success.

After the story of Jackson's arrest broke, CBS scrambled to figure out a plan for its "Number Ones" special—the musical hour pegged to the release of Jackson's new album that was set to air in less than a week, in the middle of the November sweeps period. Moonves and his lieutenants first announced that the show wouldn't air until after the case against Jackson had been fully resolved in the courts. "Given the gravity of the charges against Mr. Jackson," the network said in a press release, "we believe it would be inappropriate at this time to broadcast an entertainment special."

But Jackson's managers kept badgering Moonves to air the special; after all, the singer still had an album to sell. CBS finally relented and negotiated a new deal with Jackson to air the special on Friday, January 2, 2004—hardly a premium spot on the network schedule—in return for an interview with Jackson.

Moonves later said that the Jackson camp initially rejected CBS's suggestion of a news interview following the arrest. "The Jackson people, their first thing was, 'No, no, no, we can't talk about it,'" Moonves recalls. "Then they called back and said we might be willing to do an interview . . . with *Ed*. He trusted Ed. He liked Ed. So I spoke to Andrew [Heyward] and said, 'This is the situation.' It was all laid out, what the quid pro quo would be." As for which broadcast the interview would appear on, Hewitt conceded that it had to air that Sunday "because of an obligation" to Jackson—and admitted several weeks later that the arrangement was "unorthodox."

"Now, are you caving in to the entertainment division?" Hewitt asks, looking back. "In a way you're caving in to the corporation you work for. You're not in business for yourself. There is an entity that has a lot of arms, and I think the bind you get in sometimes, like that, the very fact that you work for this conglomerate, sometimes works to your advantage and sometimes works to your disadvantage. . . . Was the circumstance under which we aired the Jackson thing unorthodox? Yes. Unorthodox in the way we do business. Okay, he can have the special if we do this. . . . Yeah, there were a lot of caveats. Got to be on that Sunday, got to do all that stuff."

Given the now pressing deadline, Bradley reluctantly postpones a planned vacation to Mexico with his wife and travels instead to Los Angeles to conduct the Jackson interview. Initially Jackson's handlers say he'll only be available for a 10-minute interview on Christmas Eve; then Jackson doesn't even show up. On Christmas Day, Bradley, Radutzky, and a *60 Minutes* film crew—along with Jack Sussman, CBS Entertainment's executive vice president for specials and the network's chief liaison with the Jackson camp—return to the Beverly Hills Hotel suite, awaiting Jackson's rescheduled noon arrival for the interview. He and his entourage finally show up sometime after 4:00 P.M.

Bradley and Jackson sit opposite each other in armchairs, their conversation frequently punctuated by stops and starts dictated by the Jackson camp. Every time Bradley asks Jackson a specific question related to the charges, the interview stops and Jackson confers with his team. Much of the 23 minutes of taped conversation is devoted to Jackson's denials of the molestation charges.

BRADLEY: What is your response to the—the allegations that were—were brought by the district attorney in Santa Barbara that you—you molested this boy?

JACKSON: Totally false. Before I would hurt a child, I would slit my wrists. I would never hurt a child. This is totally false. I was outraged. I could never do something like that.

BRADLEY: This is a kid you knew?

JACKSON: Yes.

BRADLEY: How would you characterize your relationship with this boy?

JACKSON: I've helped many, many, many children, thousands of children—cancer kids, leukemia kids. This is one of many.

A few minutes later, Jackson alleges abuses of his own, claiming he was mistreated at the Santa Barbara police station during the booking process on November 25, a month before the Bradley interview took place.

JACKSON: They manhandled me very roughly. My shoulder is dislocated, literally. It's hurting me very badly. I'm in pain all the time. This is—see this arm? This is as far as I can reach it. Same with this side over here.
BRADLEY: Because of what happened at the police station?
JACKSON: Yeah, yeah, at the police station. And what they did to me—if you—if you saw what they did to my arms—it's very bad what they did. It's very swollen. I don't want to say.

However, it seems Jackson does want to say. The next day, Jackson, through his attorney Mark Geragos, provides Bradley with photographic evidence of his injuries. During the interview, Jackson also alleges that the police locked him in a bathroom for 45 minutes, while taunting him. The interview then turns to more discussion of Jackson's behavior toward children, before Jackson finally stops the interview. He and his entourage leave the hotel suite soon afterward.

The interview, transcribed and sent to New York within hours, whets Hewitt's appetite. Meanwhile, for the next two days, Hewitt and Howard wait anxiously for a script of the story to arrive from Los Angeles.

Finally, Radutzky e-mails a draft of the first part of the script to Howard on Sunday at 6:00 A.M. West Coast time. It is five minutes short. ("We lost a lot of time because we started with an idea in mind that this was more a chronological piece explaining his life, and then come to the conclusion that, hey, it's not about that," Bradley says, looking back on the editing process. "We probably blew most of Friday trying to sort out the form, the shape of the piece. And a lot of Saturday trying to get comment from the people we felt we needed comment from.") The draft focuses almost exclusively on the interview itself, and, from Hewitt's point of view, doesn't adequately address the response to the charges made by Jackson against the authorities. Hewitt and Howard read through the script and point out holes everywhere that need to be filled.

"Where's the fucking police department?" Hewitt keeps asking. "You have to have the goddamned police department's response, otherwise it's bullshit." With only 12 hours left, Howard reluctantly gives the team more time to fill in the gaping holes.

Knowing the dangers of presenting a one-sided story about Jackson—with every media outlet in the country watching closely to see how *60 Minutes* handles this delicate story—Howard orders changes that they promise to deliver later that day, when both he and Hewitt will be in the control room, waiting.

It isn't until 2:00 on Sunday afternoon that Radutzky and Bradley feed the first segment of the two-part piece. They've filled the five-minute gap by this time, but the piece still fails to properly address Hewitt's objections. He still wants more clarity concerning the response to Jackson's own allegations of abuse. With Howard and West nearby, he screams his instructions to Radutzky over the phone in a manner that everyone at *60 Minutes* has grown accustomed to over the years. "How the fuck can we put a piece on where the police department is giving us no fucking answer!" he rages. "It's not enough! It's fucking bullshit!"

Hewitt is profoundly frustrated by being forced to wait for an incomplete story he has no real time to fix. He can easily see the weaknesses in the piece—the questions that Bradley doesn't ask, the absence of response from those Jackson accuses of wrongdoing (let alone the child at the center of the case), and the lack of perspective on Jackson's essential oddness. It is clear to everyone in the control room that one more week would give Bradley and Radutzky the chance to turn this piece into something much stronger. But there isn't another week, or even another minute. Radutzky and Bradley need to feed a final version to the network by 5:00 P.M., to leave enough time for the extended mechanical process of readying a *60 Minutes* to go out on the airwaves. But 4:00 P.M. comes and goes, and then 4:30 P.M., and still no piece.

"Goddamnit! God-fucking-damnit!" Hewitt screams into the phone at Radutzky. "Where the fuck is the piece?!" Hoarse from yelling, Hewitt starts banging the phone against the control room table. "Don, how am I supposed to finish the story with you yelling at me?" Radutzky yells back, but to no avail—Hewitt is too enraged to listen.

There is one bright spot amid the panic that has quickly enveloped Control Room 33 at CBS News. CBS is broadcasting a professional football game that is running late—as it does most weeks—and it now appears likely that *60 Minutes* won't go on the air much before 7:30 P.M., giving Radutzky and Bradley another half-hour. In the end, with not a minute to spare, the show goes on the air that Sunday night—as though nothing had happened.

But clearly something has happened. The night has proven pivotal for Hewitt. Everything he loves and hates is on the table: Hollywood, news, drama, celebrity, sex, ratings, deadlines, and rules. It is a quintessential Hewitt moment, and one that has disrupted the smooth and uneventful final year at *60 Minutes* he planned for himself. If Hewitt is lucky, good ratings will distract everybody from the problems facing the show itself.

The next morning, Hewitt gets the overnight numbers. The episode reached the highest number of the 18-49 audience in almost four years. It scored a 12.0/20 household rating and share and a total audience of 18.8 million viewers, making it the number one show of the week. This marks the first time that *60 Minutes* has been number one on television since the March 1998 broadcast that featured Bradley's interview with Kathleen Willey—another Bradley-Radutzky collaboration that

60 Minutes had been accused of rushing onto the air without adequate reporting.

At 4:00 A.M. on New Year's Eve, Hewitt is back on the phone with Radutzky, yelling again.

"What the fuck is this about?" Hewitt demands. In that morning's edition, the *New York Times* is reporting that CBS had paid Michael Jackson an additional $1 million for the *60 Minutes* interview, and alleging that Ed Bradley promised Jackson money at their Neverland encounter the previous February. The *Times* attributes the allegations to a business associate of Jackson and a CBS executive, both anonymous.

Radutzky tries to calm Hewitt down. "I don't have any idea," he says. "We didn't pay them anything." Over the next several days, Hewitt launches an angry counterattack against the *Times*, insinuating a lack of ethical standards in its reporting.

The internal bruises from the Jackson story have been slow to heal, and some questions about the broadcast remain unanswered to the satisfaction of everyone at *60 Minutes*. "Ten years ago we wouldn't have done a Michael Jackson interview," Mike Wallace says soon afterward. "Who is he? Not a story for us."

Morley Safer is even more emphatic. "I think it's going to be very, very dangerous for this broadcast if they try making it too relevant because the pressure will be there to be doing what we shouldn't be doing," Safer says. "I think everything from Jessica Lynch to Michael Jackson . . . apart from the fact that I have serious questions about how important they are as stories, we don't do those stories very well. I don't do those stories very well. I don't do them. There's no interest."

In March 2004, one *60 Minutes* correspondent, requesting anonymity, remains uncertain of what really happened between Jackson and *60 Minutes*. Like the rest of the tigers, this correspondent has an ongoing love-hate experience with Hewitt. "I'm not sure how much Don knew about this," the correspondent says. "We were just on a roll, and Don wanted to get ratings, and I don't think he even knew about most of this stuff. I don't think he knew anything about deals. I don't think anybody in the front office would have raised that with Don because his reaction would have been so unpredictable."

The correspondent pauses for a moment and then adds: "I think that maybe I'm underestimating. Maybe Don was in it up to his ears, you know?"

As for Jeffrey Fager, poised to succeed Hewitt as executive producer of *60 Minutes* in the fall of 2004, his main reaction to the Jackson episode is relief that it didn't happen on his watch. He tells associates that he feels certain he would have been crucified for it by the news media: "They would have said, 'That sort of thing would never have happened if Don Hewitt was still around.'"

But the chase for ratings and riches has been Don Hewitt's obsession pretty much ever since he went to work in television over a half-century ago. That's when he first merged a childhood infatuation with Hildy Johnson and the movies into the dry, dull business of reporting the news—and, in the process, created something no one had ever seen before.

Epilogue

Mike Wallace has wandered back to his office from Don Hewitt's impromptu good-bye party, well ahead of most of the others still drinking champagne in the screening room and listening to their deposed boss rail against the CBS managers who have inexplicably removed him from his job.

"It's time for Don to go," Wallace whispers.

It has been a difficult winter and spring at *60 Minutes*. Hewitt has alternated between accepting his fate and denying it, frequently complaining that he still doesn't understand the reasons for his forced resignation. Even the high points of these last several months were tinged with controversy; the ratings and headlines generated by a February interview with former White House terrorism chief Richard Clarke were followed by criticisms that the show should have disclosed its corporate tie to the Free Press, Clarke's publisher, which, like CBS, is owned by Viacom. Even Ed Bradley's return to health, following last year's bypass surgery, was slowed by an emergency appendectomy. And the ratings triumphs for the broadcast from earlier in the season diminished considerably as the year progressed. By May, the show was back to its usual numbers, way down from the highs reached by the Lawrence Taylor and Michael Jackson episodes.

Hewitt's imminent replacement, Jeff Fager, has been taking producers and correspondents to lunch all spring at Gabriel's to discuss the show's future. He has told people he doesn't want to make wholesale changes, but it is clear he wants to make *60 Minutes* more timely and relevant. After the Tyco mistrial in March, Hewitt had passed on a Bradley interview with the infamous Juror Number Four who stood in the way of a guilty verdict. Fager, at *60 Minutes II*, immediately scheduled a two-part interview of the juror by his star correspondent, anchorman Dan Rather. (It didn't do anything in the ratings, CBS chief Leslie Moonves mutters afterward.) Most people expect that Rather will play an integral role next season in Fager's *60 Minutes*. (One week after taking over the show, Fager used a Rather piece on his June 13, 2004, Reagan special following the former president's death—instead of using one by Lesley Stahl, for example, who covered the Reagan administration. The following week, Rather appeared in a special one-hour *60 Minutes* interview with Bill Clinton.)

Meanwhile, Hewitt has managed to displease his correspondents with one final decision, endorsing the removal of the "II" that has followed the name of the Wednesday-night broadcast since it launched in 1998: from now on, it will be known as *60 Minutes*. When that decision is announced, the correspondents complain bitterly that their show has been devalued and voice concerns that pieces from *60 Minutes II* will now compete with theirs for placement on the prestigious Sunday broadcast. No one quite understands why Hewitt has agreed to this, except perhaps to make the Wednesday show less likely to get canceled—and somehow reflect poorly on his legacy. It may also be a parting gift to Josh Howard, who had been his personal choice to succeed him at *60 Minutes* and who instead has been named executive producer of *60 Minutes II*.

"Everyone was very upset about that," Wallace says. "It made no sense."

But Wallace, like his fellow correspondents, is focused on the future. He has agreed to devote at least one more season to *60 Minutes,* producing 10 stories for Fager; after that, he'll see how he's feeling. "What else am I going to do?" he says, with a twinge of sadness.

Wallace knew nothing about Hewitt's plans for next season until his surprise announcement at the party a few minutes earlier—Hewitt's revelation of the *30 Minutes* concept he claims to have sold to 19 CBS owned-and-operated stations. It will be a locally produced news-magazine under Hewitt's oversight—*30 New York Minutes, 30 Miami Minutes,* etc. Wallace holds out no hope at all for its success.

"How do you control an idea like that?" Wallace asks. "Nineteen different shows. How can he run all of them? Nineteen! How does he plan to make sure of the quality? He's squandering the name."

Wallace then shakes his head dismissively. "Terrible idea," he says. "Terrible."

It is pointed out that 36 years ago, Wallace had a similar opinion of another crazy Hewitt idea, a show called *60 Minutes.* Wallace turns away, lost for a moment in the memory. "True," he says, looking out his office window. "That one worked."

Note on Sources

This narrative account of the history of *60 Minutes* incorporates in-person interviews with present and former producers, correspondents, support personnel, and executives connected with the broadcast, as well as others who worked alongside Don Hewitt at CBS in the years that preceded its premiere in 1968. It also draws on several books, articles, and memoirs that chronicled various parts of the show's history.

Tell Me a Story by Don Hewitt (Public Affairs; 2002) proved an invaluable resource, in particular for the chapters concerning Hewitt's early years, as did his earlier memoir, *Minute by Minute* (Random House; 1985). In cases where Hewitt's verbal retelling of his life story differed from his written account, I've chosen his memoir as the definitive version. In cases where the two memoirs offered differing accounts, I've used his 2002 memoir as the definitive source, except as noted in the text. Thus the facts and dialogue used in the telling of several key anecdotes in Hewitt's life depend heavily on his published account—in particular, details of his upbringing, the blackboard discovery at the 1952 convention that led to the creation of the super, the near-theft of the NBC truck in Iowa during the Khrushchev visit to an Iowa farm in 1959, and his dealings with Dan Rather concerning Abraham Zapruder on November 22, 1963. I have also used the books as a reference for key facts and dates from his early years as a journalist, and as a factual backup on later incidents at *60 Minutes*.

Similarly, Mike Wallace's memoir, *Close Encounters* (William Morrow; 1984), offers a detailed account of several important moments in Wallace's life, as recalled with the help of his collaborator, Gary Paul Gates. I have used his written recollections as a source for several episodes described in the narrative, in particular his early years in broadcasting, the death of his son Peter, and his journey through television news to the staff of *60 Minutes*. Lesley Stahl's memoir, *Reporting Live* (Simon & Schuster; 1999), provided the factual basis for my narrative of her pre–*60 Minutes* life, as well as the discussion of her relationship with her mother. Dan Rather's memoirs (written with collaborator Mickey Herskowitz) were valuable chronicles of key moments in his career: *The Camera Never Blinks* (William Morrow; 1977) and *The Camera Never Blinks Twice* (William Morrow; 1994). The former covered details of Rather's early life and career, in particular his conflicts with Richard Nixon and his early years at CBS, and the latter included a detailed account of his 1980 Afghanistan piece for *60 Minutes* that contributed information to my narrative. *Before the Colors Fade*, by Harry Reasoner (Alfred A Knopf; 1981) proved a valuable account of Reasoner's career at CBS and *60 Minutes*.

Two important, independent histories of CBS News helped to establish the context of Hewitt's rise and that of *60 Minutes*: *Air Time: The Inside Story of CBS News* by Gary Paul Gates (Harper & Row; 1978) and *Who Killed CBS?: The Undoing of America's Number One News Network* by Peter J. Boyer (Random House; 1988). The memoir of CBS News president William Leonard, *In the Storm of the Eye: A Lifetime at CBS* (Putnam; 1987), included detail and dialogue contained in the account of Walter Cronkite's departure as anchorman, and his replacement by Dan Rather, as well as Leonard's version of the start-up of *60 Minutes*. A CBS-approved history of *60 Minutes*, *60 Minutes: 25 Years of Television's Finest Hour* (General Publishing Group; 1993), was a handy resource for facts and details.

Also helpful were *The Decade That Shaped Television News: CBS in the 1950s,* by CBS News president Sig Mickelson (Praeger; 1998), and *Salant, CBS and the Battle for the Soul of Broadcast Journalism: The Memoirs of Richard S. Salant,* edited by Susan and Bill Buzanberg (Westview Press; 1999). I owe a considerable debt to the reporting of Elsa Walsh, whose thorough analysis of Meredith Vieira's struggles at *60 Minutes* were included in her fascinating book, *Divided Lives: The Public and Private Struggles of 3 Accomplished Women* (Simon & Schuster; 1995). I also depended on *We're Going to Make You a Star,* by Sally Quinn (Simon & Schuster; 1975), for Quinn's account of her sexual-harassment by Hewitt.

The television beat reporters and critics from the *New York Times* from the 1950s through 2004—Jack Gould, John O'Connor, Peter J. Boyer, Peter Kaplan, Jeremy Gerard, Tony Schwartz, Sally Bedell Smith, Lawrie Mifflin, Jim Rutenberg, and Bill Carter—provided a contemporaneous and valuable record of many significant events in *60 Minutes* history. A January 1978 profile of *60 Minutes* in *Rolling Stone* by Donovan Moore offered useful perspective, as did Harry Stein's look at the show in May 1979 for the *New York Times Magazine.* Mark Hertsgaard's insightful May 1991 *Rolling Stone* article, "The Sixty-Minute Man," proved especially helpful, particularly as the source of Hewitt's stinging 1990 memo to the staff. I learned much from Susan Steinberg's informative 1998 *American Masters* documentary, "90 Minutes on *60 Minutes.*" "The Man Who Knew Too Much," by Marie Brenner in the May 1996 *Vanity Fair,* offered a comprehensive account of the Wigand controversy. Of additional help were "Fast & Flawed," Howard Kurtz's account of Ed Bradley's interview with Kathleen Willey in the August 1998 *Brill's Content,* and "Real to Reel," D. M. Osborne's report on the *60 Minutes*–Jeffrey Wigand controversy in the July/August 1999 *Brill's Content.*

Acknowledgments

Don Hewitt agreed to cooperate with this book before I even had a publisher, and without any control over its content. He encouraged friends and associates to talk to me, and opened many doors. For his courage and willingness to do so, I'm enormously grateful. The decision of Andrew Heyward, the president of CBS News, to lend his approval to this project—again, with no promises made in return—made a huge difference to my efforts. I owe special thanks to Ed Bradley, Jeffrey Fager, Patti Hassler, Josh Howard, Steve Kroft, Andy Rooney, Morley Safer, Diane Sawyer, Bob Simon, Meredith Vieira, Mike Wallace, and Betsy West for contributing their time to my *60 Minutes* education. To the rest of the vast *60 Minutes* and CBS News family, both present and former, who helped me along the way, many thanks. Thanks also to Gil Schwartz and Kevin Tedesco for their assistance.

My eternal gratitude goes to Alice Martell, for her incomparable gifts as an agent and as a human being.

Thanks to David Hirshey, my friend and editor, whose smart judgments shaped every page; to Nick Trautwein for his thoughtful insights and superior editing skills; and to Larkin Warren, for her valuable editorial input. I'm also grateful for the research assistance of Kate Pickert and Jacqueline Reeves.

I got ideas, suggestions, diversion, and the feigned appearance of interest in my endless chatter about *60 Minutes* from many family members and friends. I owe them thanks: Bill Abrams, Tony Gilroy, Bill Hamilton, Neal Jacobsen, Donald Katz, David Koepp, Leslie Larson, Jane Mayer, Joan and Howard Minsky, Jeffrey Minsky, Maura Minsky, Olya Minsky, Patricia Morrisroe, Julie Salamon, Joanna Scheier, Melissa Thomas, Michael Wadman, and Matt Wagner. Peter Cohn read an early draft and gave me valuable notes and suggestions. Thanks to Mary Fontenelle and Tom Carr for their ongoing help to my family and me.

The idea for this book came from my father, Albert Blum, an extraordinary historian and teacher. I'm grateful for the inspiration he's given me over the years. My brother, Steven, offered considerable help and kindness along the way.

My children, Sam and Annie, knew just the right moment to say "tick . . . tick . . . tick . . ." for maximum amusement. They frequently kept my priorities straight by shifting my attention to the New York Mets' pennant prospects, or my favorite *American Idol* contestant.

Oh yes, and about Terri Minsky: her love, support, and faith in me have made more things possible than I ever dreamed of, including this book.

Index